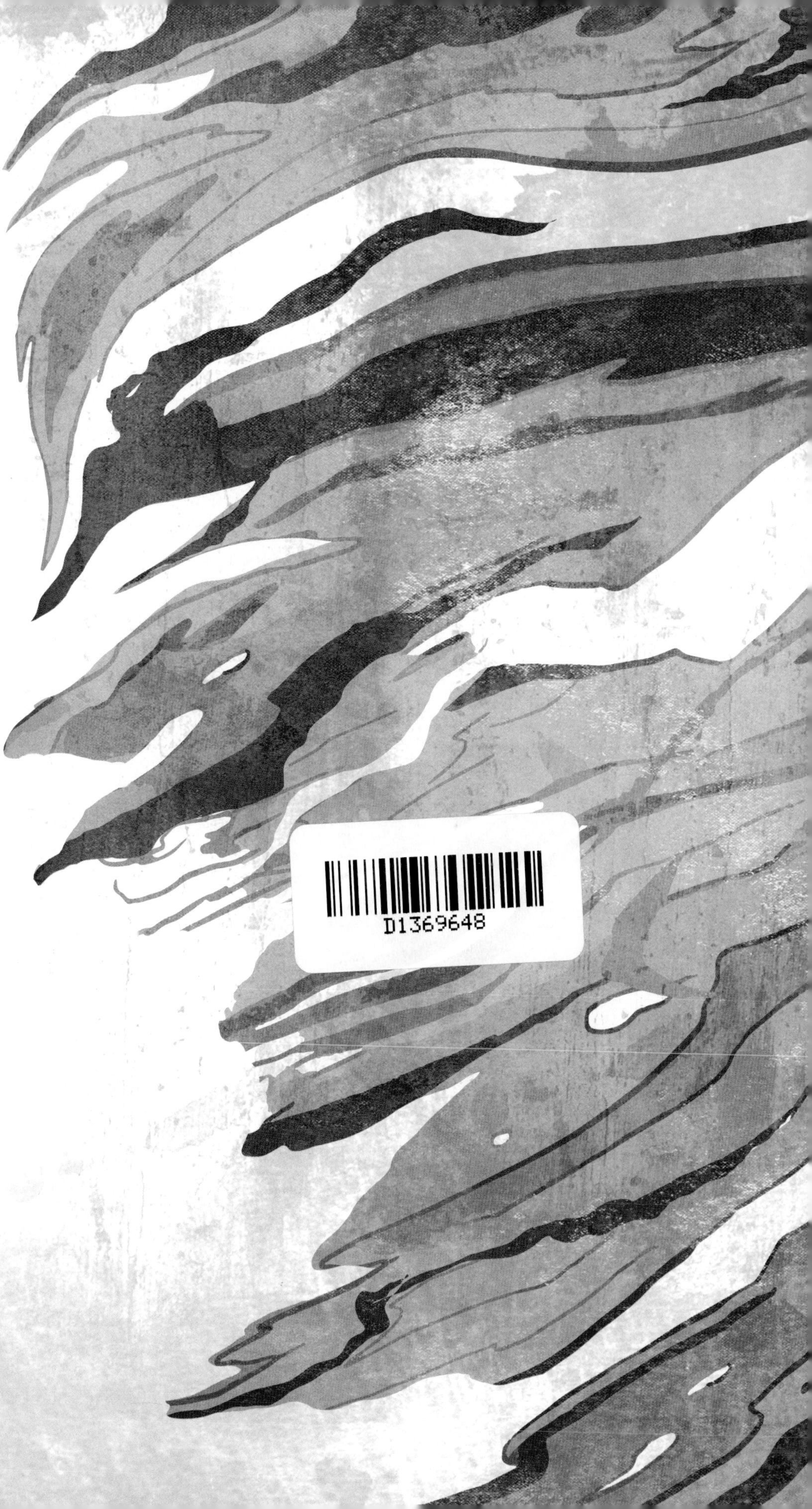

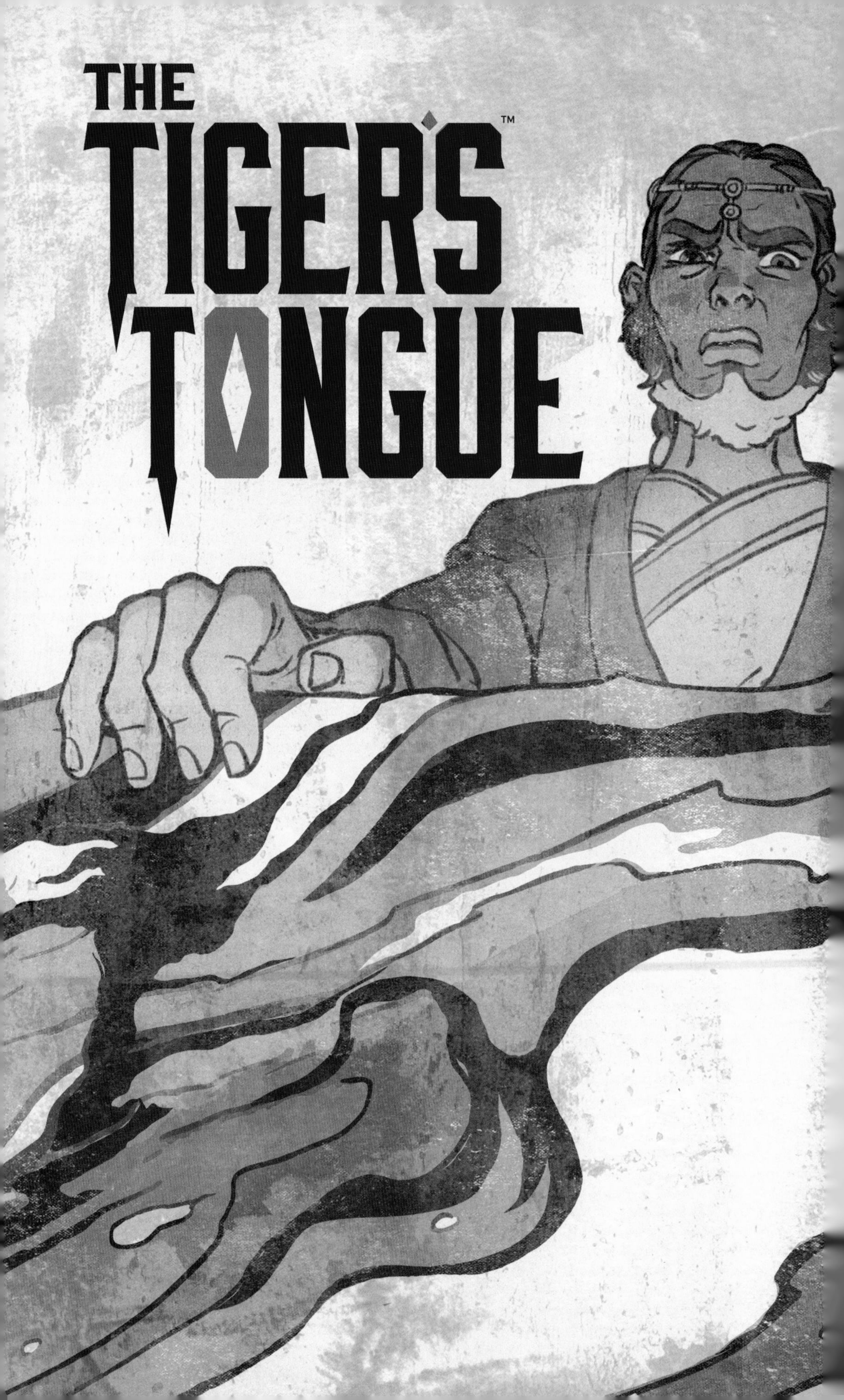
THE
TIGER'S™
TONGUE

OLIVIA STEPHENS
WRITER

ODERA IGBOKWE
COVER ARTIST

DIANSAKHU BANTON-PERRY
ARTIST

JOAMETTE GIL
LETTERER

BEX GLENDINING
INKER & COLORIST

MICHAEL MOCCIO
EDITOR

DAVID REYES
BOOK & LOGO DESIGNER

The Tiger's Tongue™ published by Mad Cave Studios, Inc. 8838 SW 129th St. Miami, FL 33176. Contains materials originally published in single magazine form as The Tiger's Tongue™ (2022) #1- 5.

First Printing. Printed in Canada.
ISBN: 978-1-952303-32-6

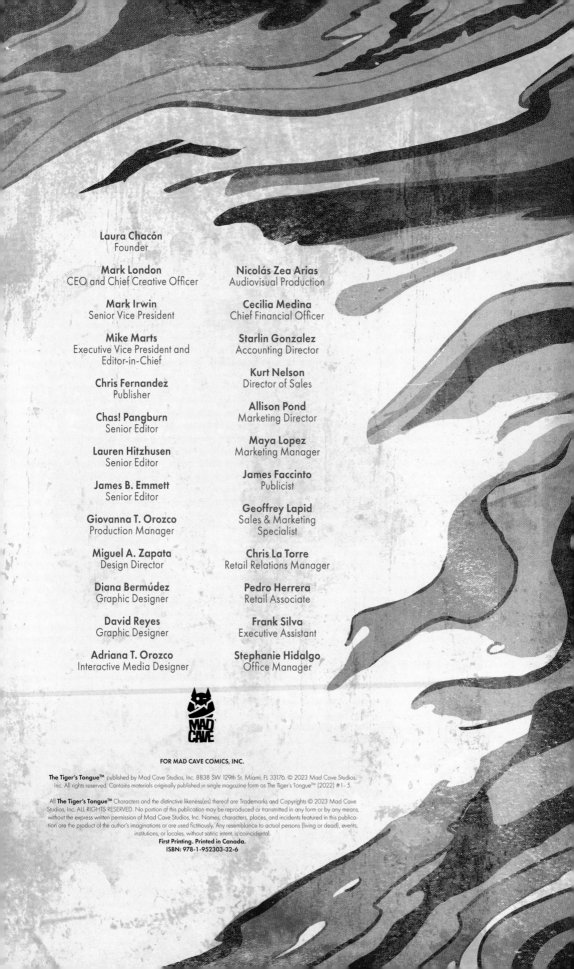

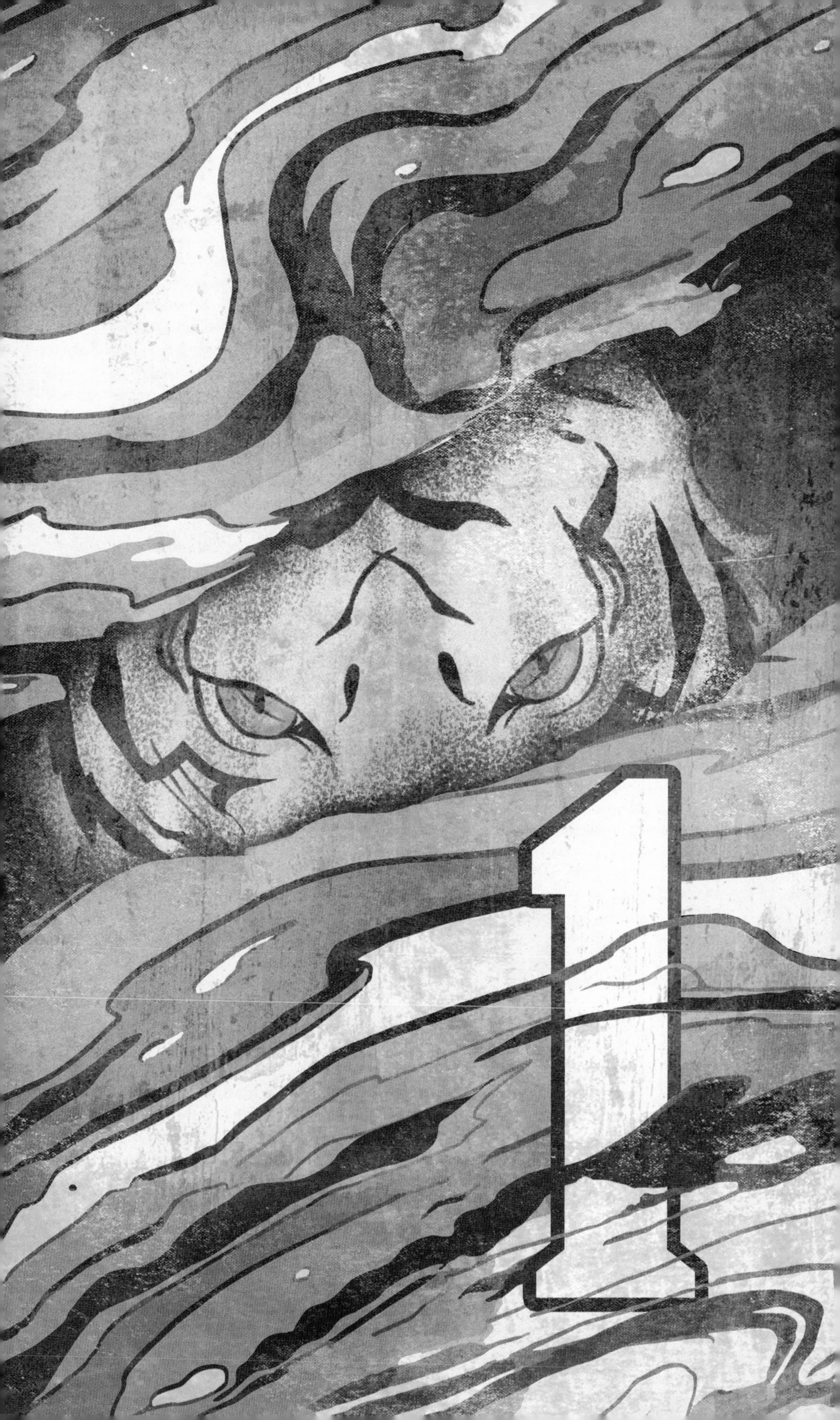
1

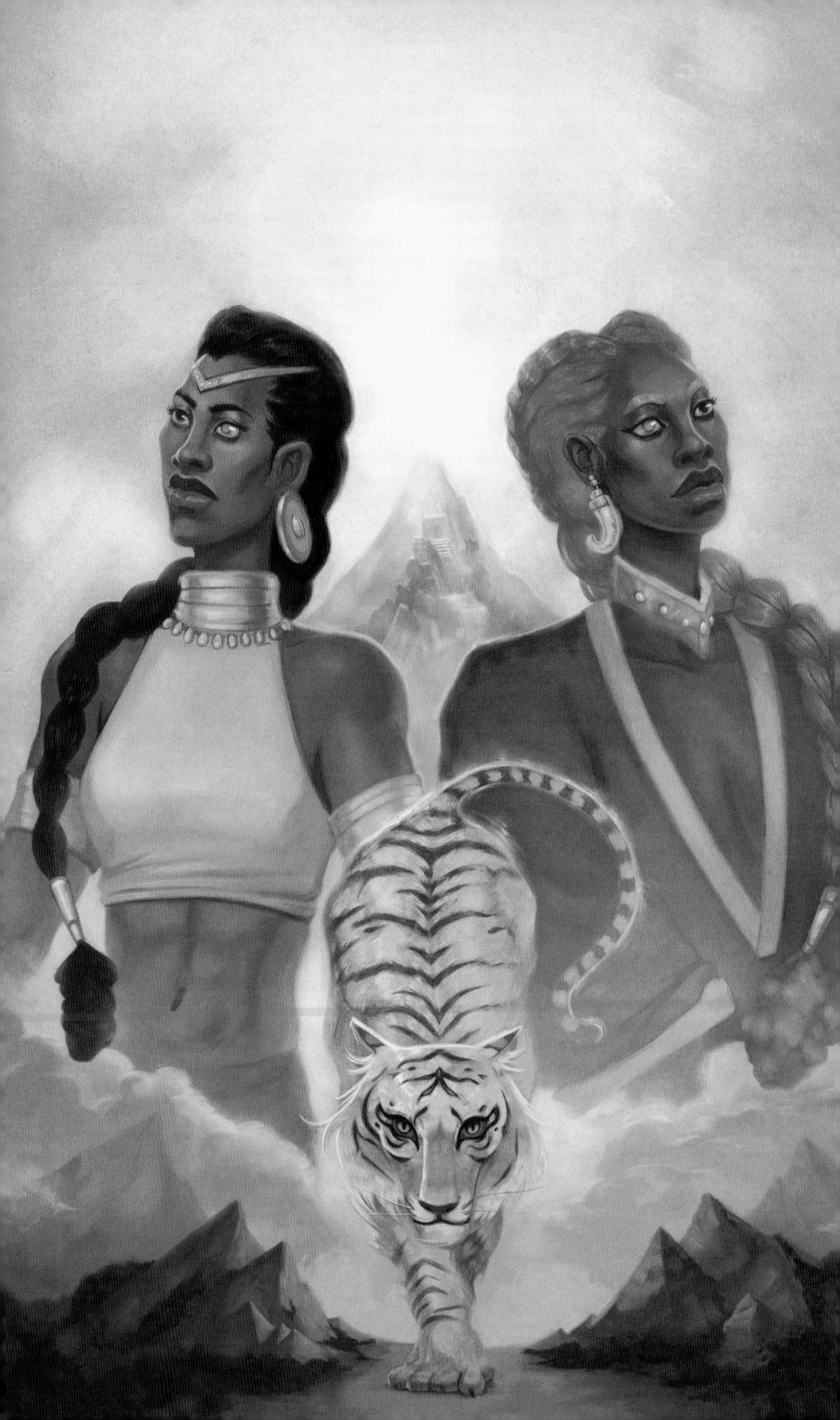

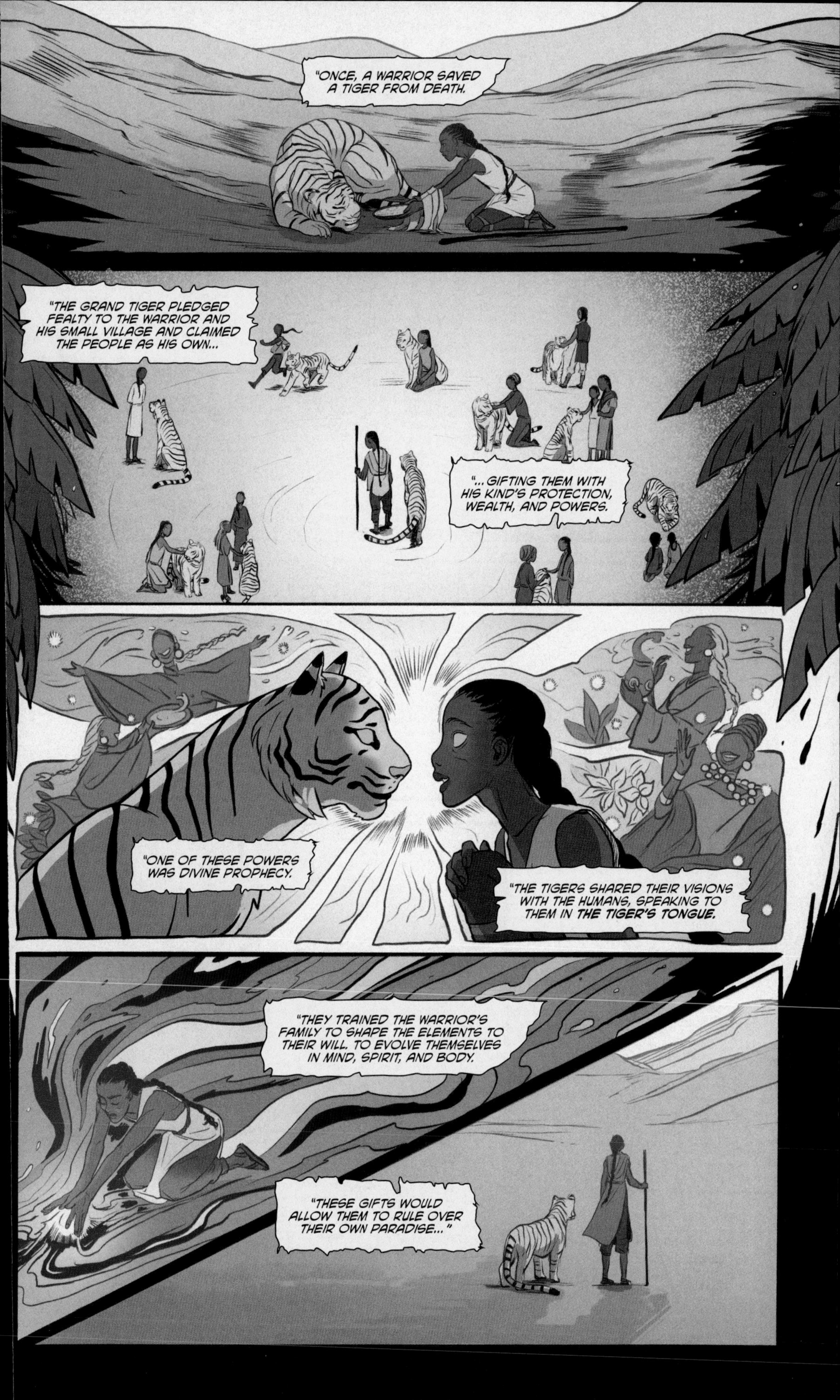
"ONCE, A WARRIOR SAVED A TIGER FROM DEATH.
"THE GRAND TIGER PLEDGED FEALTY TO THE WARRIOR AND HIS SMALL VILLAGE AND CLAIMED THE PEOPLE AS HIS OWN...
"...GIFTING THEM WITH HIS KIND'S PROTECTION, WEALTH, AND POWERS.
"ONE OF THESE POWERS WAS DIVINE PROPHECY.
"THE TIGERS SHARED THEIR VISIONS WITH THE HUMANS, SPEAKING TO THEM IN **THE TIGER'S TONGUE.**
"THEY TRAINED THE WARRIOR'S FAMILY TO SHAPE THE ELEMENTS TO THEIR WILL. TO EVOLVE THEMSELVES IN MIND, SPIRIT, AND BODY.
"THESE GIFTS WOULD ALLOW THEM TO RULE OVER THEIR OWN PARADISE..."

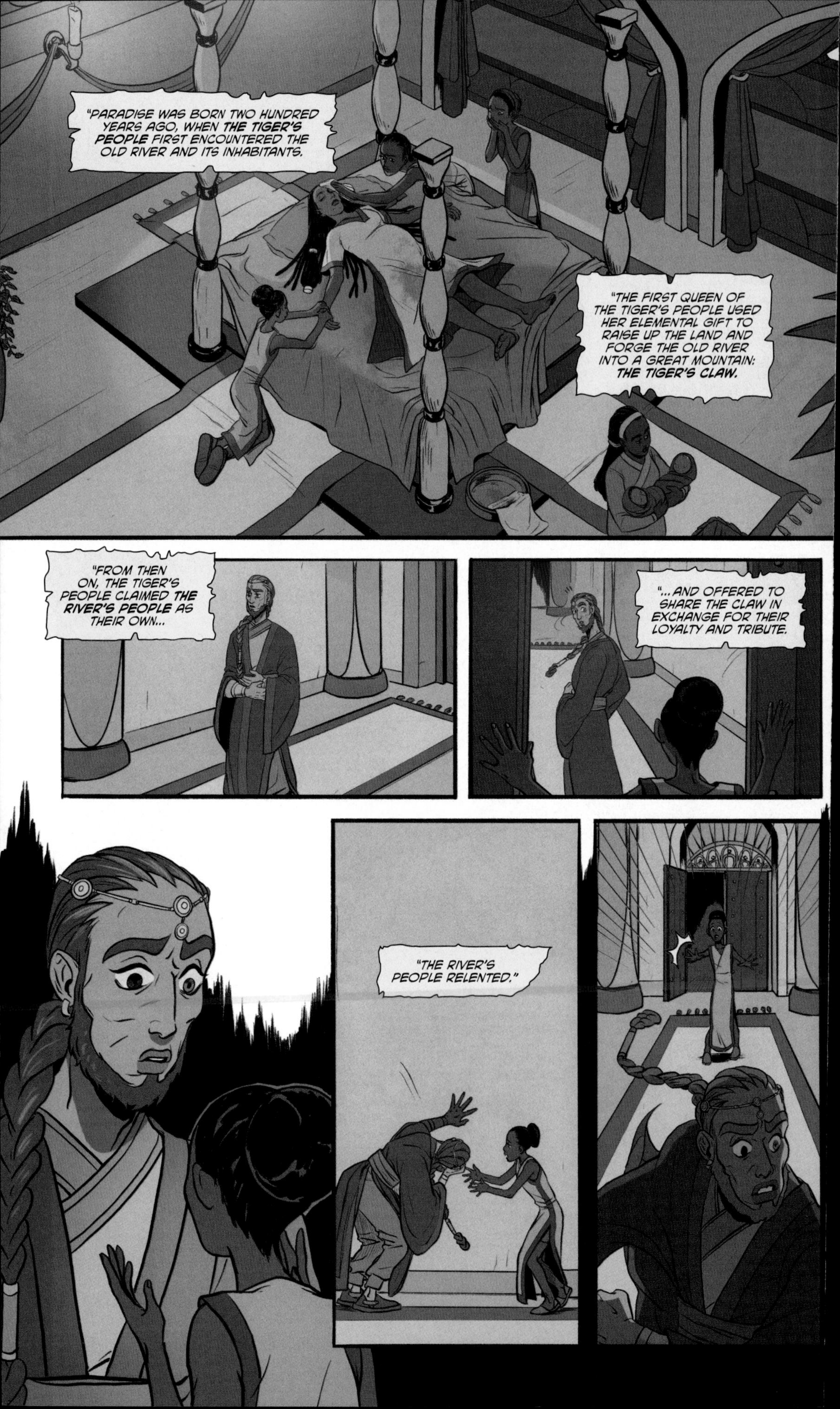
"PARADISE WAS BORN TWO HUNDRED YEARS AGO, WHEN **THE TIGER'S PEOPLE** FIRST ENCOUNTERED THE OLD RIVER AND ITS INHABITANTS.
"THE FIRST QUEEN OF THE TIGER'S PEOPLE USED HER ELEMENTAL GIFT TO RAISE UP THE LAND AND FORGE THE OLD RIVER INTO A GREAT MOUNTAIN: **THE TIGER'S CLAW.**
"FROM THEN ON, THE TIGER'S PEOPLE CLAIMED **THE RIVER'S PEOPLE** AS THEIR OWN...
"...AND OFFERED TO SHARE THE CLAW IN EXCHANGE FOR THEIR LOYALTY AND TRIBUTE.
"THE RIVER'S PEOPLE RELENTED."

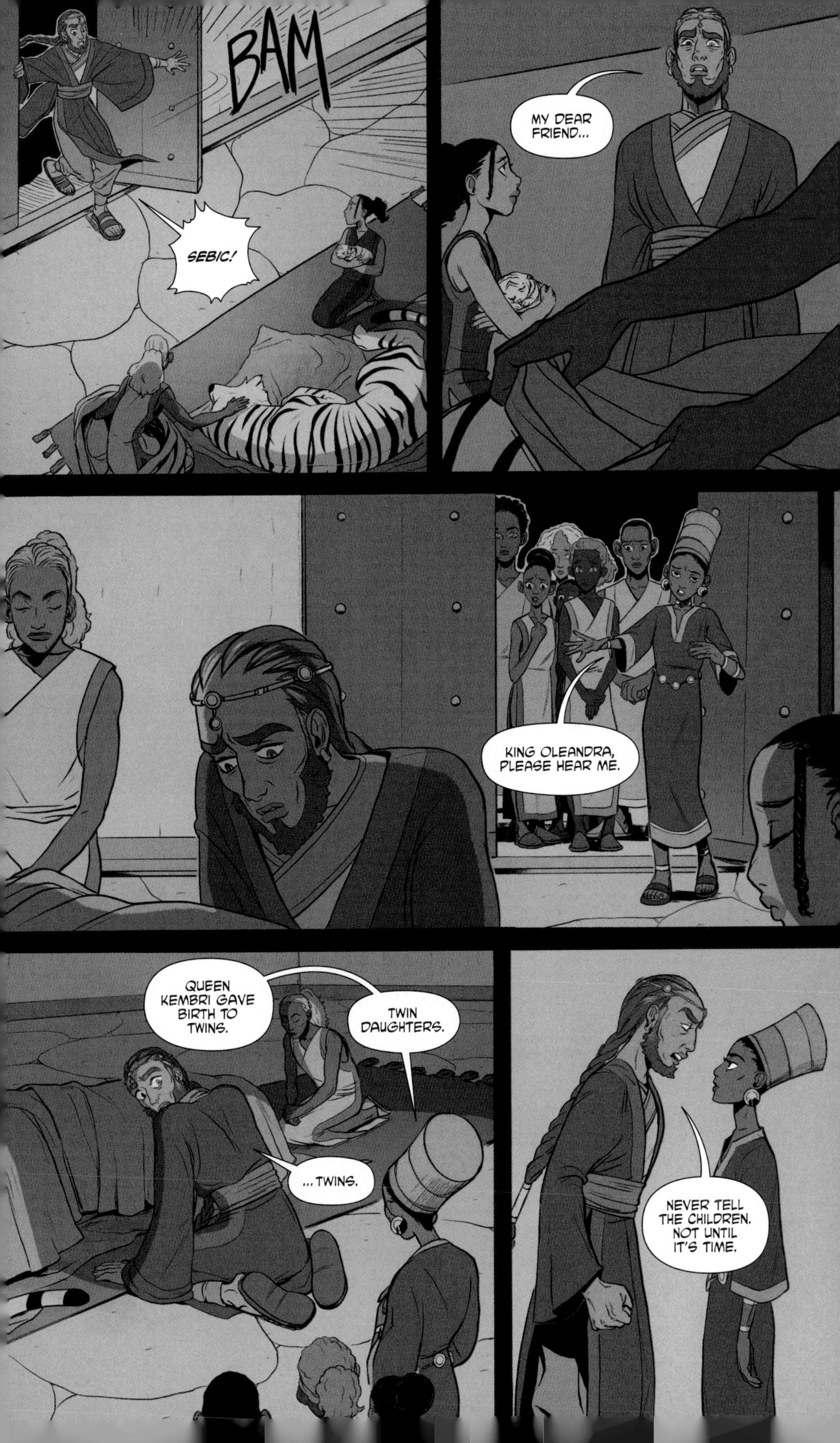
BAM
SEBIC!
MY DEAR FRIEND...
KING OLEANDRA, PLEASE HEAR ME.
QUEEN KEMBRI GAVE BIRTH TO TWINS.
TWIN DAUGHTERS.
...TWINS.
NEVER TELL THE CHILDREN. NOT UNTIL IT'S TIME.

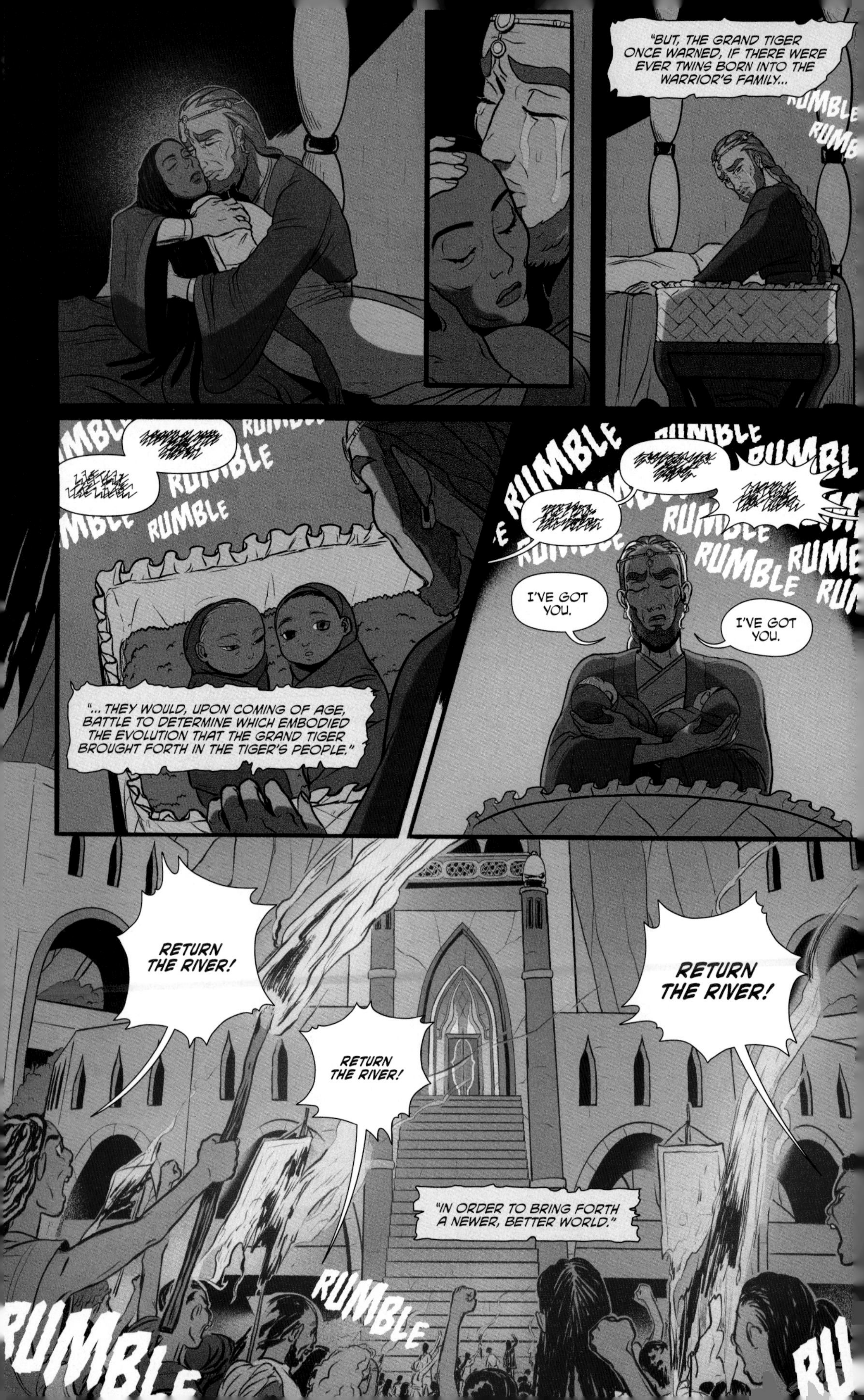
"BUT, THE GRAND TIGER ONCE WARNED, IF THERE WERE EVER TWINS BORN INTO THE WARRIOR'S FAMILY...
RUMBLE
RUMBLE
RUMBLE
RUMBLE
"... THEY WOULD, UPON COMING OF AGE, BATTLE TO DETERMINE WHICH EMBODIED THE EVOLUTION THAT THE GRAND TIGER BROUGHT FORTH IN THE TIGER'S PEOPLE."
RUMBLE
RUMBLE
RUMBLE
I'VE GOT YOU.
I'VE GOT YOU.
RETURN THE RIVER!
RETURN THE RIVER!
RETURN THE RIVER!
"IN ORDER TO BRING FORTH A NEWER, BETTER WORLD."
RUMBLE
RUMBLE

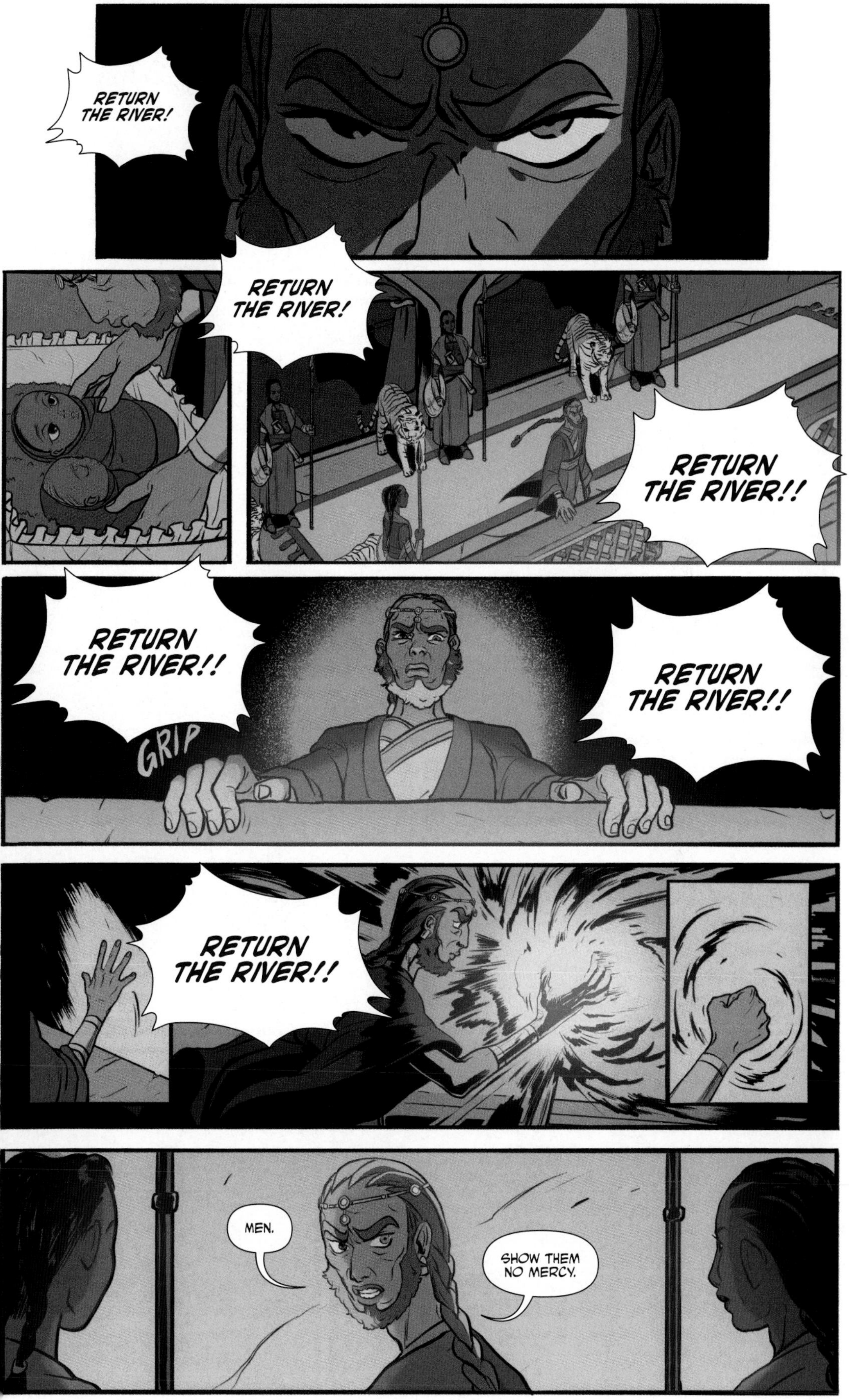
RETURN THE RIVER!
RETURN THE RIVER!
RETURN THE RIVER!!
RETURN THE RIVER!!
RETURN THE RIVER!!
GRIP
RETURN THE RIVER!!
MEN.
SHOW THEM NO MERCY.

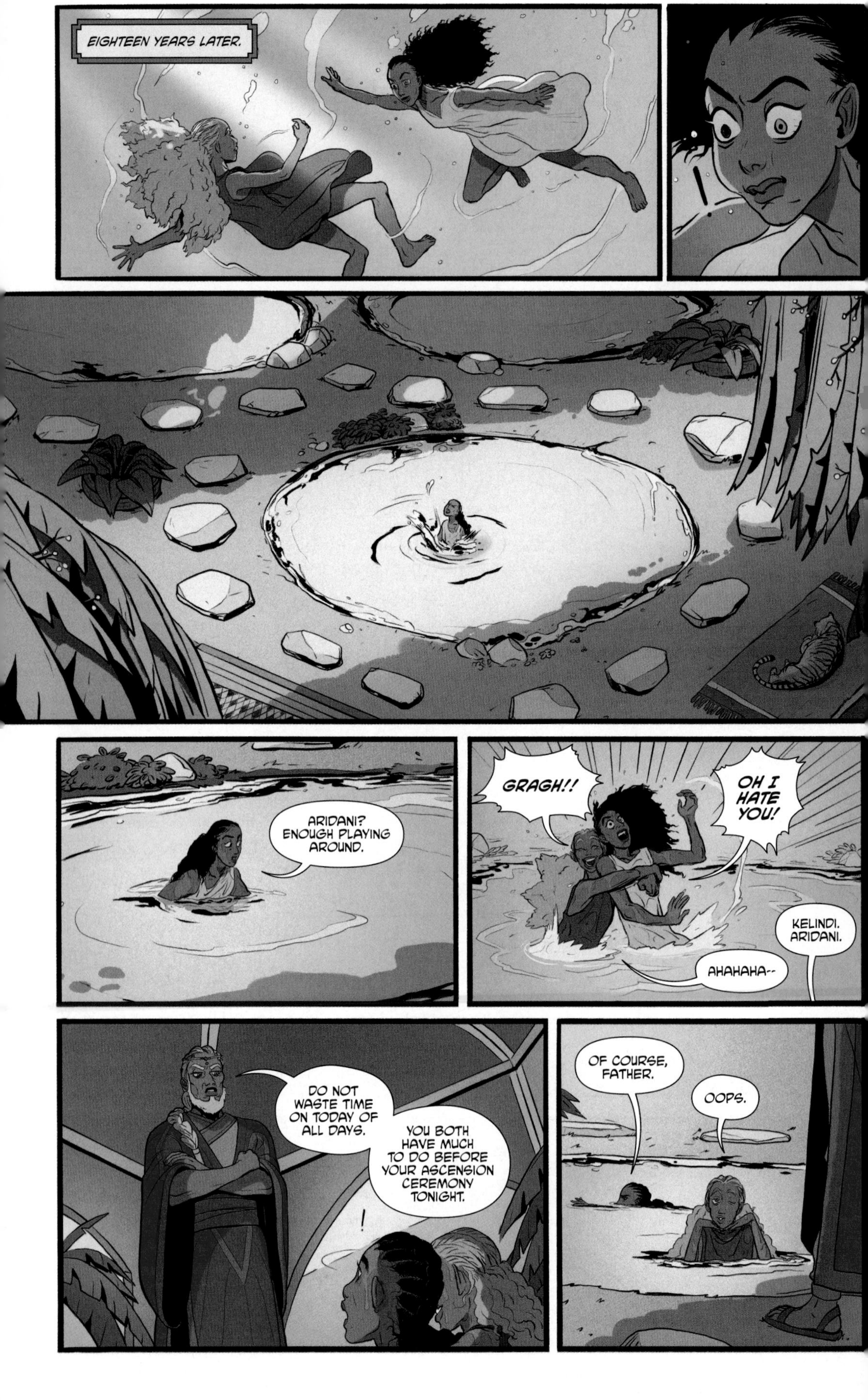
EIGHTEEN YEARS LATER.
!
ARIDANI? ENOUGH PLAYING AROUND.
GRAGH!!
OH I HATE YOU!
KELINDI. ARIDANI.
AHAHAHA--
DO NOT WASTE TIME ON TODAY OF ALL DAYS.
YOU BOTH HAVE MUCH TO DO BEFORE YOUR ASCENSION CEREMONY TONIGHT.
!
OF COURSE, FATHER.
OOPS.

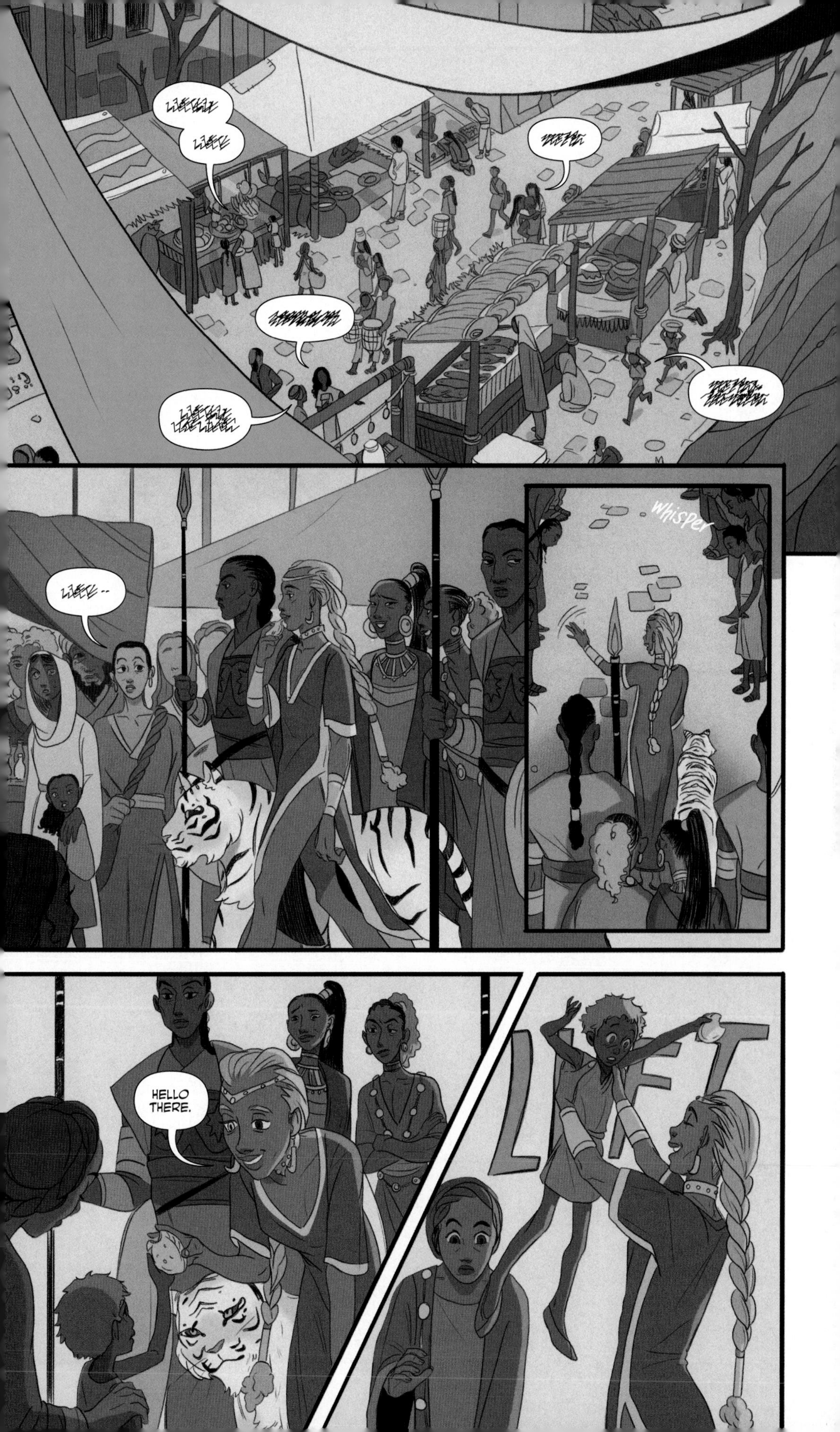
whisper
HELLO THERE.

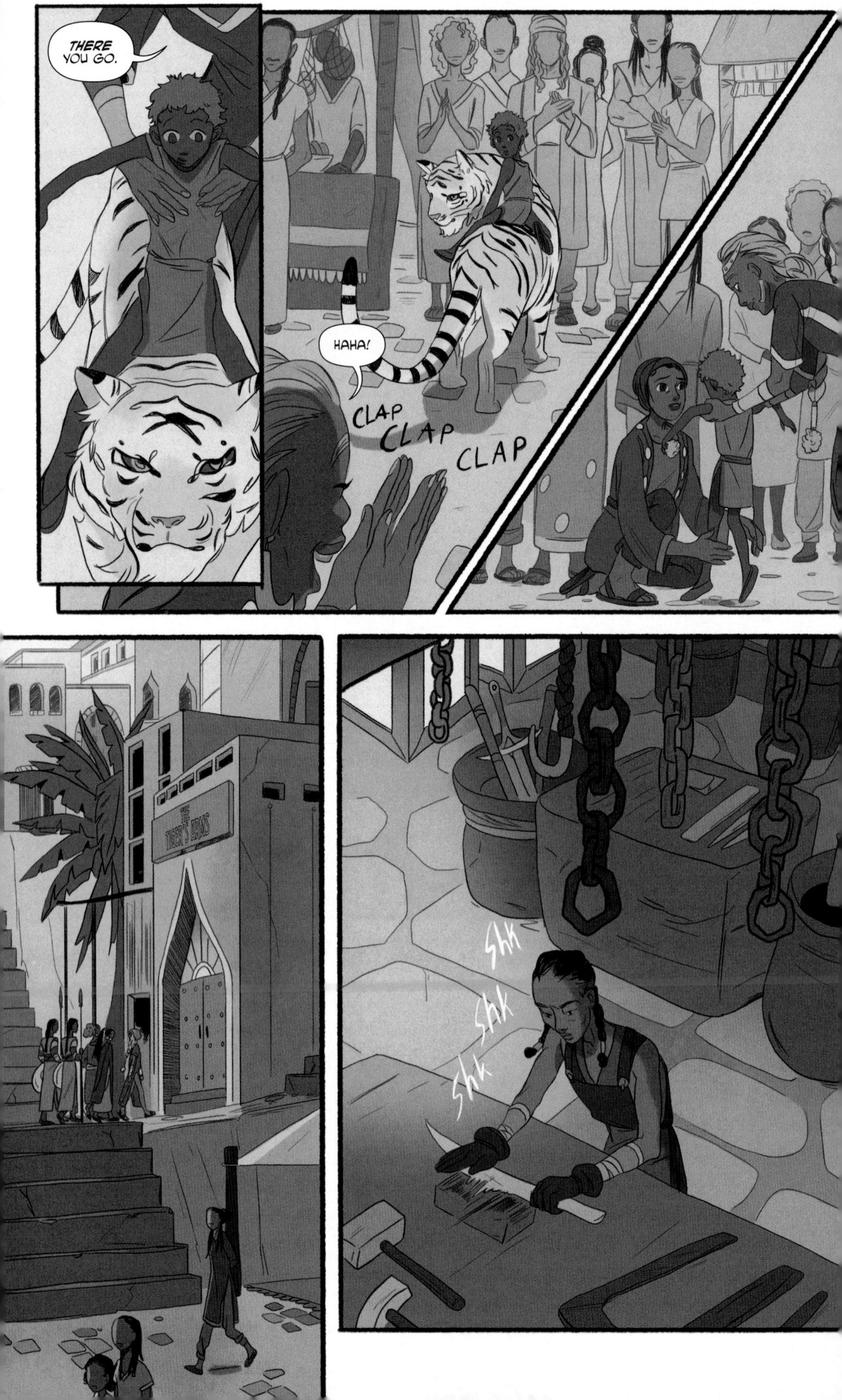
THERE YOU GO.
HAHA!
CLAP
CLAP
CLAP
THE TIGER'S ARMS
Shk
Shk
Shk

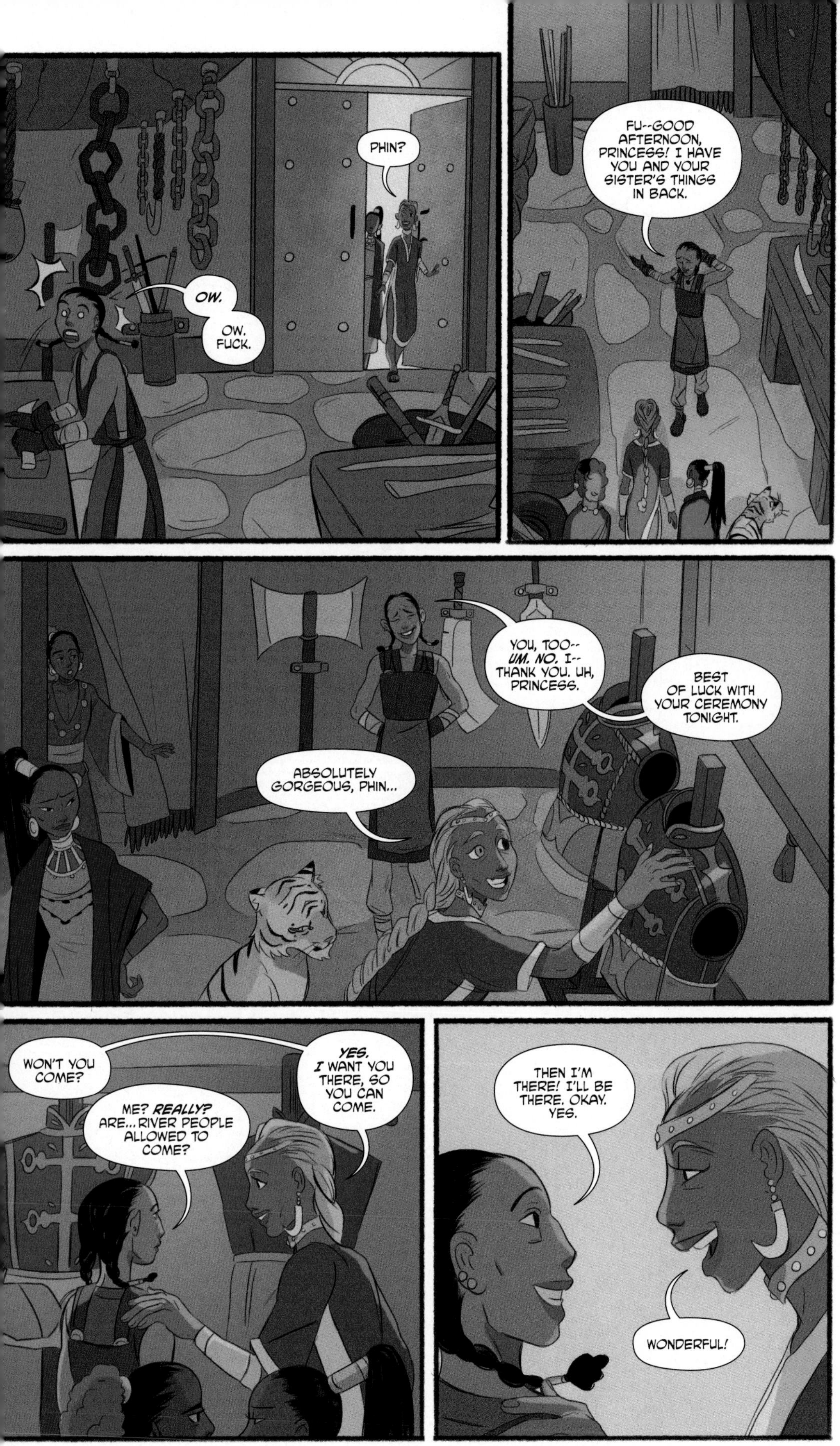
PHIN?
OW.
OW. FUCK.
FU--GOOD AFTERNOON, PRINCESS! I HAVE YOU AND YOUR SISTER'S THINGS IN BACK.
ABSOLUTELY GORGEOUS, PHIN...
YOU, TOO-- UM. NO. I-- THANK YOU. UH, PRINCESS.
BEST OF LUCK WITH YOUR CEREMONY TONIGHT.
WON'T YOU COME?
ME? REALLY? ARE... RIVER PEOPLE ALLOWED TO COME?
YES. I WANT YOU THERE, SO YOU CAN COME.
THEN I'M THERE! I'LL BE THERE. OKAY. YES.
WONDERFUL!

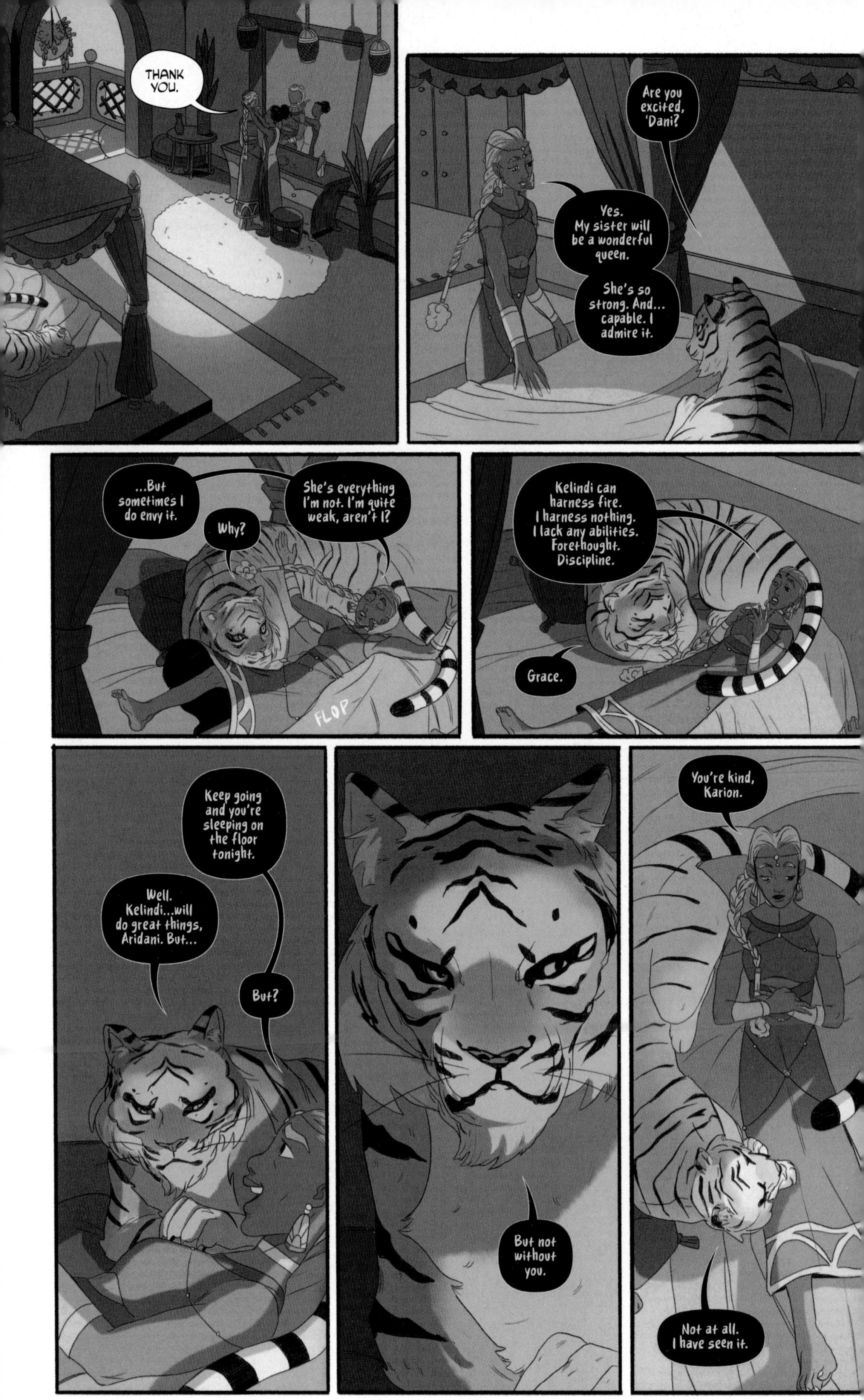
THANK YOU.
Are you excited, 'Dani?
Yes. My sister will be a wonderful queen.
She's so strong. And... capable. I admire it.
...But sometimes I do envy it.
Why?
She's everything I'm not. I'm quite weak, aren't I?
FLOP
Kelindi can harness fire. I harness nothing. I lack any abilities. Forethought. Discipline.
Grace.
Keep going and you're sleeping on the floor tonight.
Well. Kelindi...will do great things, Aridani. But...
But?
But not without you.
You're kind, Karion.
Not at all. I have seen it.

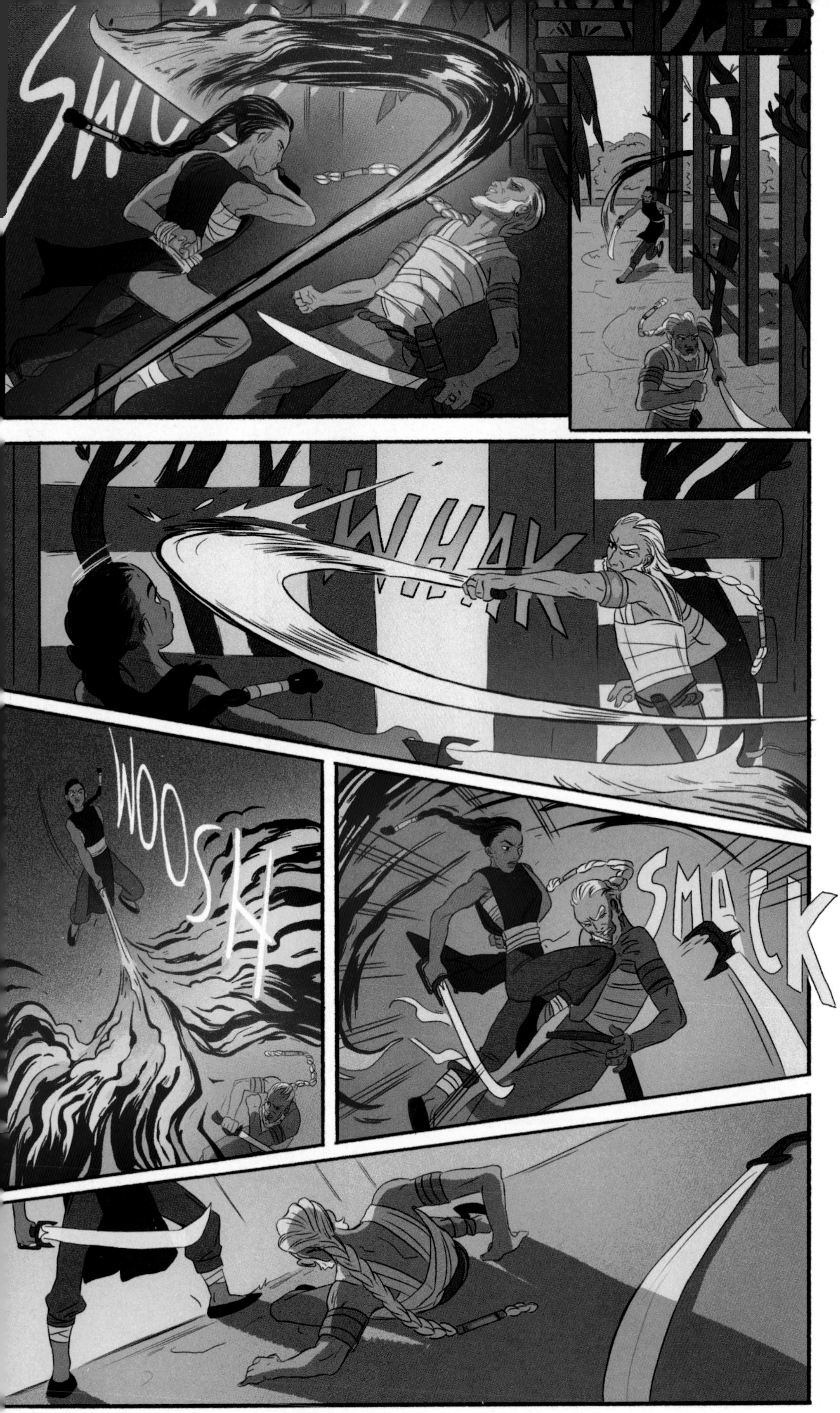
WHAK
WOOSH
SMACK

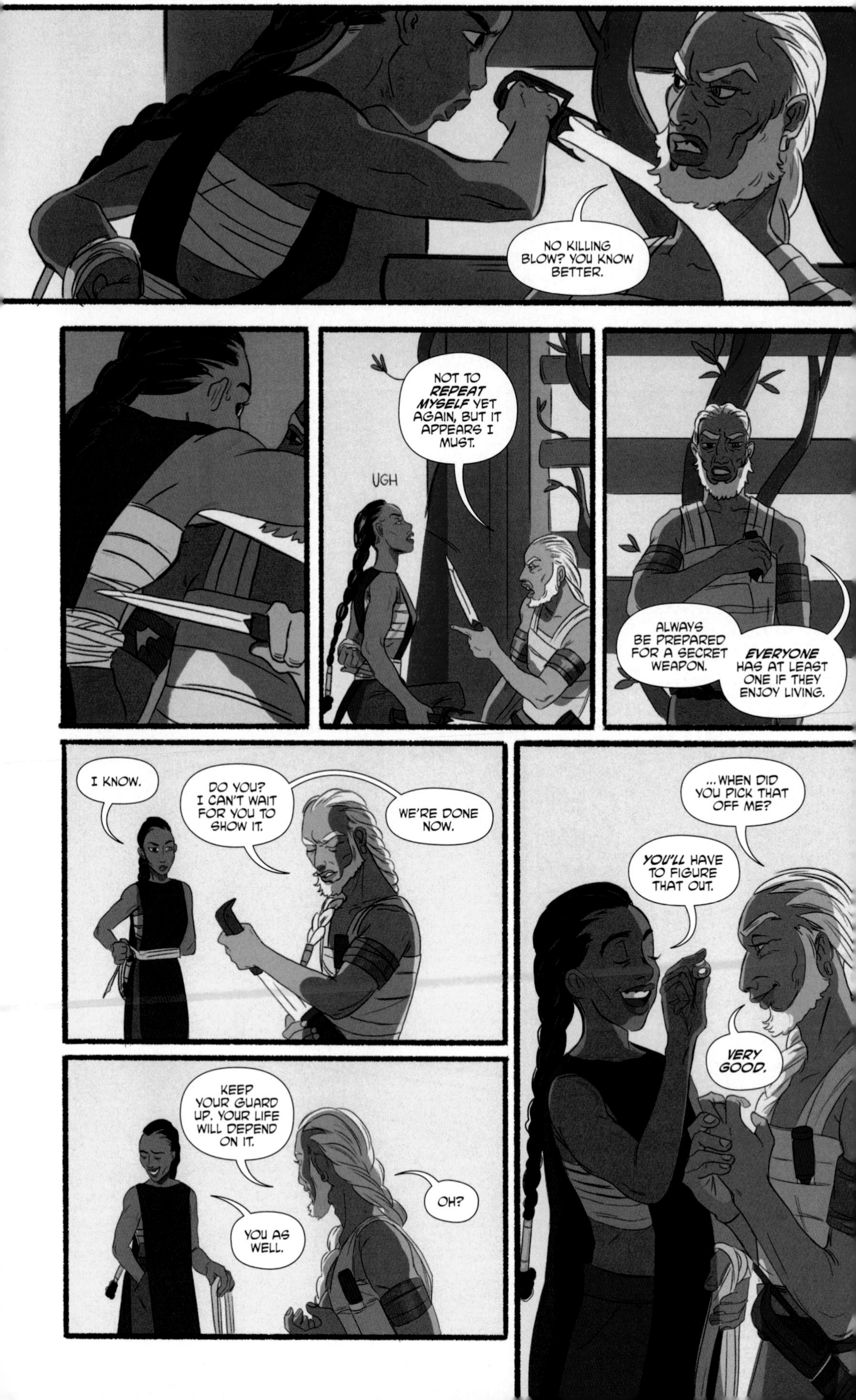
NO KILLING BLOW? YOU KNOW BETTER.
NOT TO REPEAT MYSELF YET AGAIN, BUT IT APPEARS I MUST.
UGH
ALWAYS BE PREPARED FOR A SECRET WEAPON.
EVERYONE HAS AT LEAST ONE IF THEY ENJOY LIVING.
I KNOW.
DO YOU? I CAN'T WAIT FOR YOU TO SHOW IT.
WE'RE DONE NOW.
KEEP YOUR GUARD UP. YOUR LIFE WILL DEPEND ON IT.
YOU AS WELL.
OH?
...WHEN DID YOU PICK THAT OFF ME?
YOU'LL HAVE TO FIGURE THAT OUT.
VERY GOOD.

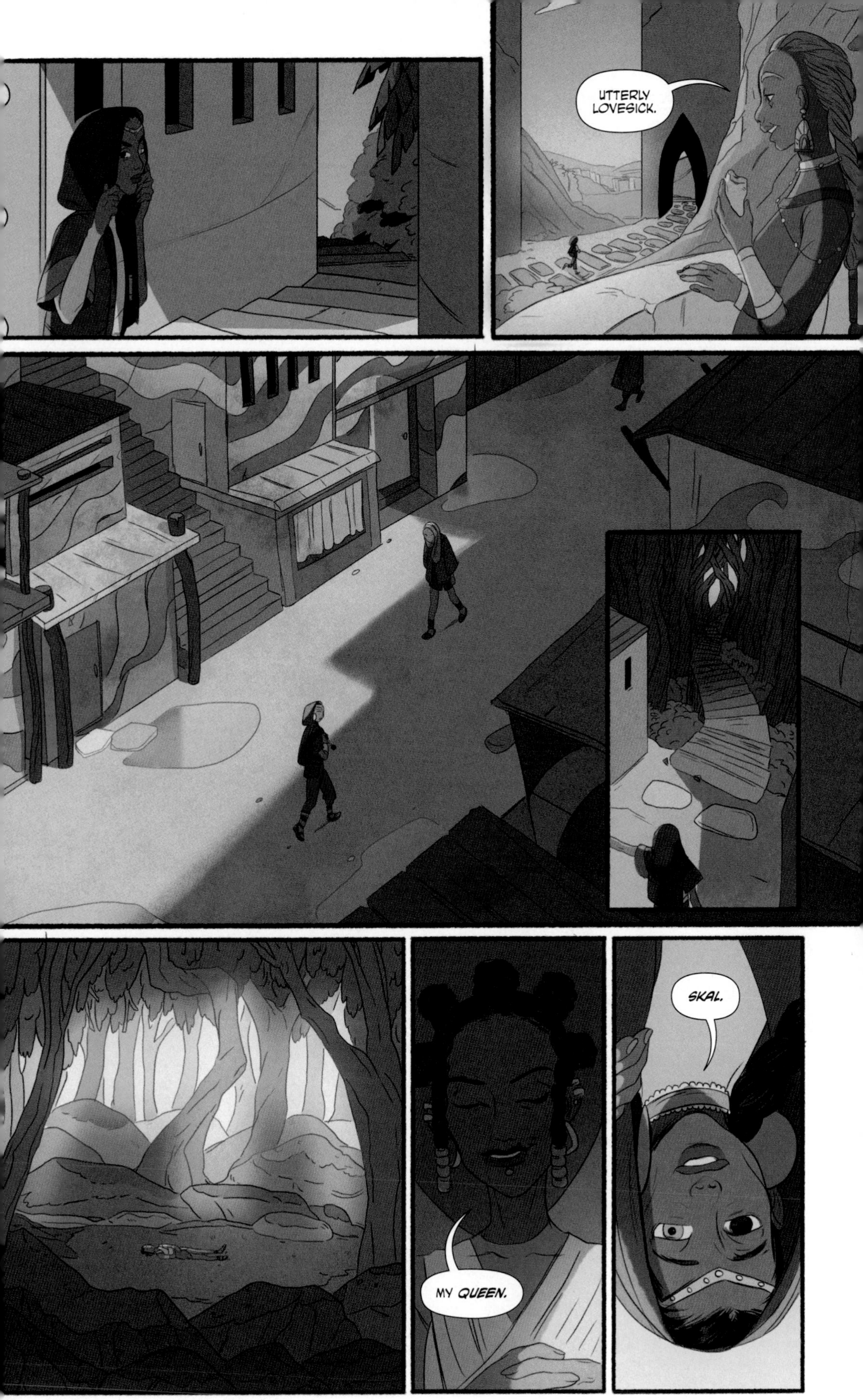
UTTERLY LOVESICK.
MY QUEEN.
SKAL.

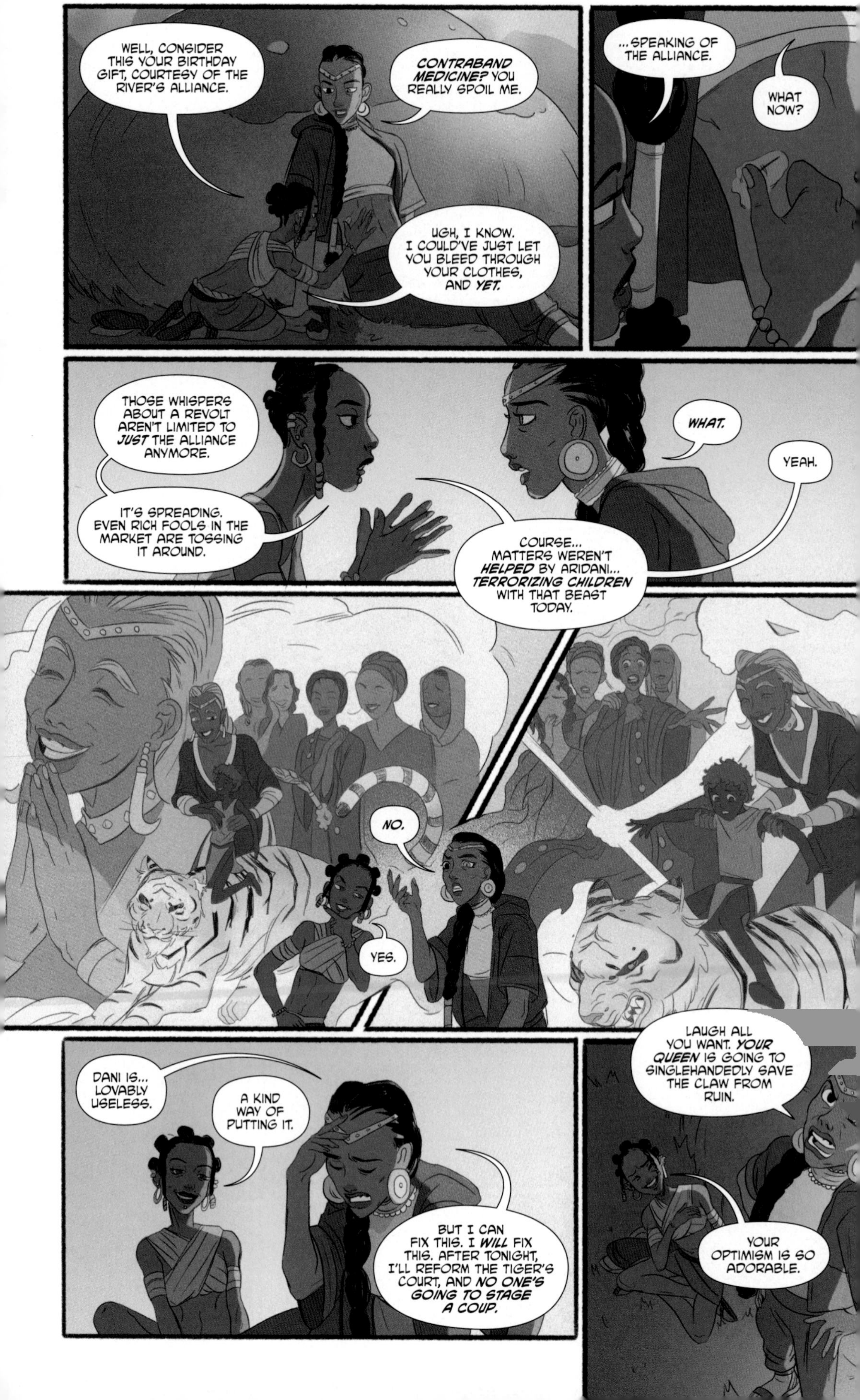
WELL, CONSIDER THIS YOUR BIRTHDAY GIFT, COURTESY OF THE RIVER'S ALLIANCE.
CONTRABAND MEDICINE? YOU REALLY SPOIL ME.
UGH, I KNOW. I COULD'VE JUST LET YOU BLEED THROUGH YOUR CLOTHES, AND YET.
...SPEAKING OF THE ALLIANCE.
WHAT NOW?
THOSE WHISPERS ABOUT A REVOLT AREN'T LIMITED TO JUST THE ALLIANCE ANYMORE.
IT'S SPREADING. EVEN RICH FOOLS IN THE MARKET ARE TOSSING IT AROUND.
WHAT.
YEAH.
COURSE... MATTERS WEREN'T HELPED BY ARIDANI... TERRORIZING CHILDREN WITH THAT BEAST TODAY.
NO.
YES.
DANI IS... LOVABLY USELESS.
A KIND WAY OF PUTTING IT.
BUT I CAN FIX THIS. I WILL FIX THIS. AFTER TONIGHT, I'LL REFORM THE TIGER'S COURT, AND NO ONE'S GOING TO STAGE A COUP.
LAUGH ALL YOU WANT. YOUR QUEEN IS GOING TO SINGLEHANDEDLY SAVE THE CLAW FROM RUIN.
YOUR OPTIMISM IS SO ADORABLE.

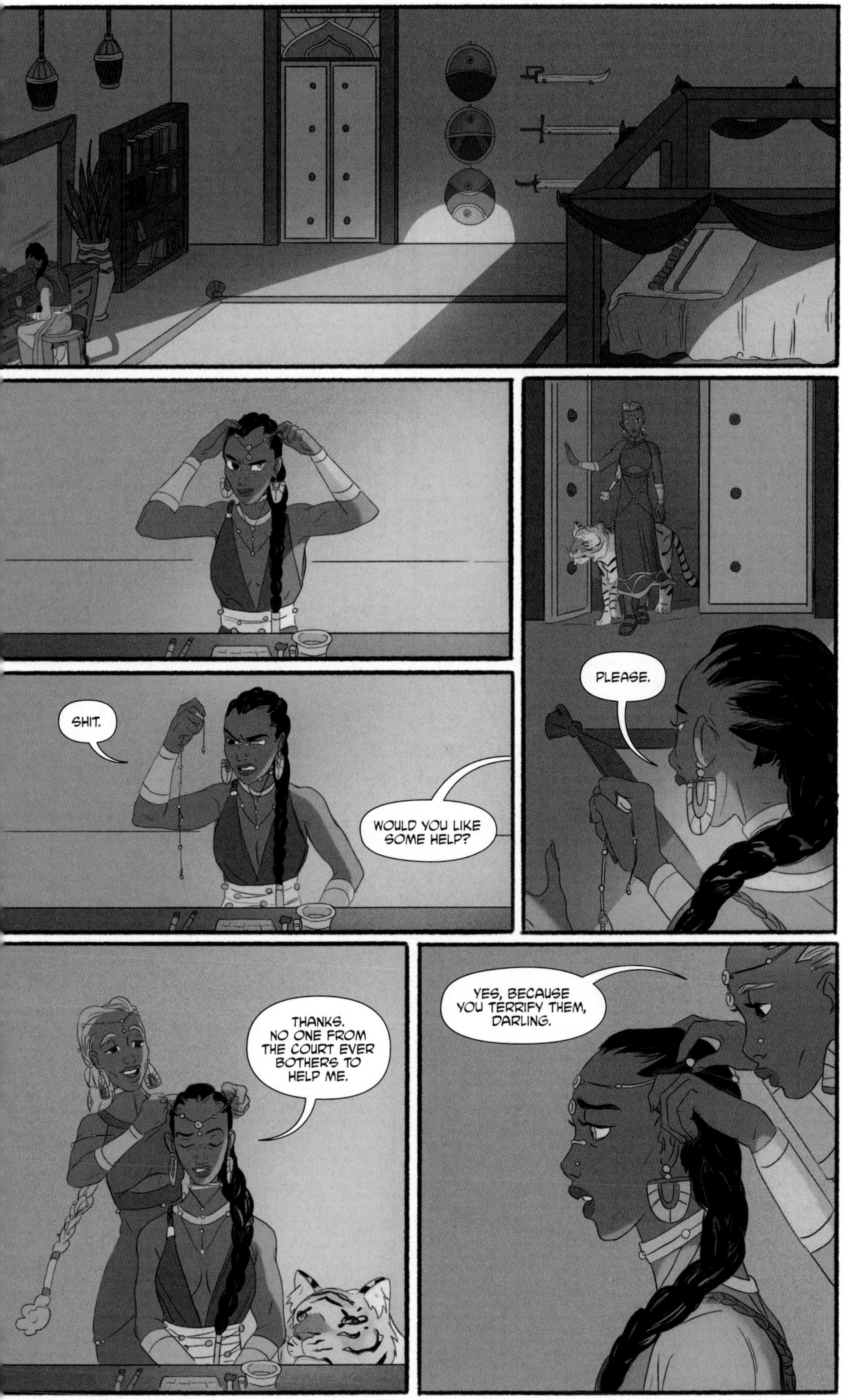
SHIT.
WOULD YOU LIKE SOME HELP?
PLEASE.
THANKS. NO ONE FROM THE COURT EVER BOTHERS TO HELP ME.
YES, BECAUSE YOU TERRIFY THEM, DARLING.

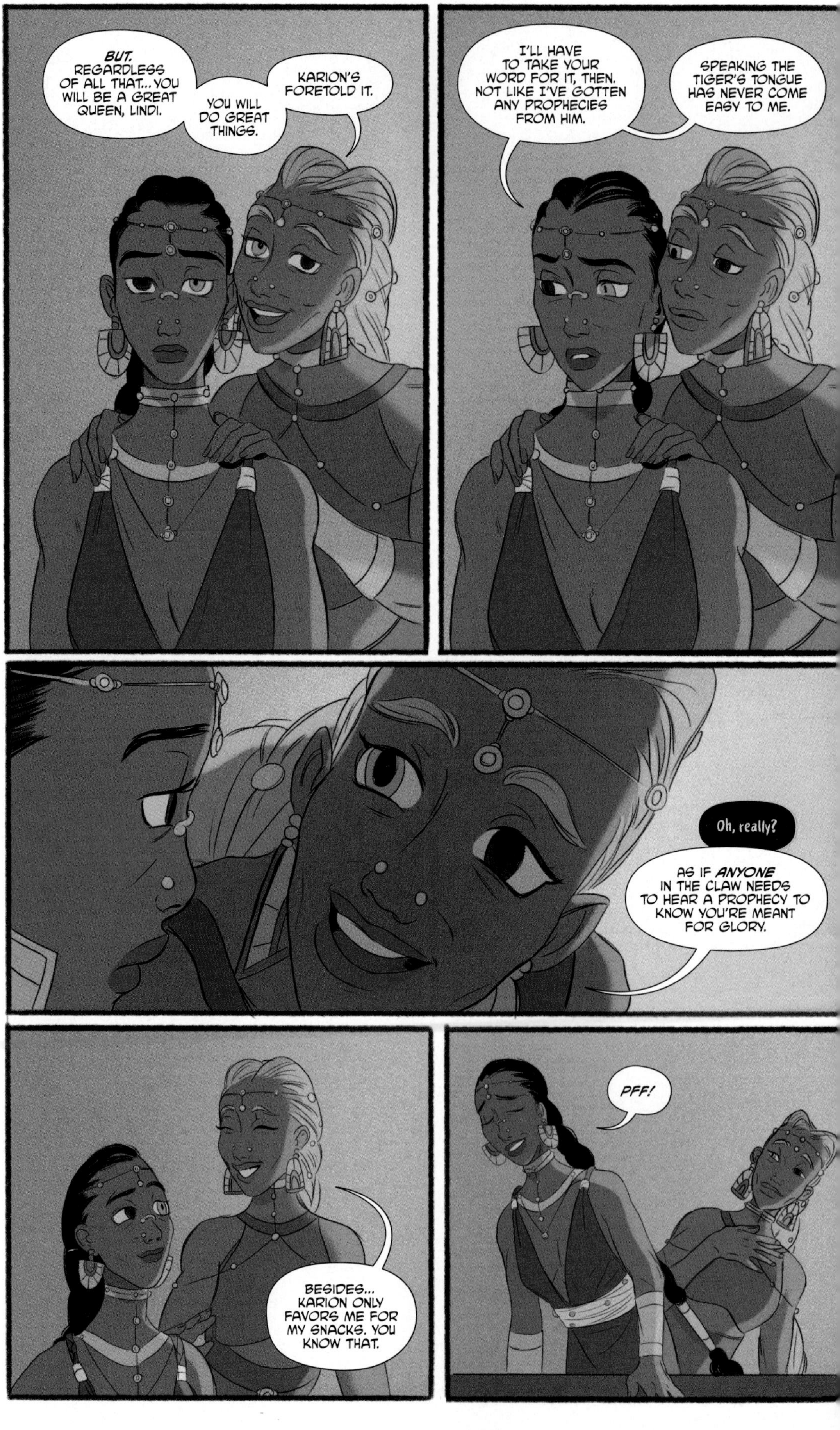
BUT. REGARDLESS OF ALL THAT... YOU WILL BE A GREAT QUEEN, LINDI.
YOU WILL DO GREAT THINGS.
KARION'S FORETOLD IT.
I'LL HAVE TO TAKE YOUR WORD FOR IT, THEN. NOT LIKE I'VE GOTTEN ANY PROPHECIES FROM HIM.
SPEAKING THE TIGER'S TONGUE HAS NEVER COME EASY TO ME.
Oh, really?
AS IF *ANYONE* IN THE CLAW NEEDS TO HEAR A PROPHECY TO KNOW YOU'RE MEANT FOR GLORY.
BESIDES... KARION ONLY FAVORS ME FOR MY SNACKS. YOU KNOW THAT.
PFF!

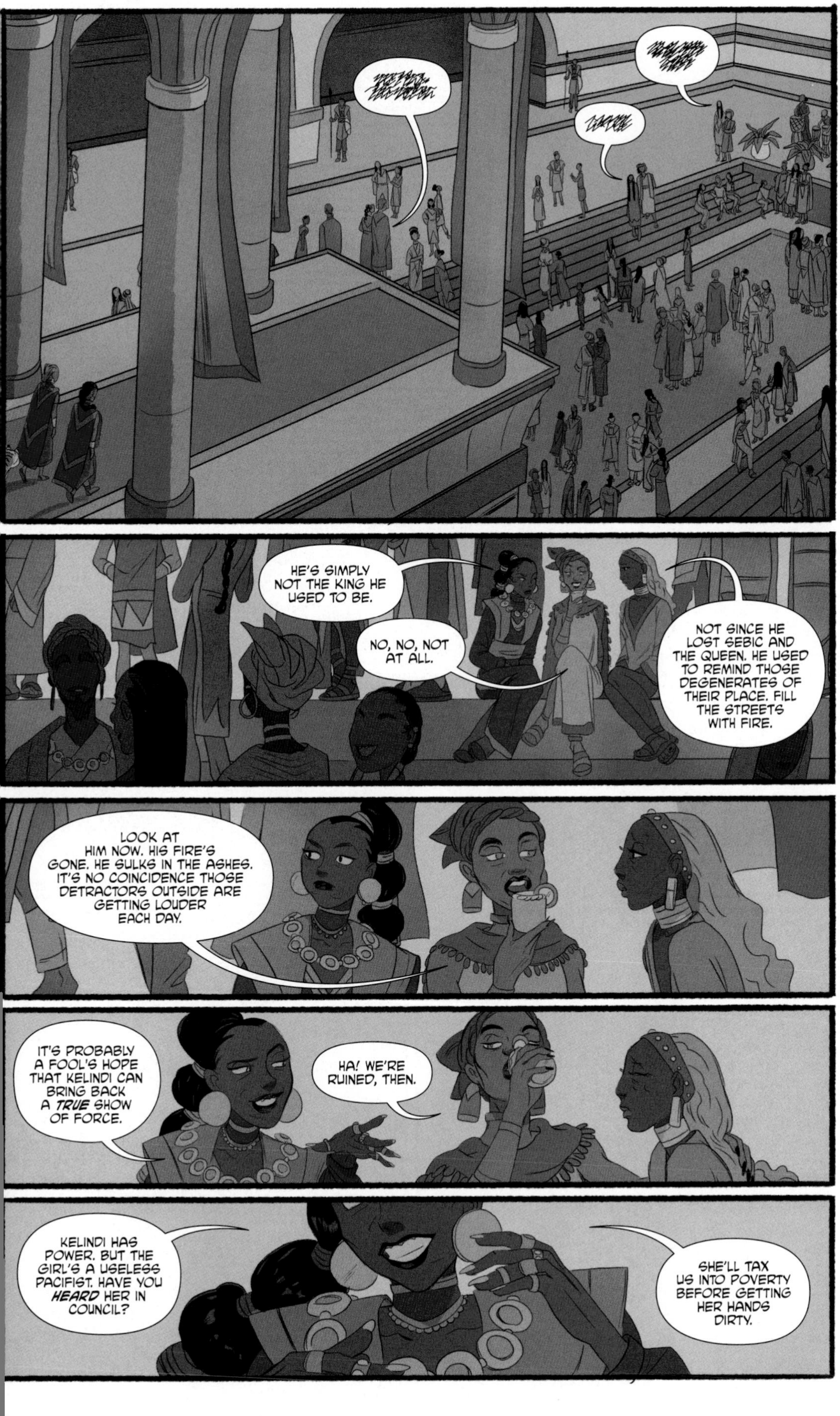
HE'S SIMPLY NOT THE KING HE USED TO BE.
NO, NO, NOT AT ALL.
NOT SINCE HE LOST SEBIC AND THE QUEEN. HE USED TO REMIND THOSE DEGENERATES OF THEIR PLACE. FILL THE STREETS WITH FIRE.
LOOK AT HIM NOW. HIS FIRE'S GONE. HE SULKS IN THE ASHES. IT'S NO COINCIDENCE THOSE DETRACTORS OUTSIDE ARE GETTING LOUDER EACH DAY.
IT'S PROBABLY A FOOL'S HOPE THAT KELINDI CAN BRING BACK A *TRUE* SHOW OF FORCE.
HA! WE'RE RUINED, THEN.
KELINDI HAS POWER. BUT THE GIRL'S A USELESS PACIFIST. HAVE YOU *HEARD* HER IN COUNCIL?
SHE'LL TAX US INTO POVERTY BEFORE GETTING HER HANDS DIRTY.

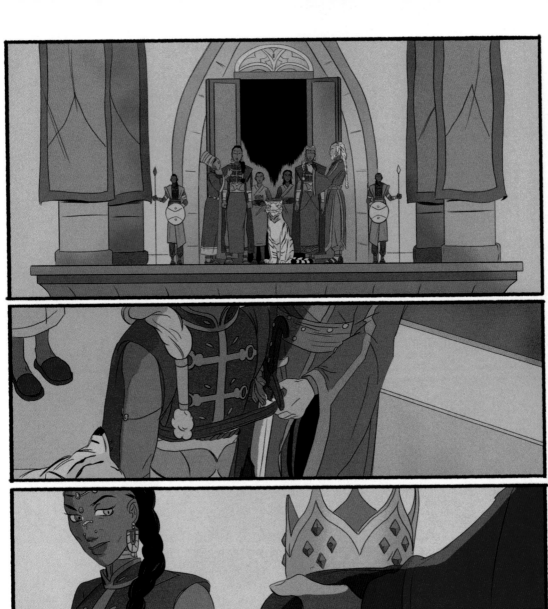

...FATHER?

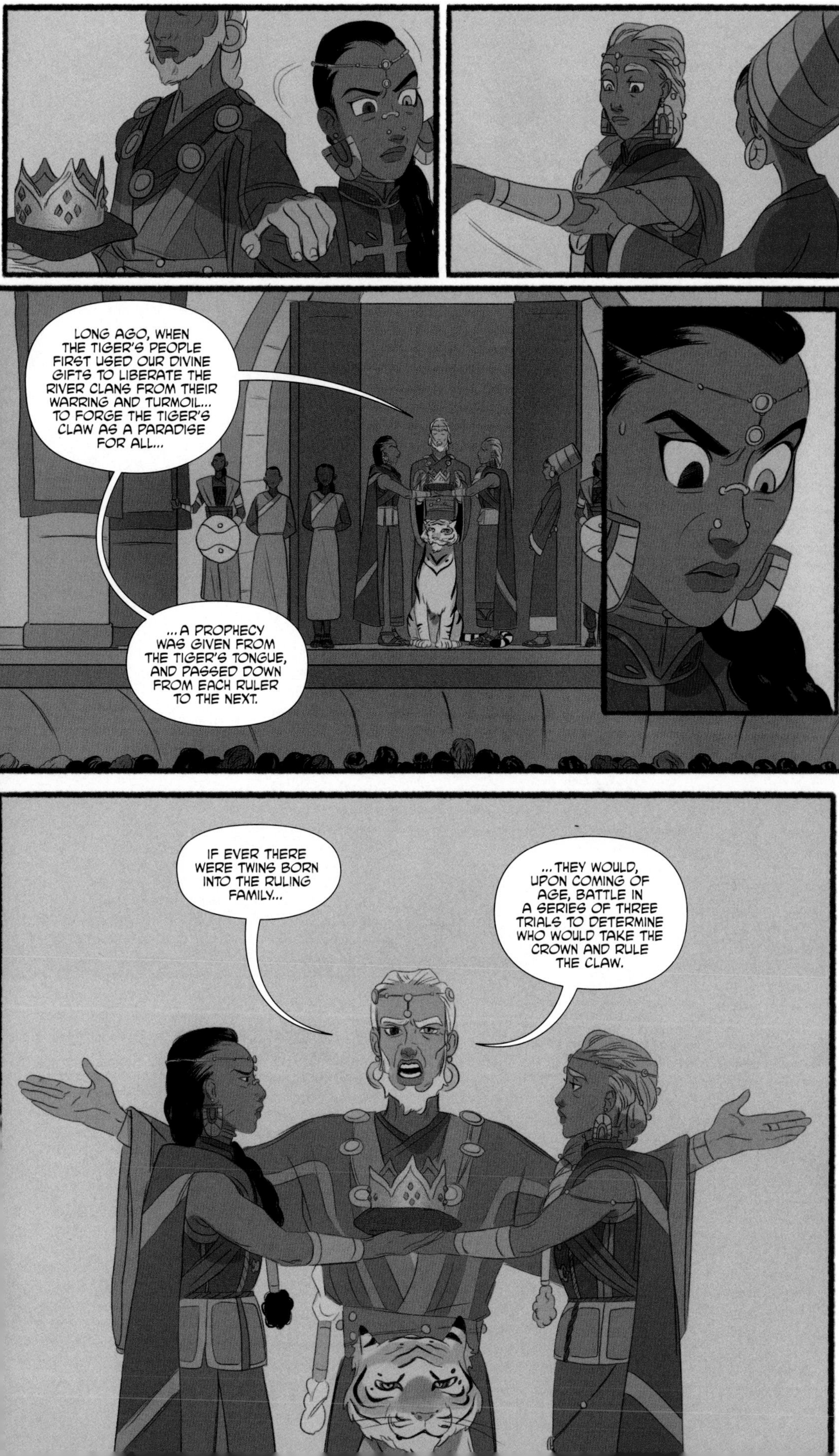
LONG AGO, WHEN THE TIGER'S PEOPLE FIRST USED OUR DIVINE GIFTS TO LIBERATE THE RIVER CLANS FROM THEIR WARRING AND TURMOIL... TO FORGE THE TIGER'S CLAW AS A PARADISE FOR ALL...
...A PROPHECY WAS GIVEN FROM THE TIGER'S TONGUE, AND PASSED DOWN FROM EACH RULER TO THE NEXT.
IF EVER THERE WERE TWINS BORN INTO THE RULING FAMILY...
...THEY WOULD, UPON COMING OF AGE, BATTLE IN A SERIES OF THREE TRIALS TO DETERMINE WHO WOULD TAKE THE CROWN AND RULE THE CLAW.

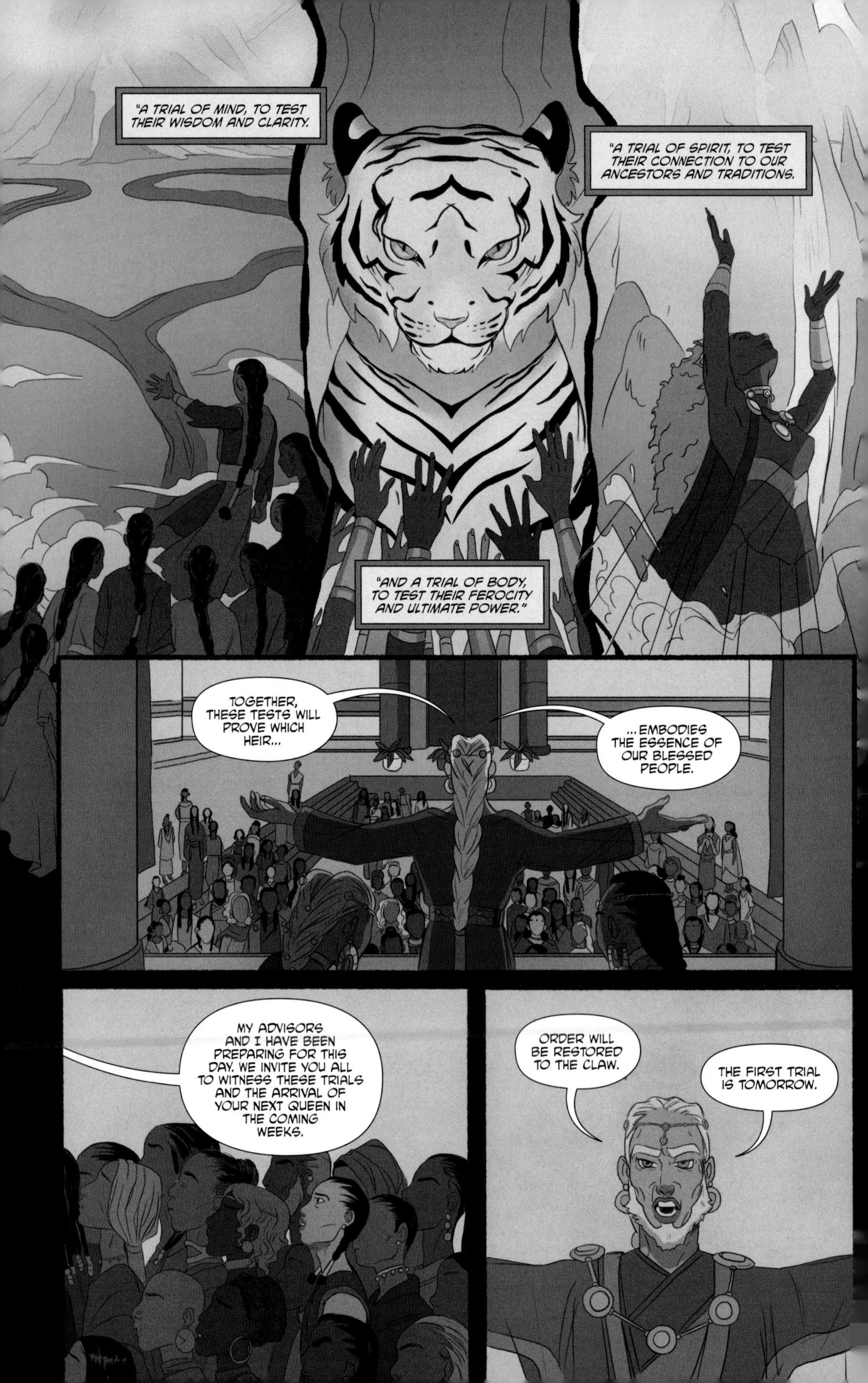
"A TRIAL OF MIND, TO TEST THEIR WISDOM AND CLARITY.
"A TRIAL OF SPIRIT, TO TEST THEIR CONNECTION TO OUR ANCESTORS AND TRADITIONS.
"AND A TRIAL OF BODY, TO TEST THEIR FEROCITY AND ULTIMATE POWER."
TOGETHER, THESE TESTS WILL PROVE WHICH HEIR...
...EMBODIES THE ESSENCE OF OUR BLESSED PEOPLE.
MY ADVISORS AND I HAVE BEEN PREPARING FOR THIS DAY. WE INVITE YOU ALL TO WITNESS THESE TRIALS AND THE ARRIVAL OF YOUR NEXT QUEEN IN THE COMING WEEKS.
ORDER WILL BE RESTORED TO THE CLAW.
THE FIRST TRIAL IS TOMORROW.

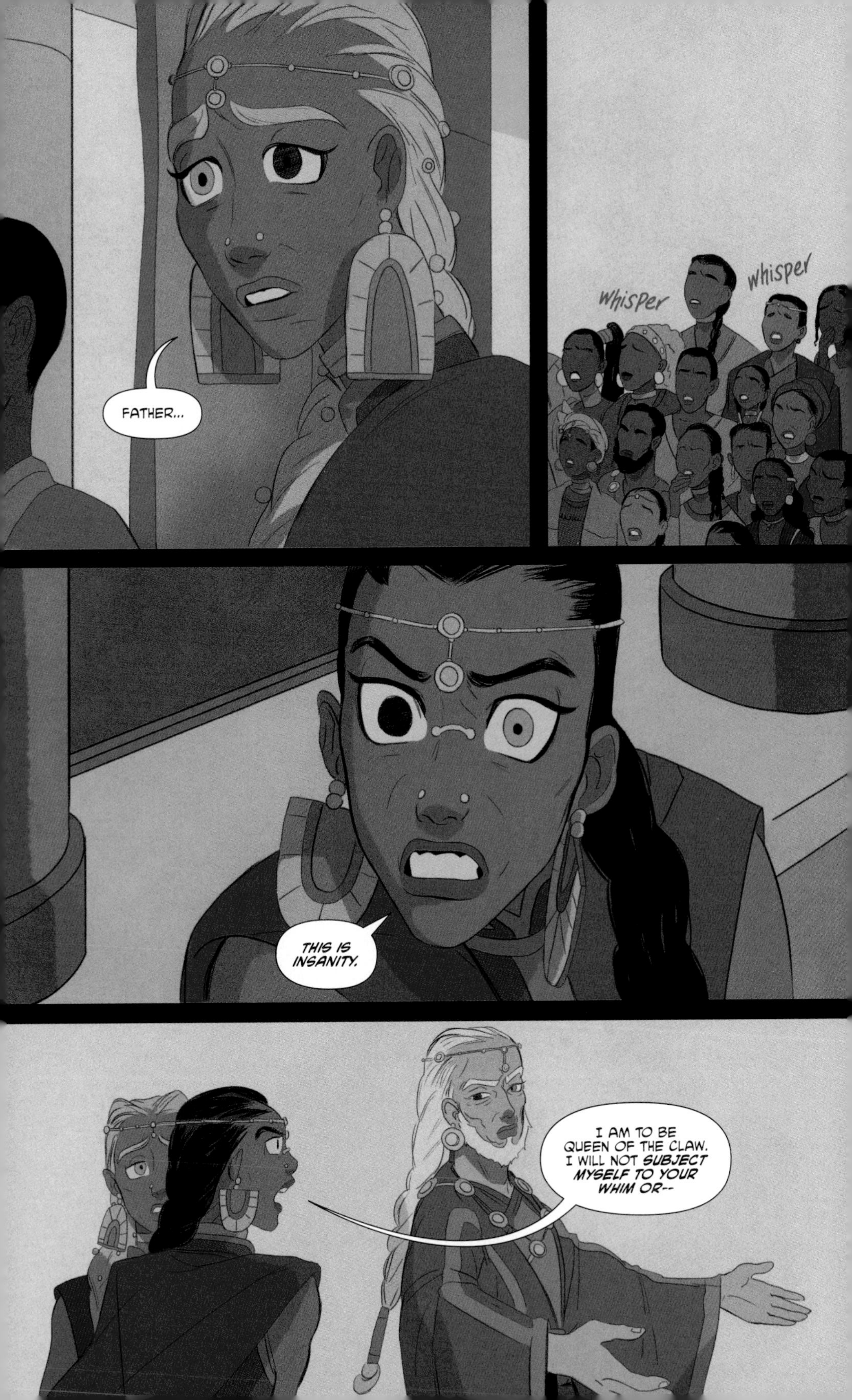
FATHER...
whisper
whisper
THIS IS INSANITY.
I AM TO BE QUEEN OF THE CLAW. I WILL NOT SUBJECT MYSELF TO YOUR WHIM OR--

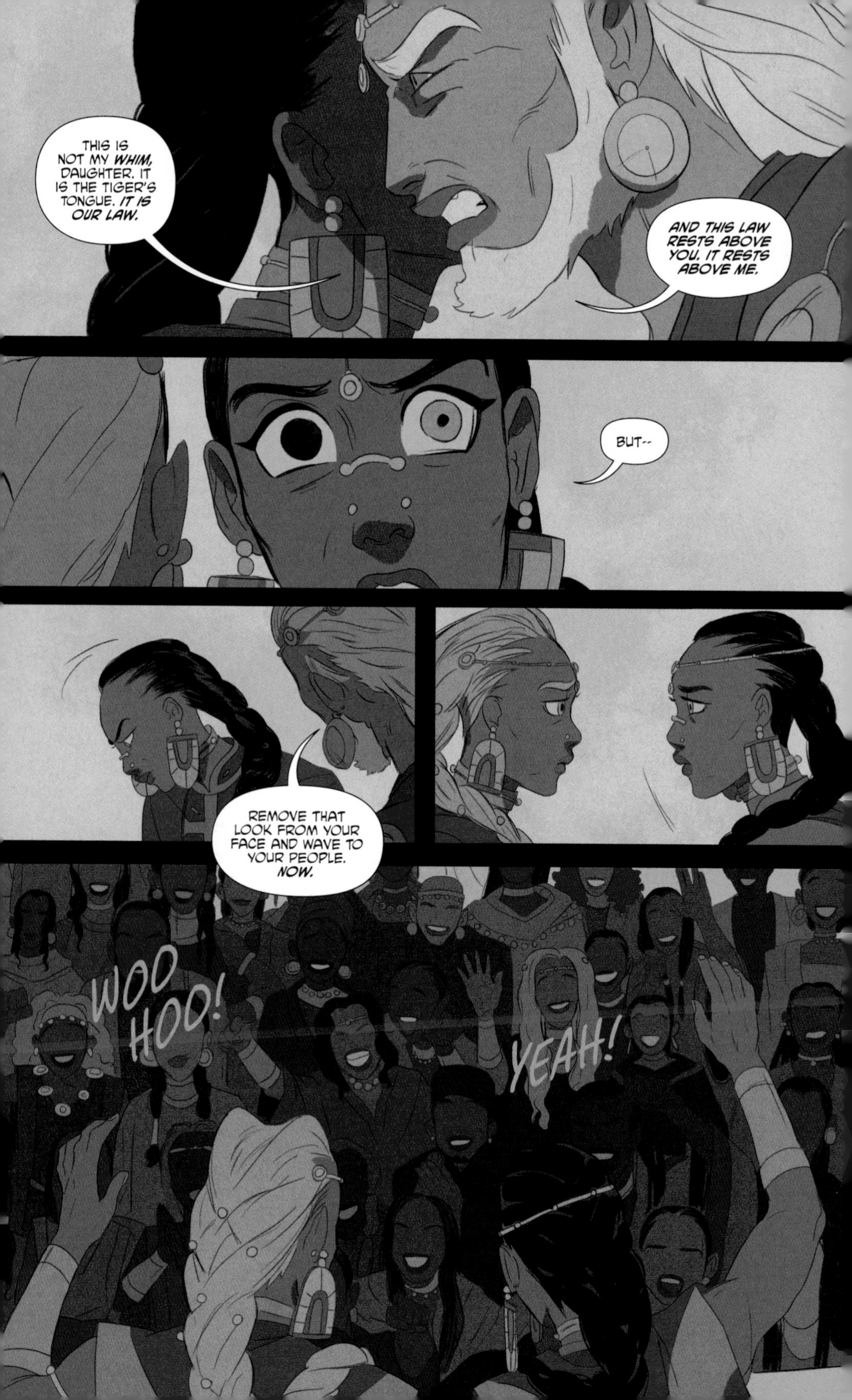
THIS IS NOT MY WHIM, DAUGHTER. IT IS THE TIGER'S TONGUE. IT IS OUR LAW.
AND THIS LAW RESTS ABOVE YOU. IT RESTS ABOVE ME.
BUT--
REMOVE THAT LOOK FROM YOUR FACE AND WAVE TO YOUR PEOPLE. NOW.
WOO HOO!
YEAH!

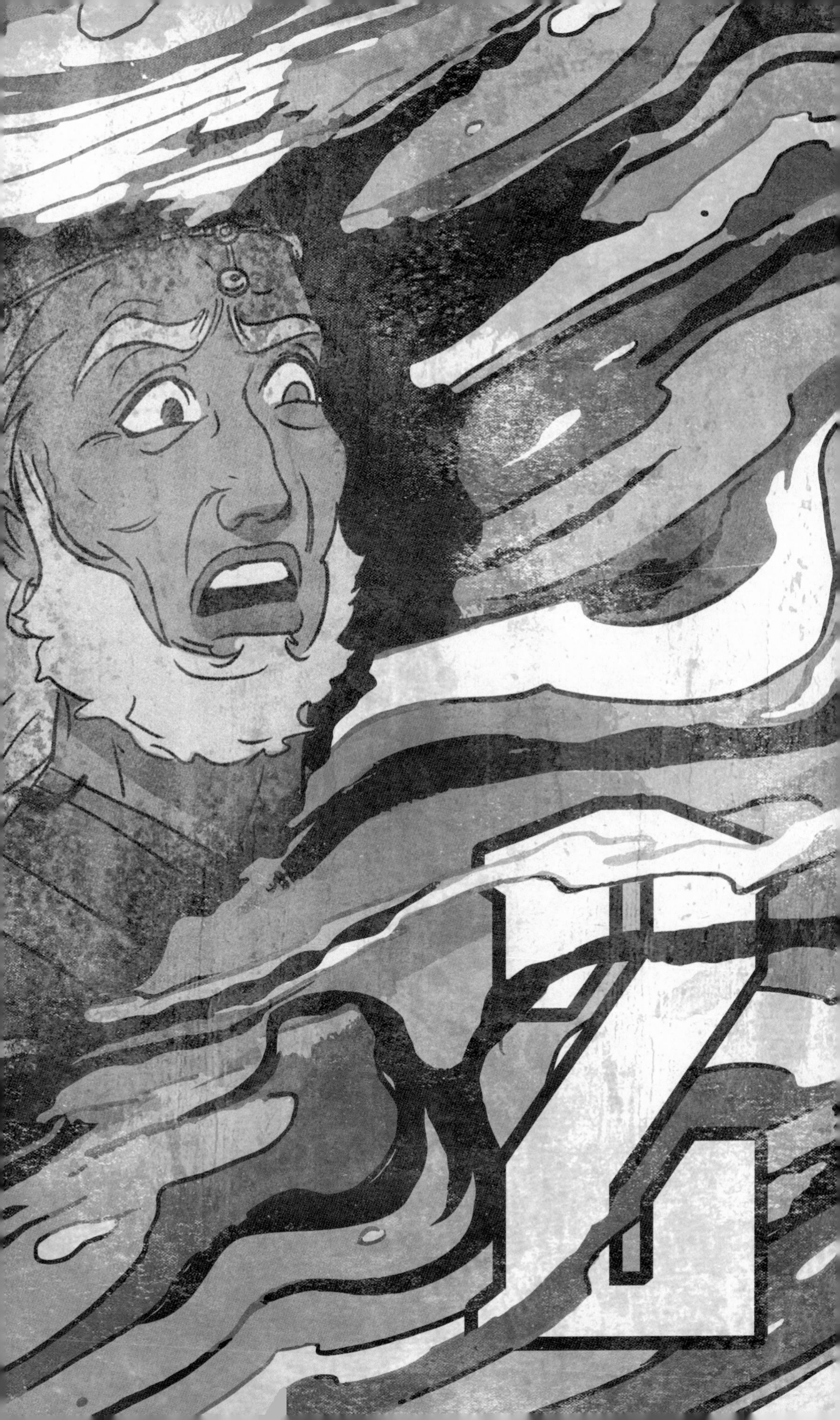
7

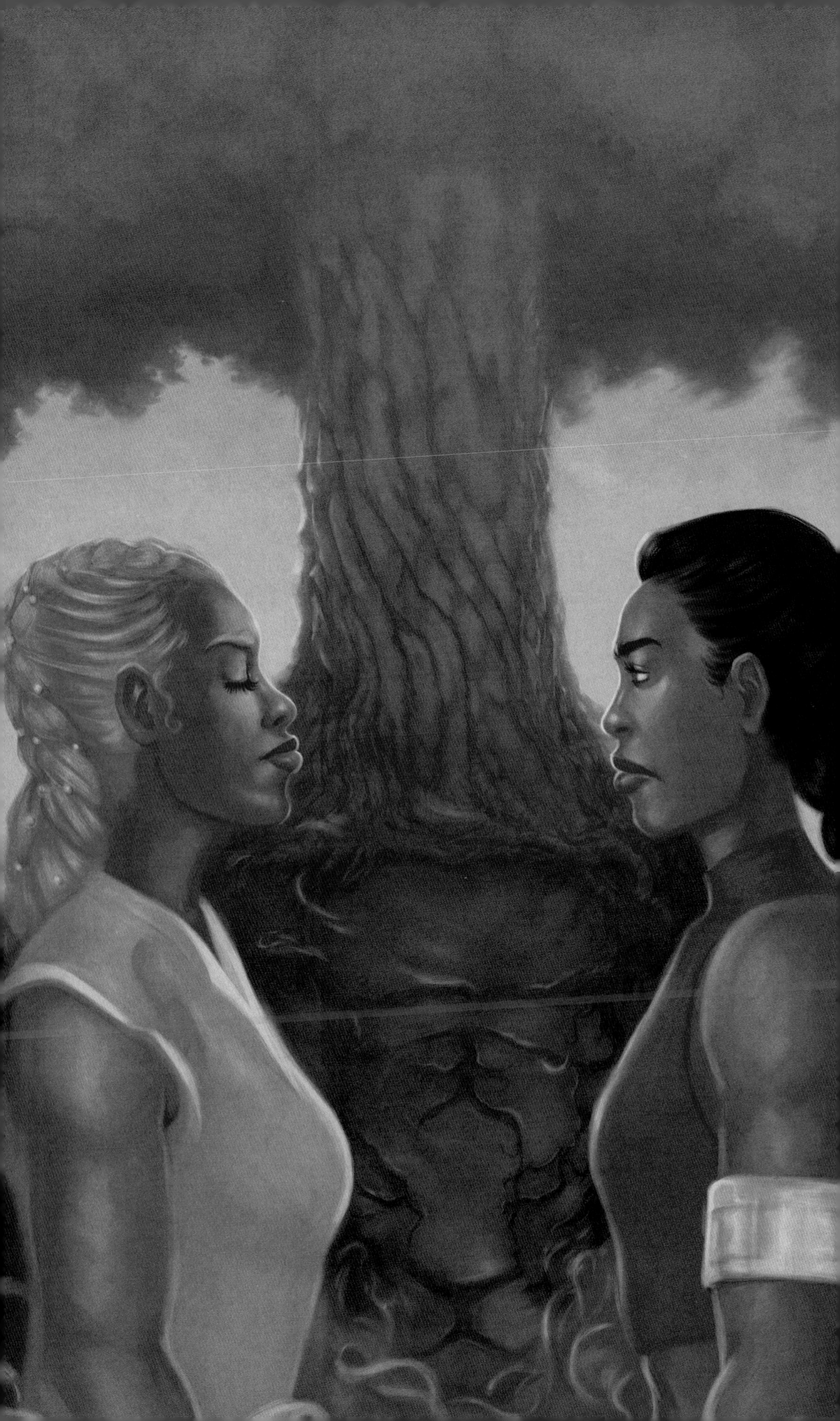

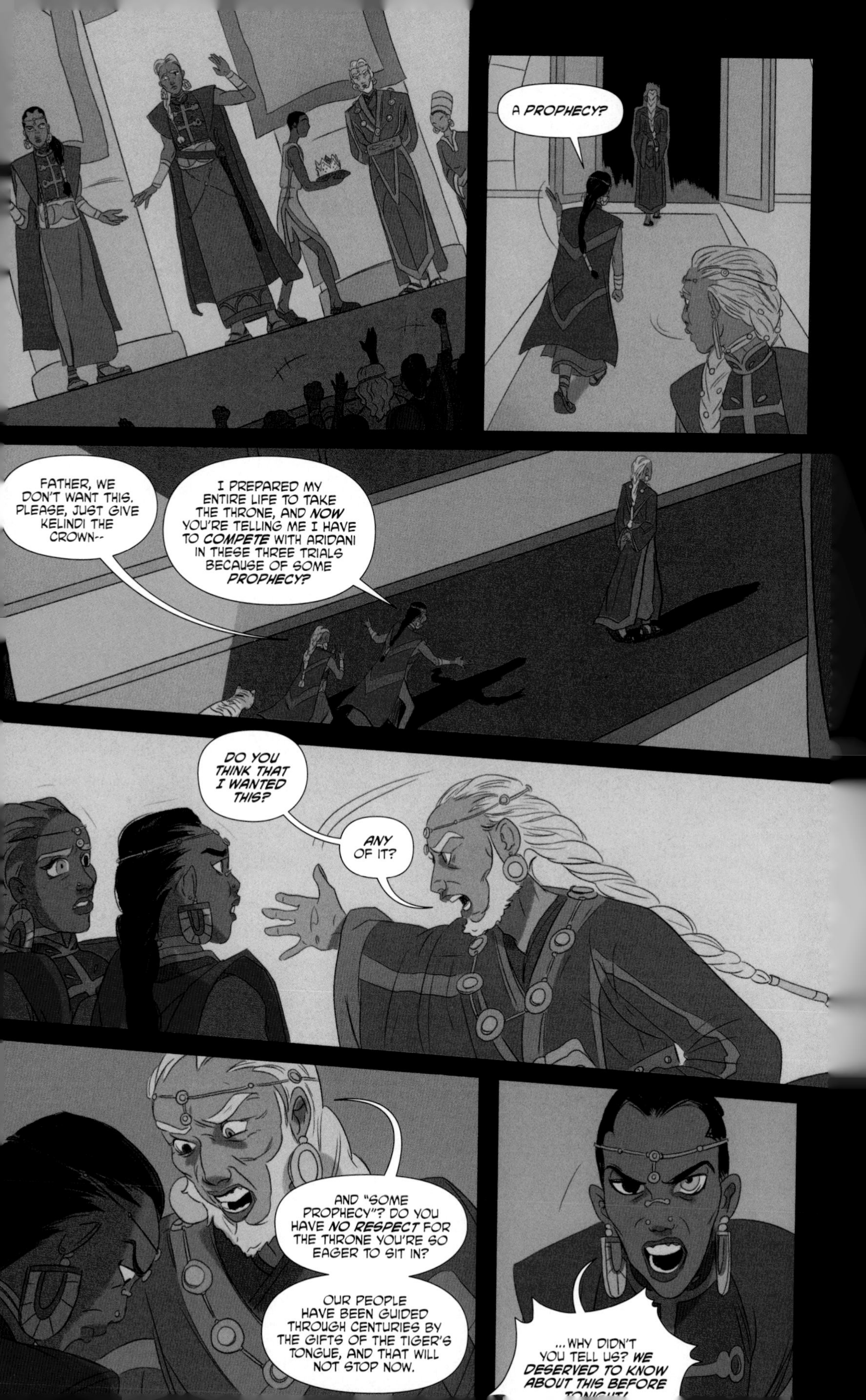
A PROPHECY?
FATHER, WE DON'T WANT THIS. PLEASE, JUST GIVE KELINDI THE CROWN--
I PREPARED MY ENTIRE LIFE TO TAKE THE THRONE, AND NOW YOU'RE TELLING ME I HAVE TO COMPETE WITH ARIDANI IN THESE THREE TRIALS BECAUSE OF SOME PROPHECY?
DO YOU THINK THAT I WANTED THIS?
ANY OF IT?
AND "SOME PROPHECY"? DO YOU HAVE NO RESPECT FOR THE THRONE YOU'RE SO EAGER TO SIT IN?
OUR PEOPLE HAVE BEEN GUIDED THROUGH CENTURIES BY THE GIFTS OF THE TIGER'S TONGUE, AND THAT WILL NOT STOP NOW.
...WHY DIDN'T YOU TELL US? WE DESERVED TO KNOW ABOUT THIS BEFORE

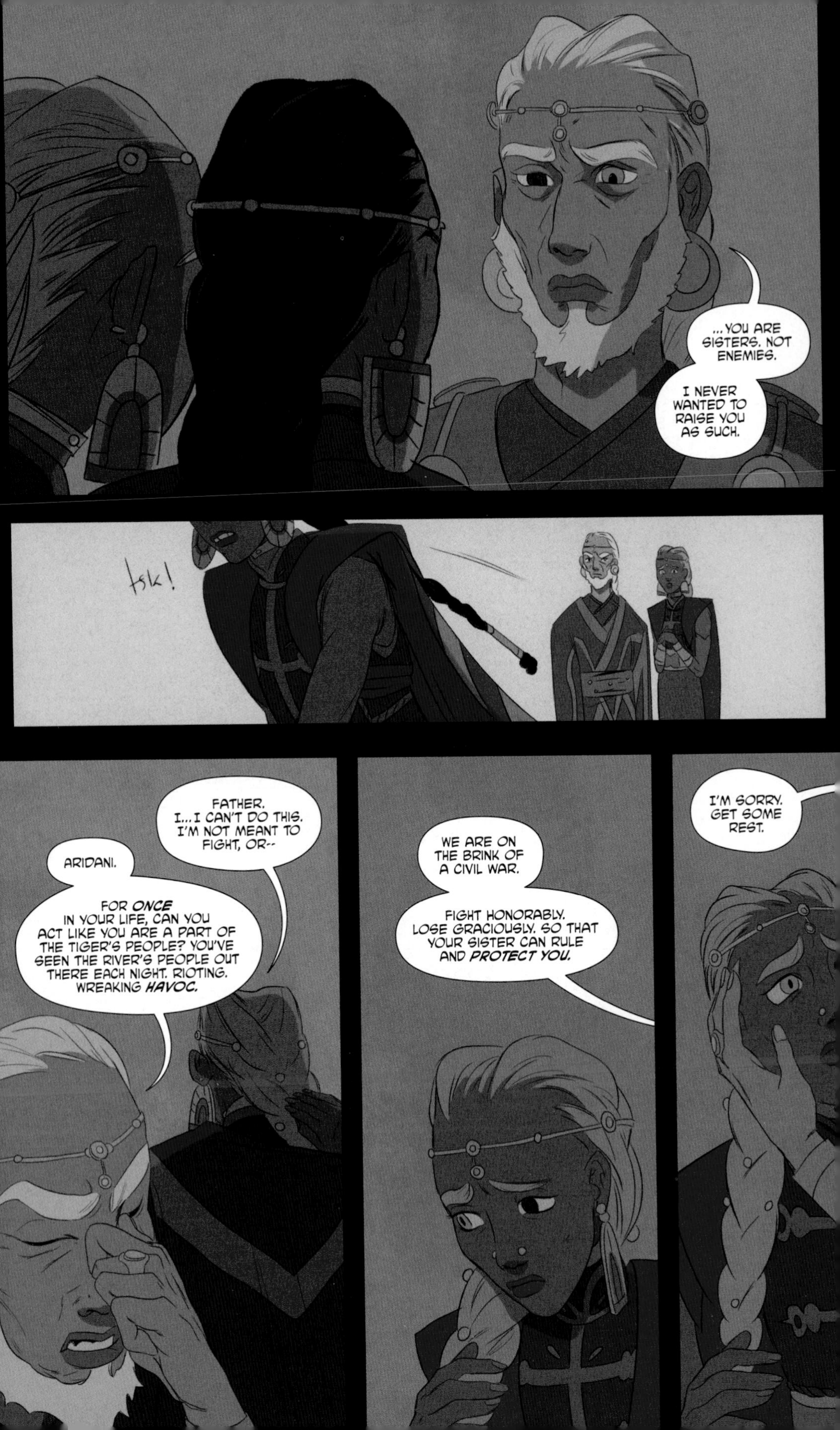
...YOU ARE SISTERS. NOT ENEMIES.
I NEVER WANTED TO RAISE YOU AS SUCH.
tsk!
FATHER. I...I CAN'T DO THIS. I'M NOT MEANT TO FIGHT, OR--
ARIDANI.
FOR *ONCE* IN YOUR LIFE, CAN YOU ACT LIKE YOU ARE A PART OF THE TIGER'S PEOPLE? YOU'VE SEEN THE RIVER'S PEOPLE OUT THERE EACH NIGHT. RIOTING. WREAKING *HAVOC.*
WE ARE ON THE BRINK OF A CIVIL WAR.
FIGHT HONORABLY. LOSE GRACIOUSLY. SO THAT YOUR SISTER CAN RULE AND *PROTECT YOU.*
I'M SORRY. GET SOME REST.

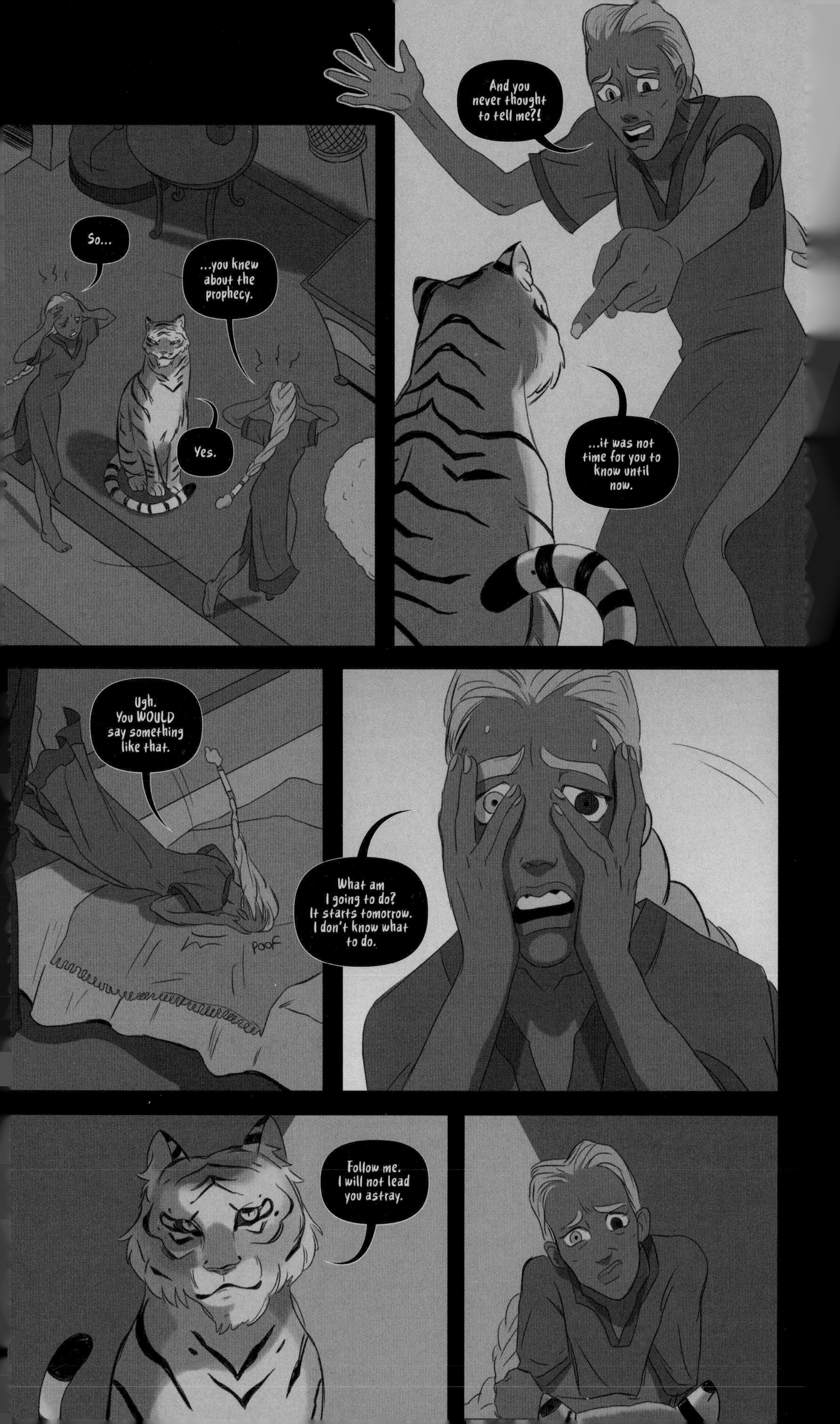
So...
...you knew about the prophecy.
Yes.
And you never thought to tell me?!
...it was not time for you to know until now.
Ugh. You WOULD say something like that.
poof
What am I going to do? It starts tomorrow. I don't know what to do.
Follow me. I will not lead you astray.

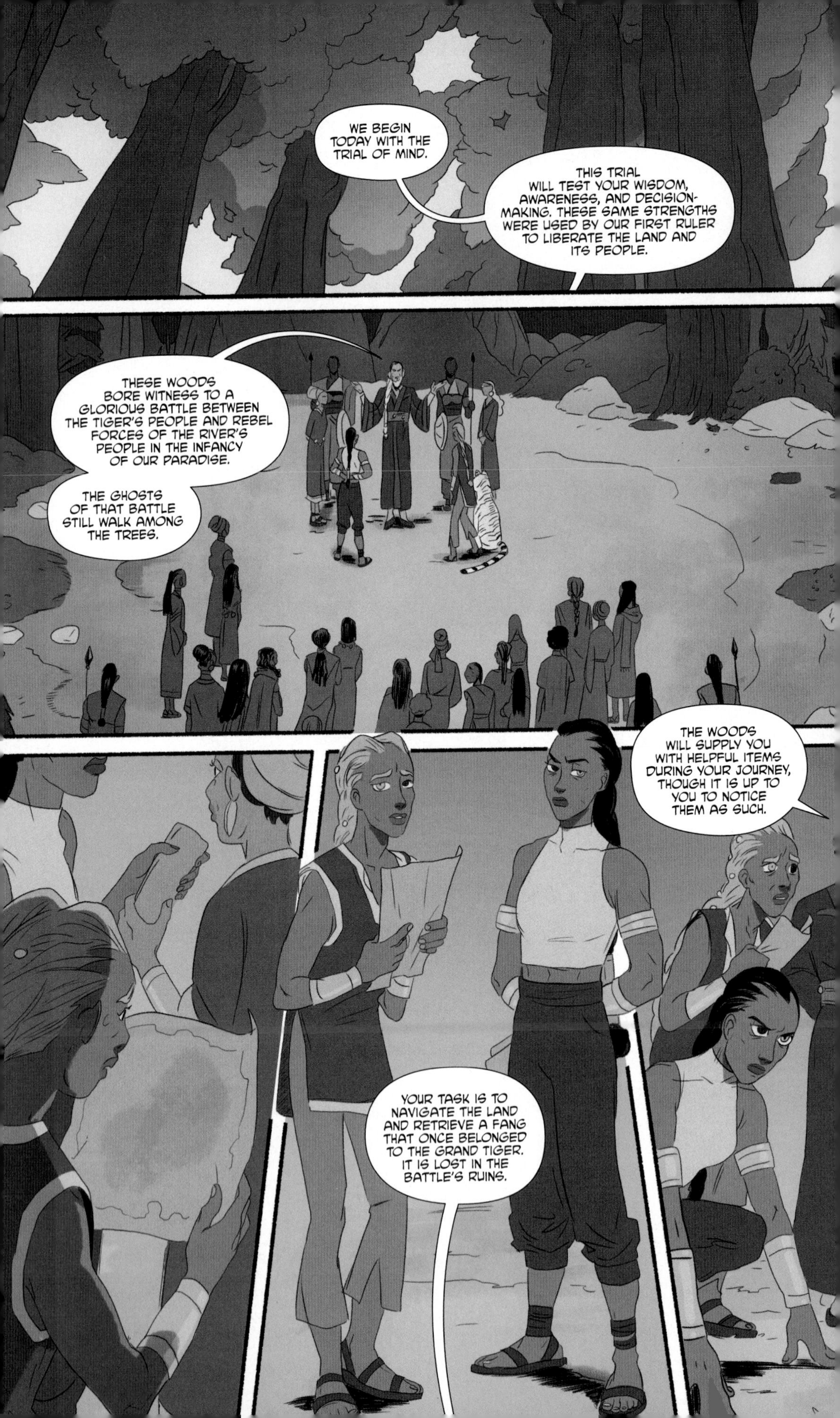
WE BEGIN TODAY WITH THE TRIAL OF MIND.
THIS TRIAL WILL TEST YOUR WISDOM, AWARENESS, AND DECISION-MAKING. THESE SAME STRENGTHS WERE USED BY OUR FIRST RULER TO LIBERATE THE LAND AND ITS PEOPLE.
THESE WOODS BORE WITNESS TO A GLORIOUS BATTLE BETWEEN THE TIGER'S PEOPLE AND REBEL FORCES OF THE RIVER'S PEOPLE IN THE INFANCY OF OUR PARADISE.
THE GHOSTS OF THAT BATTLE STILL WALK AMONG THE TREES.
THE WOODS WILL SUPPLY YOU WITH HELPFUL ITEMS DURING YOUR JOURNEY, THOUGH IT IS UP TO YOU TO NOTICE THEM AS SUCH.
YOUR TASK IS TO NAVIGATE THE LAND AND RETRIEVE A FANG THAT ONCE BELONGED TO THE GRAND TIGER. IT IS LOST IN THE BATTLE'S RUINS.

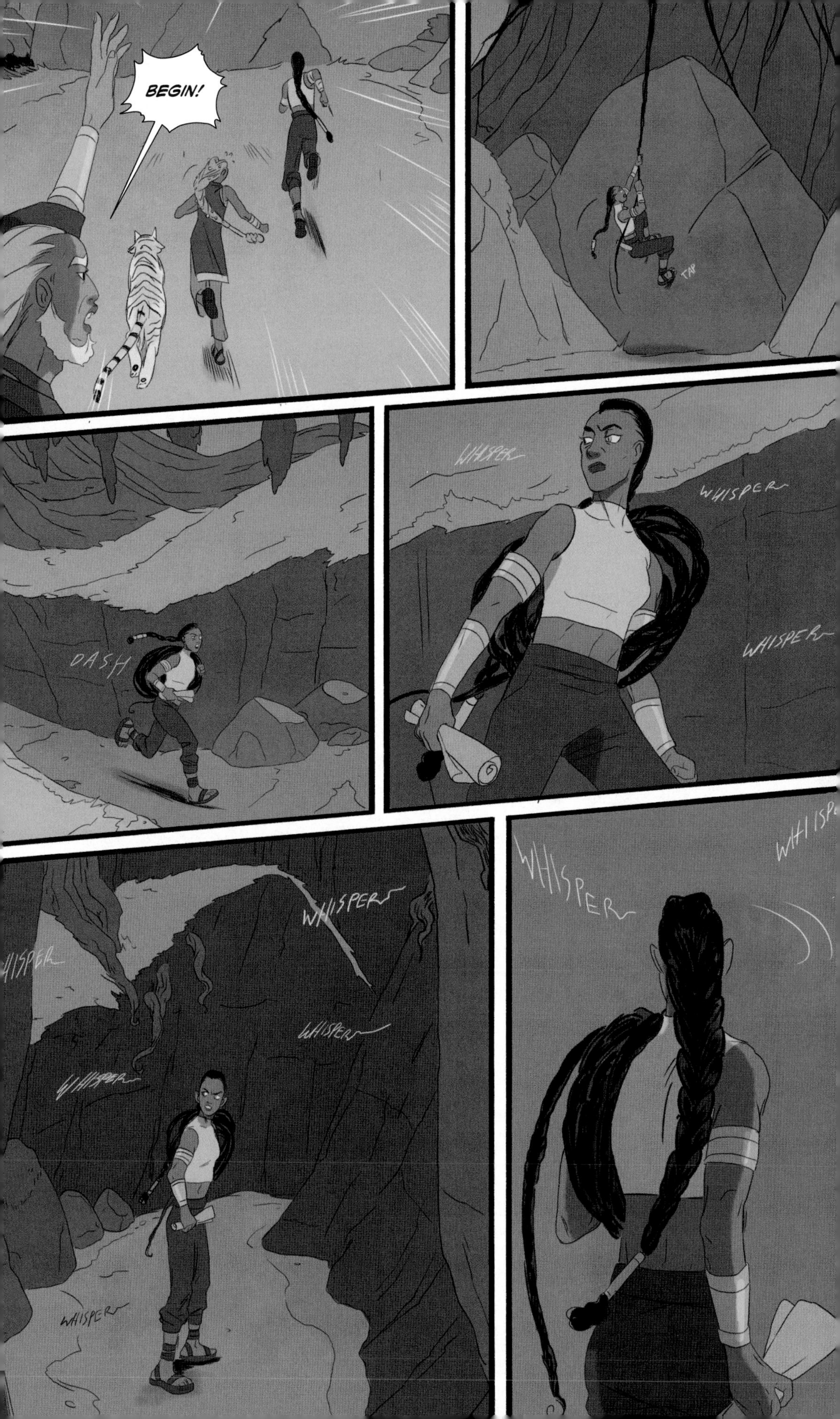
BEGIN!
TAP
DASH
WHISPER
WHISPER
WHISPER
WHISPER
WHISPER
WHISPER
WHISPER
WHISPER
WHISPER
WHISPER

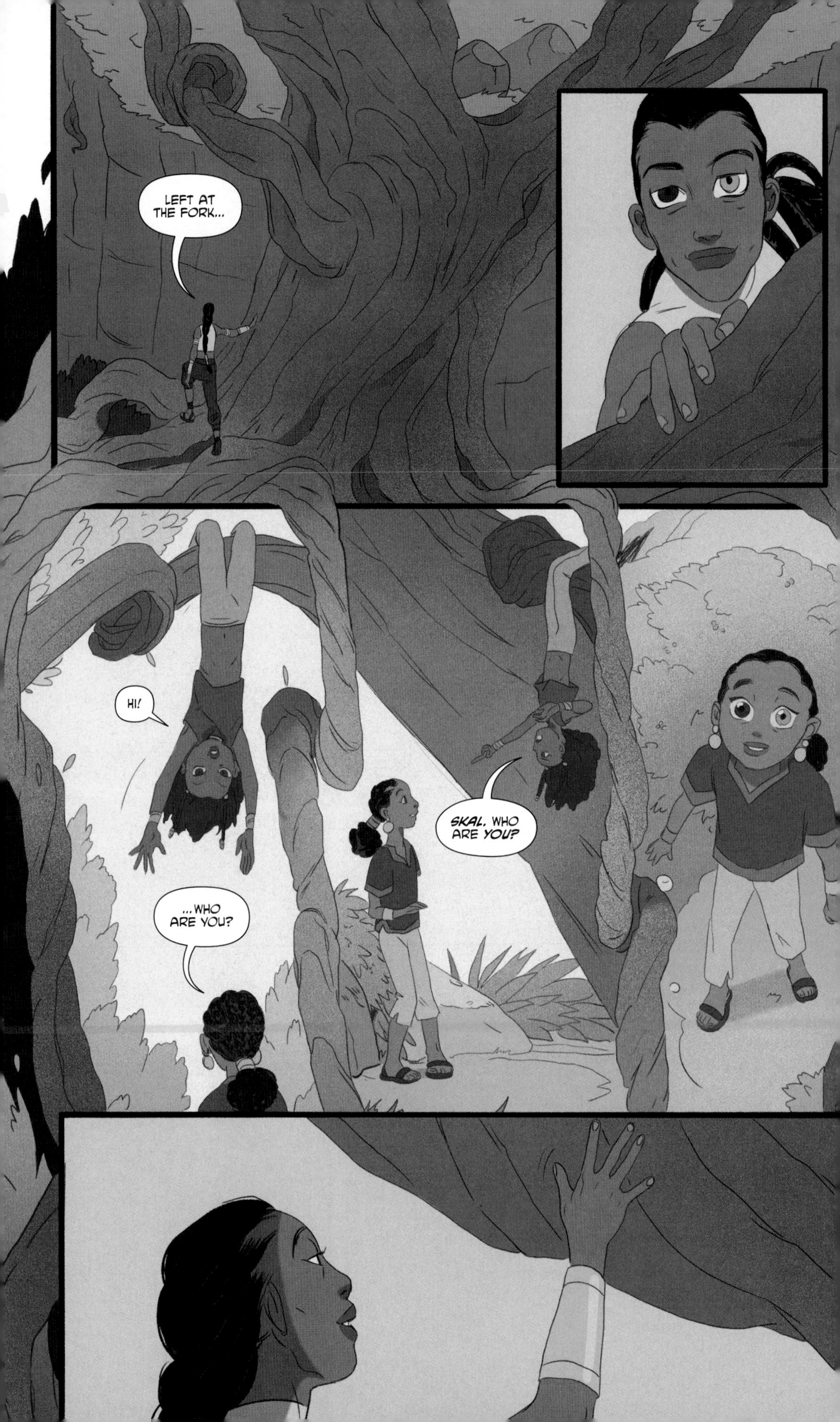
LEFT AT THE FORK...
HI!
SKAL. WHO ARE YOU?
...WHO ARE YOU?

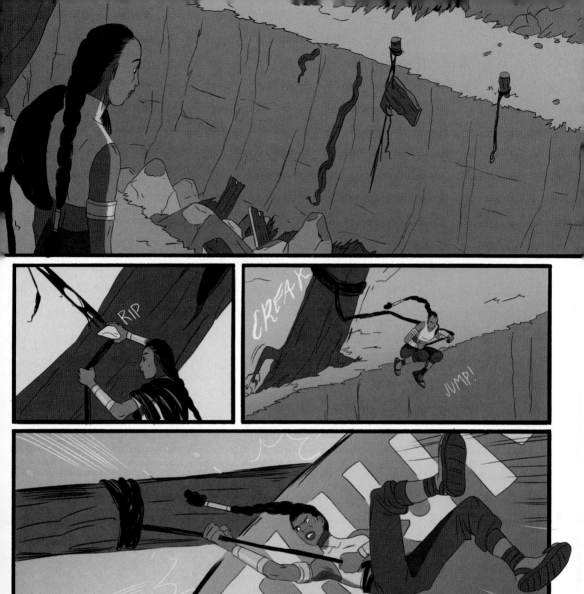

RIP

CREAK

JUMP!

...SLAUGHTERED.

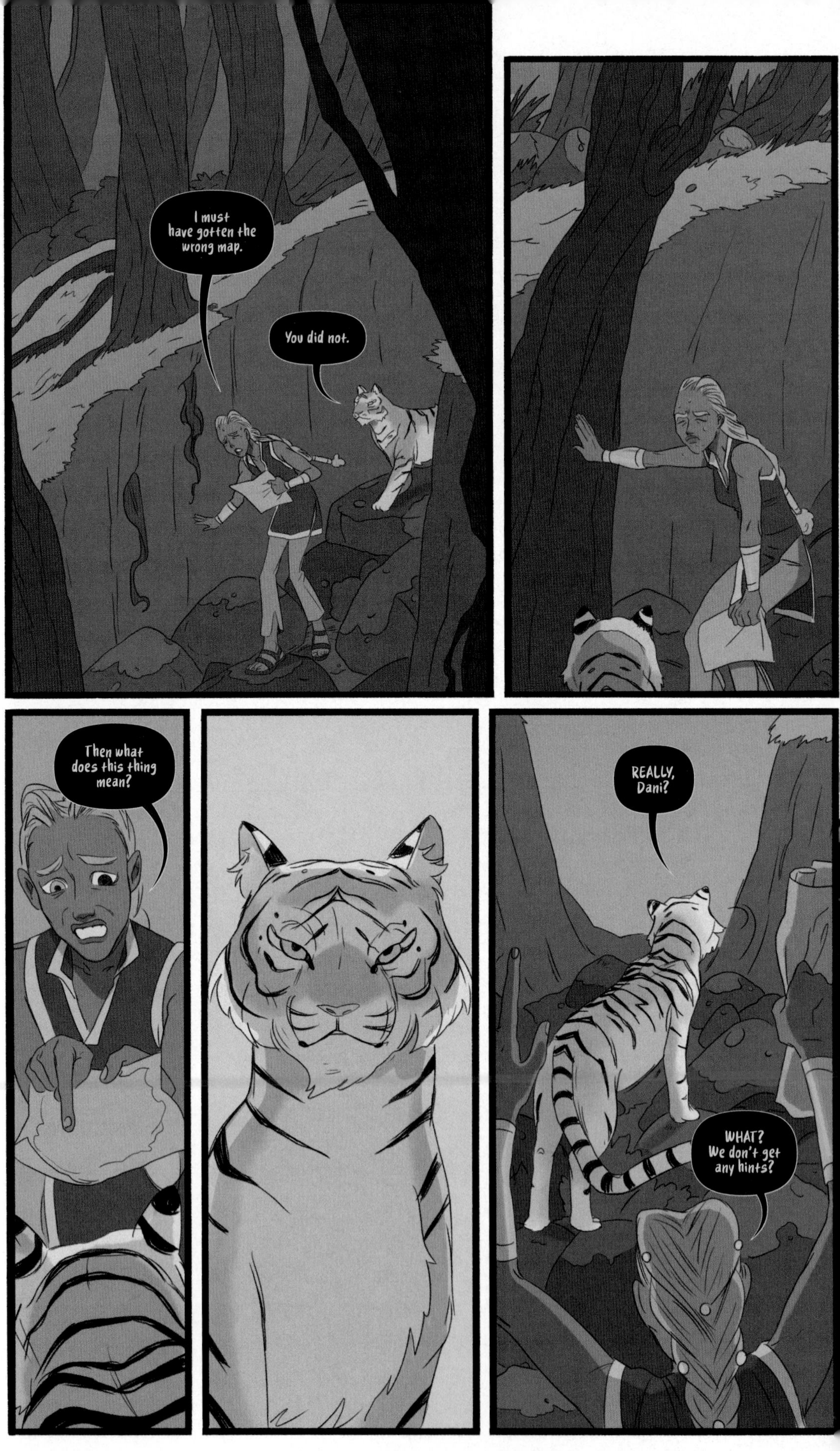

I must have gotten the wrong map.
You did not.
Then what does this thing mean?
REALLY, Dani?
WHAT? We don't get any hints?

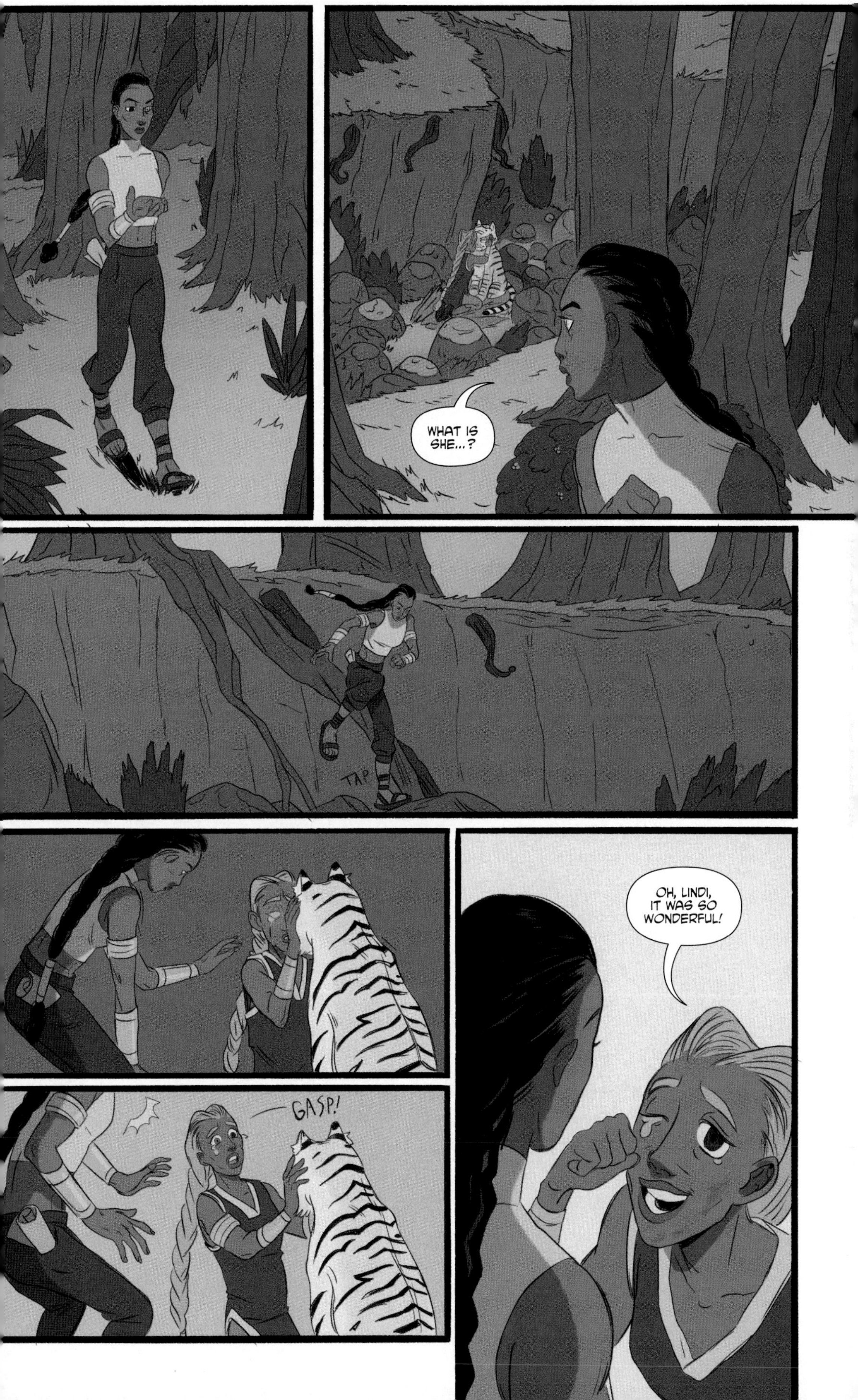
WHAT IS SHE...?
TAP
OH, LINDI, IT WAS SO WONDERFUL!
GASP!

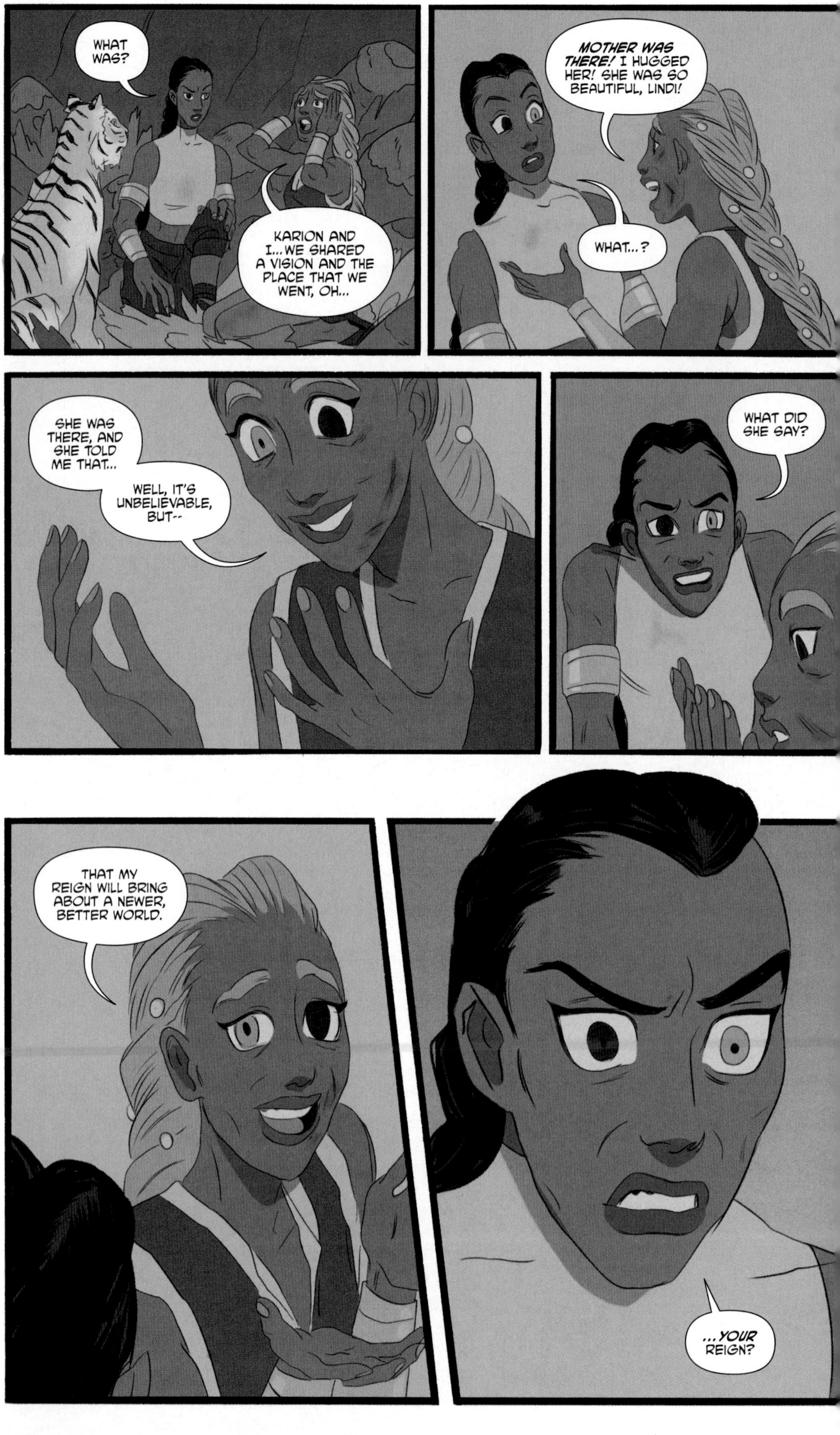
WHAT WAS?
KARION AND I...WE SHARED A VISION AND THE PLACE THAT WE WENT, OH...
MOTHER WAS THERE! I HUGGED HER! SHE WAS SO BEAUTIFUL, LINDI!
WHAT...?
SHE WAS THERE, AND SHE TOLD ME THAT...
WELL, IT'S UNBELIEVABLE, BUT--
WHAT DID SHE SAY?
THAT MY REIGN WILL BRING ABOUT A NEWER, BETTER WORLD.
...YOUR REIGN?

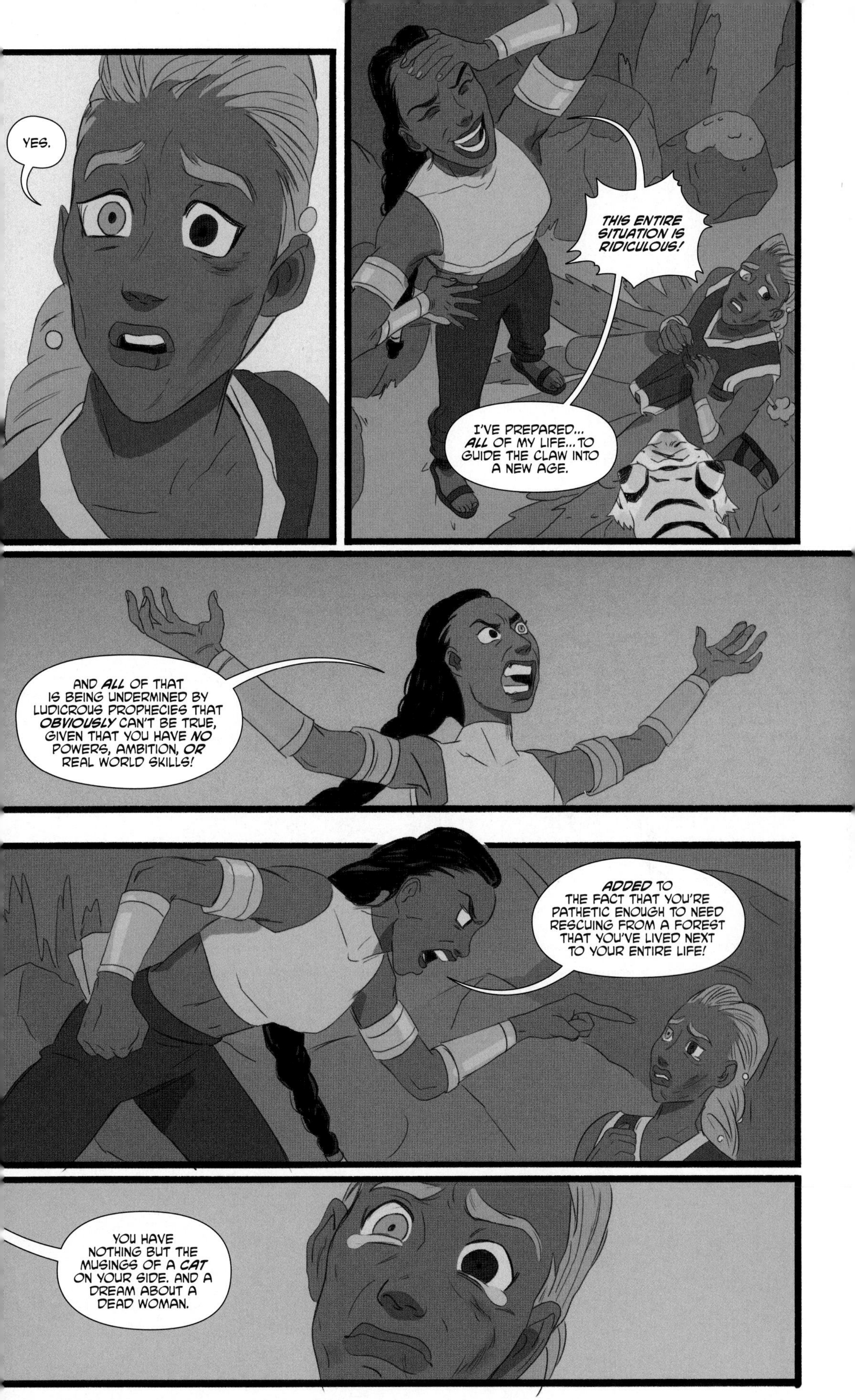
YES.
THIS ENTIRE SITUATION IS RIDICULOUS!
I'VE PREPARED... ALL OF MY LIFE... TO GUIDE THE CLAW INTO A NEW AGE.
AND ALL OF THAT IS BEING UNDERMINED BY LUDICROUS PROPHECIES THAT OBVIOUSLY CAN'T BE TRUE, GIVEN THAT YOU HAVE NO POWERS, AMBITION, OR REAL WORLD SKILLS!
ADDED TO THE FACT THAT YOU'RE PATHETIC ENOUGH TO NEED RESCUING FROM A FOREST THAT YOU'VE LIVED NEXT TO YOUR ENTIRE LIFE!
YOU HAVE NOTHING BUT THE MUSINGS OF A CAT ON YOUR SIDE. AND A DREAM ABOUT A DEAD WOMAN.

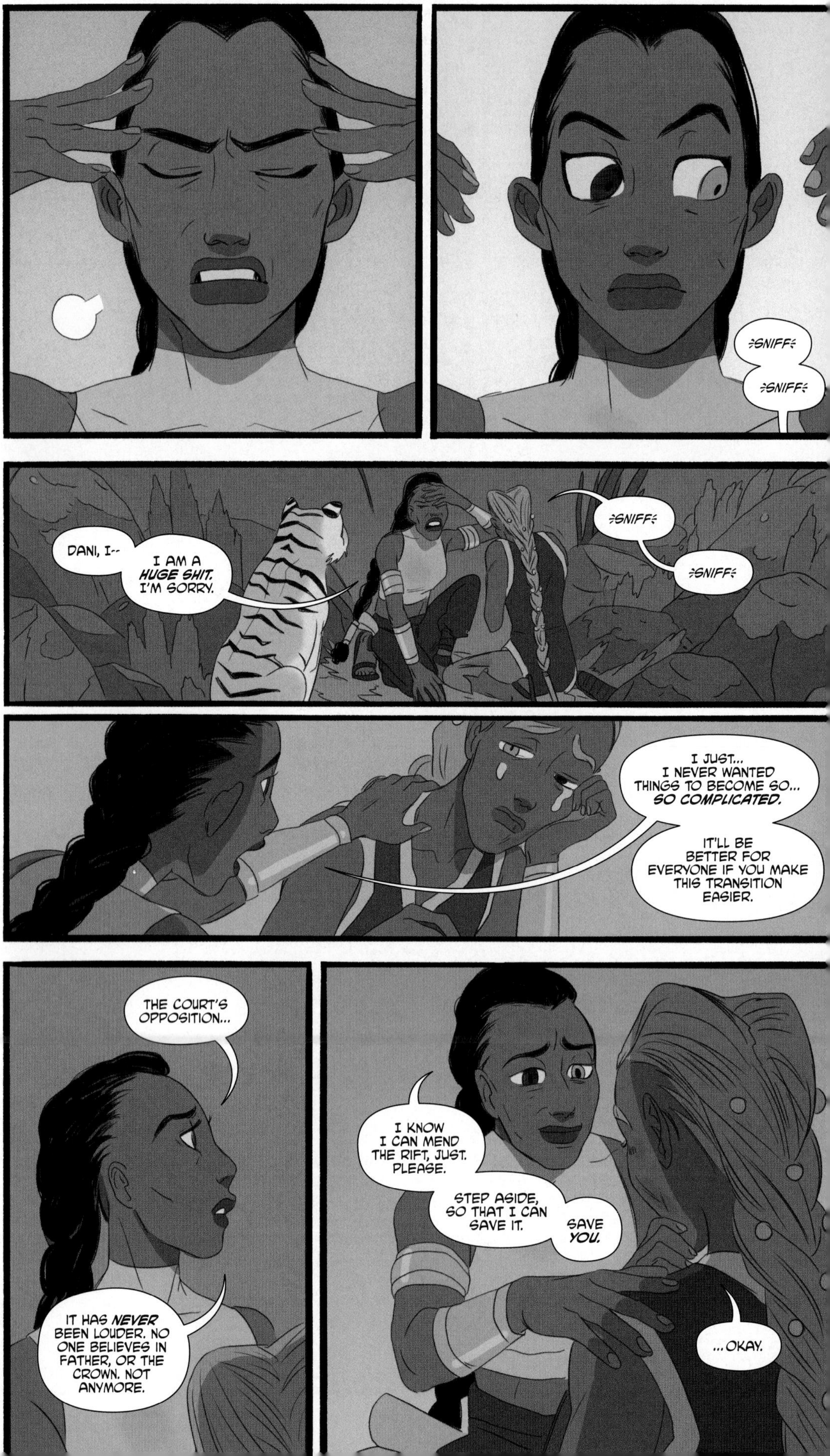

SNIFF
SNIFF
DANI, I--
I AM A HUGE SHIT. I'M SORRY.
SNIFF
SNIFF
I JUST... I NEVER WANTED THINGS TO BECOME SO... SO COMPLICATED.
IT'LL BE BETTER FOR EVERYONE IF YOU MAKE THIS TRANSITION EASIER.
THE COURT'S OPPOSITION...
IT HAS NEVER BEEN LOUDER. NO ONE BELIEVES IN FATHER, OR THE CROWN. NOT ANYMORE.
I KNOW I CAN MEND THE RIFT, JUST. PLEASE.
STEP ASIDE, SO THAT I CAN SAVE IT.
SAVE YOU.
...OKAY.

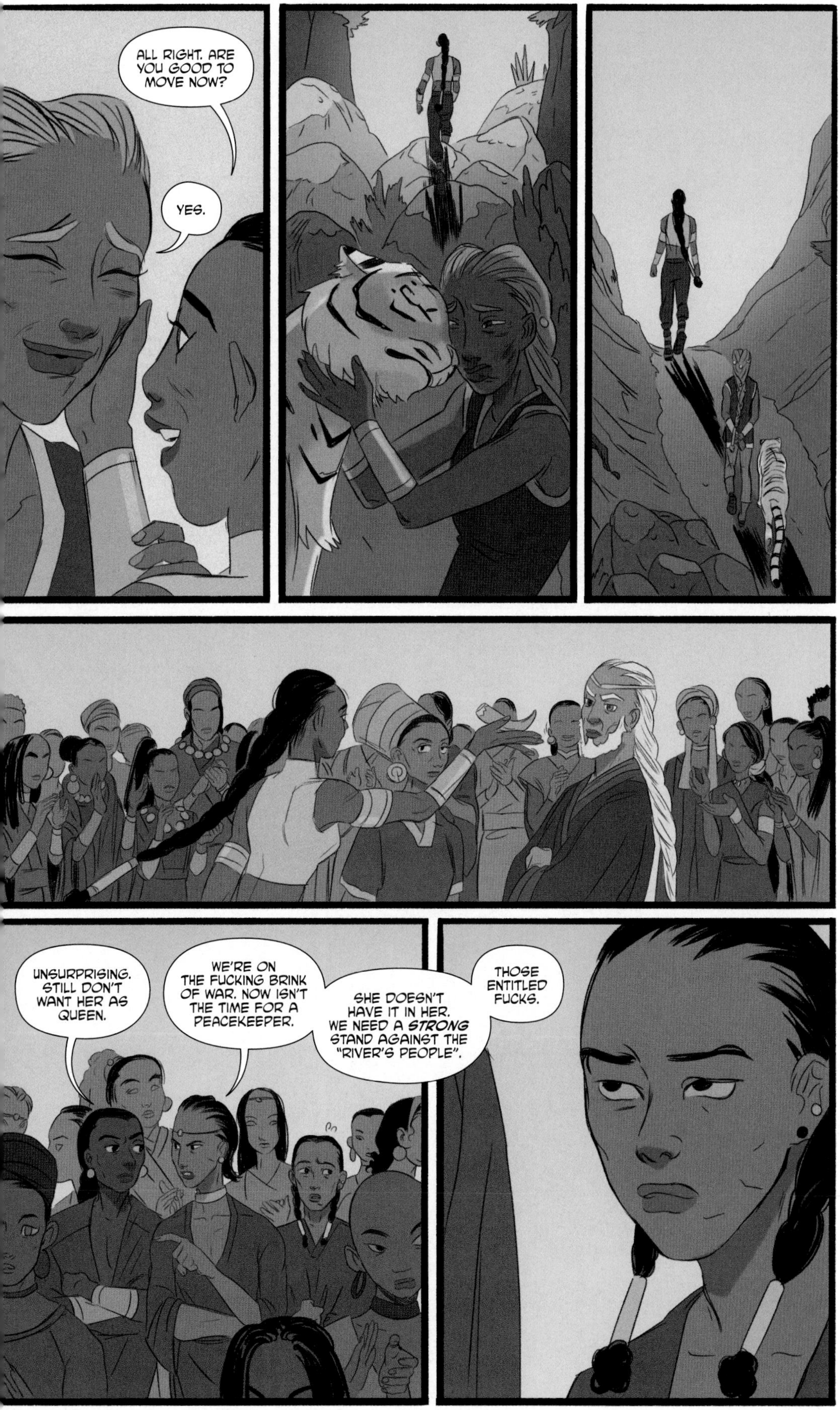
ALL RIGHT. ARE YOU GOOD TO MOVE NOW?
YES.
UNSURPRISING. STILL DON'T WANT HER AS QUEEN.
WE'RE ON THE FUCKING BRINK OF WAR. NOW ISN'T THE TIME FOR A PEACEKEEPER.
SHE DOESN'T HAVE IT IN HER. WE NEED A *STRONG* STAND AGAINST THE "RIVER'S PEOPLE".
THOSE ENTITLED FUCKS.

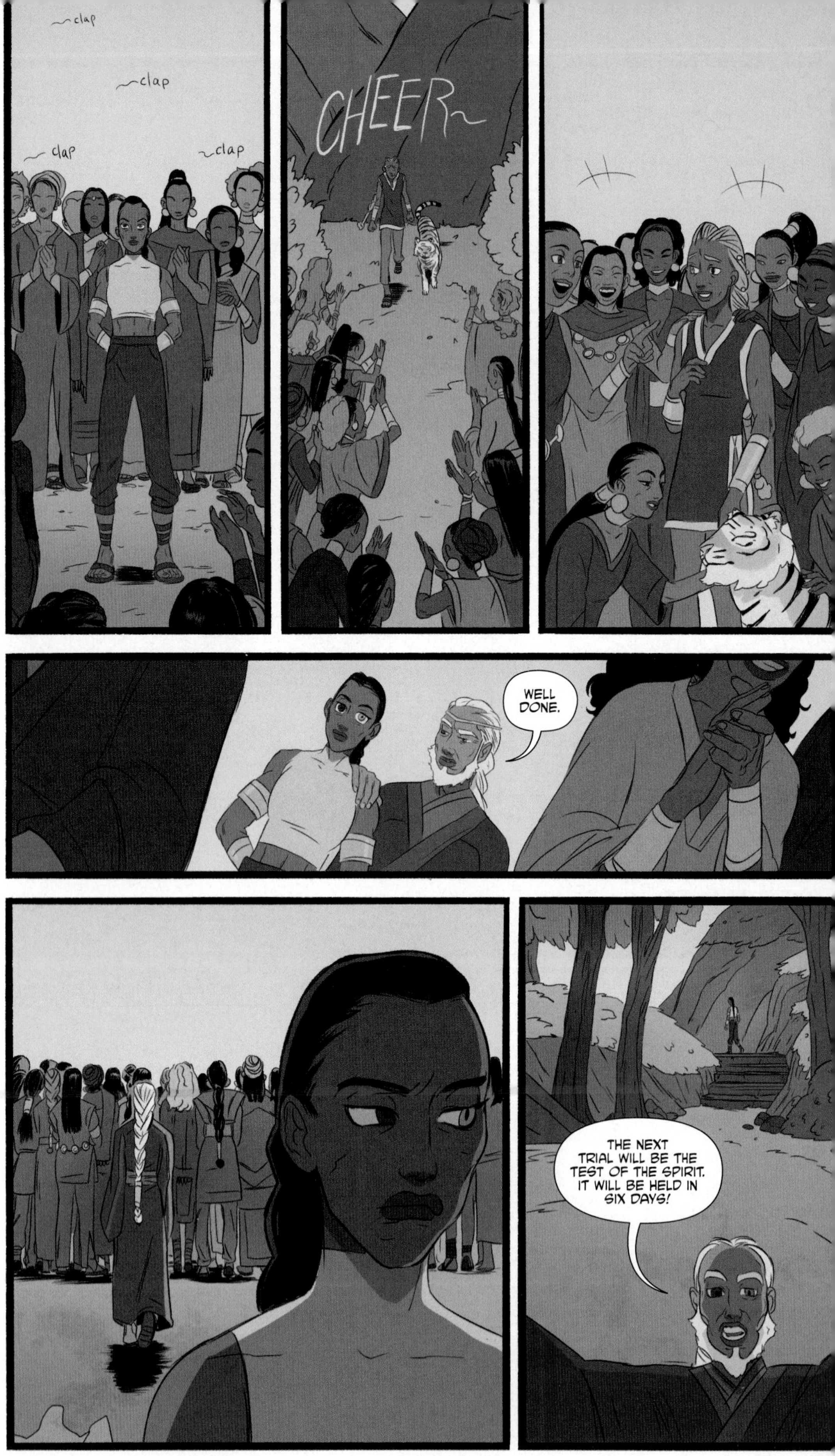
clap
clap
clap
clap
CHEER
WELL DONE.
THE NEXT TRIAL WILL BE THE TEST OF THE SPIRIT. IT WILL BE HELD IN SIX DAYS!

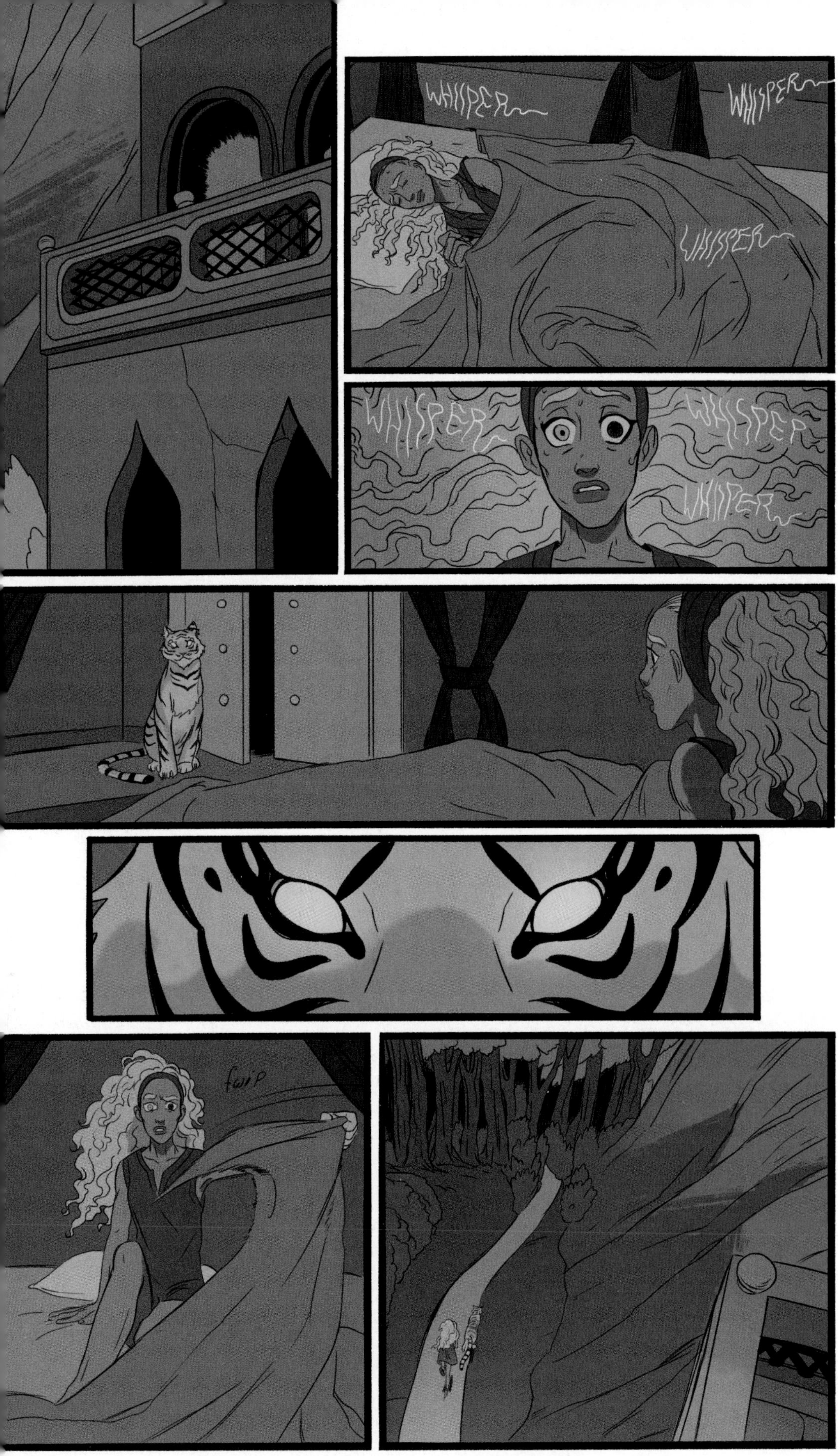
WHISPER
WHISPER
WHISPER
WHISPER
WHISPER
WHISPER
fwip

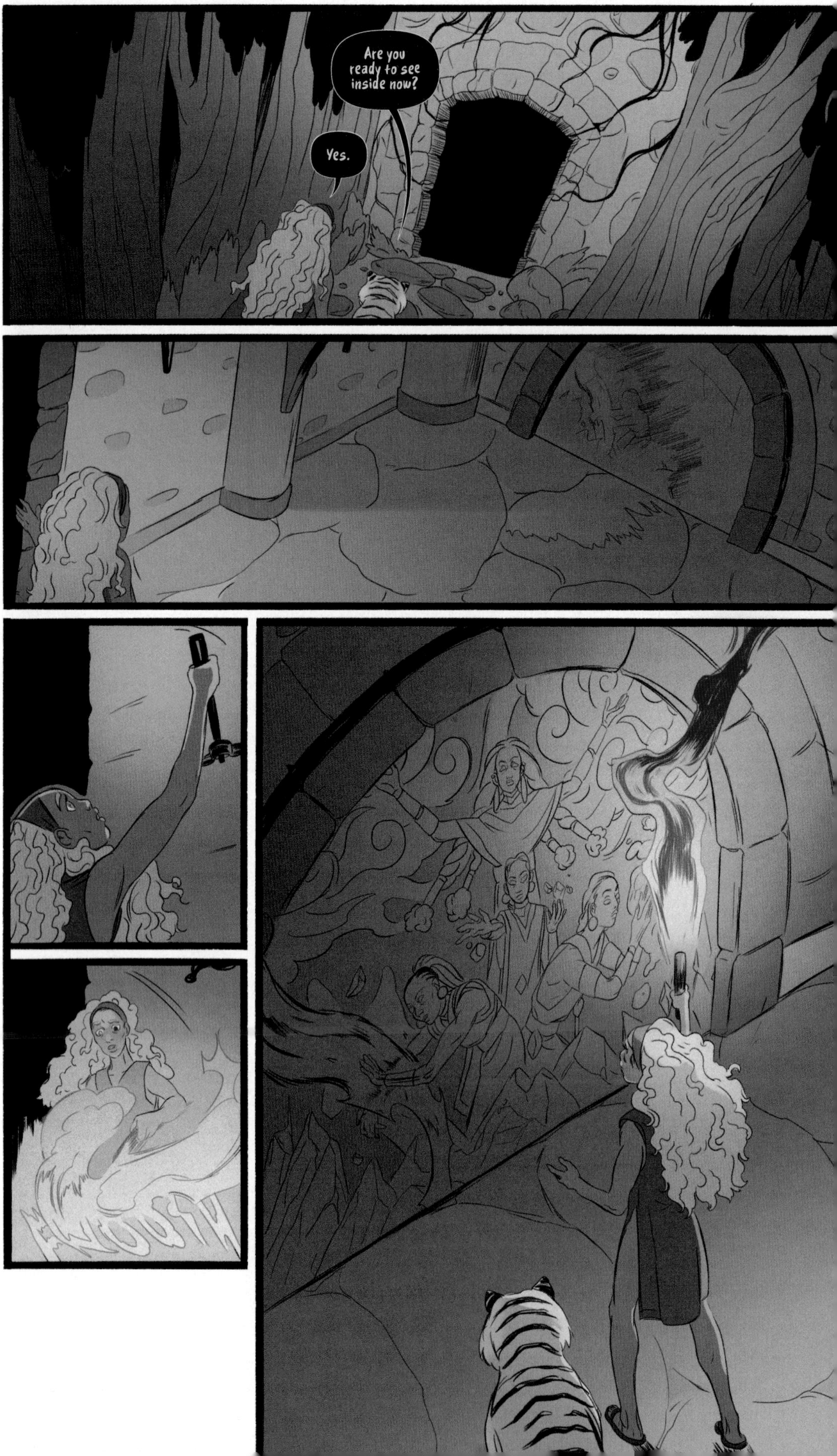
Are you ready to see inside now?
Yes.
FWOOSH

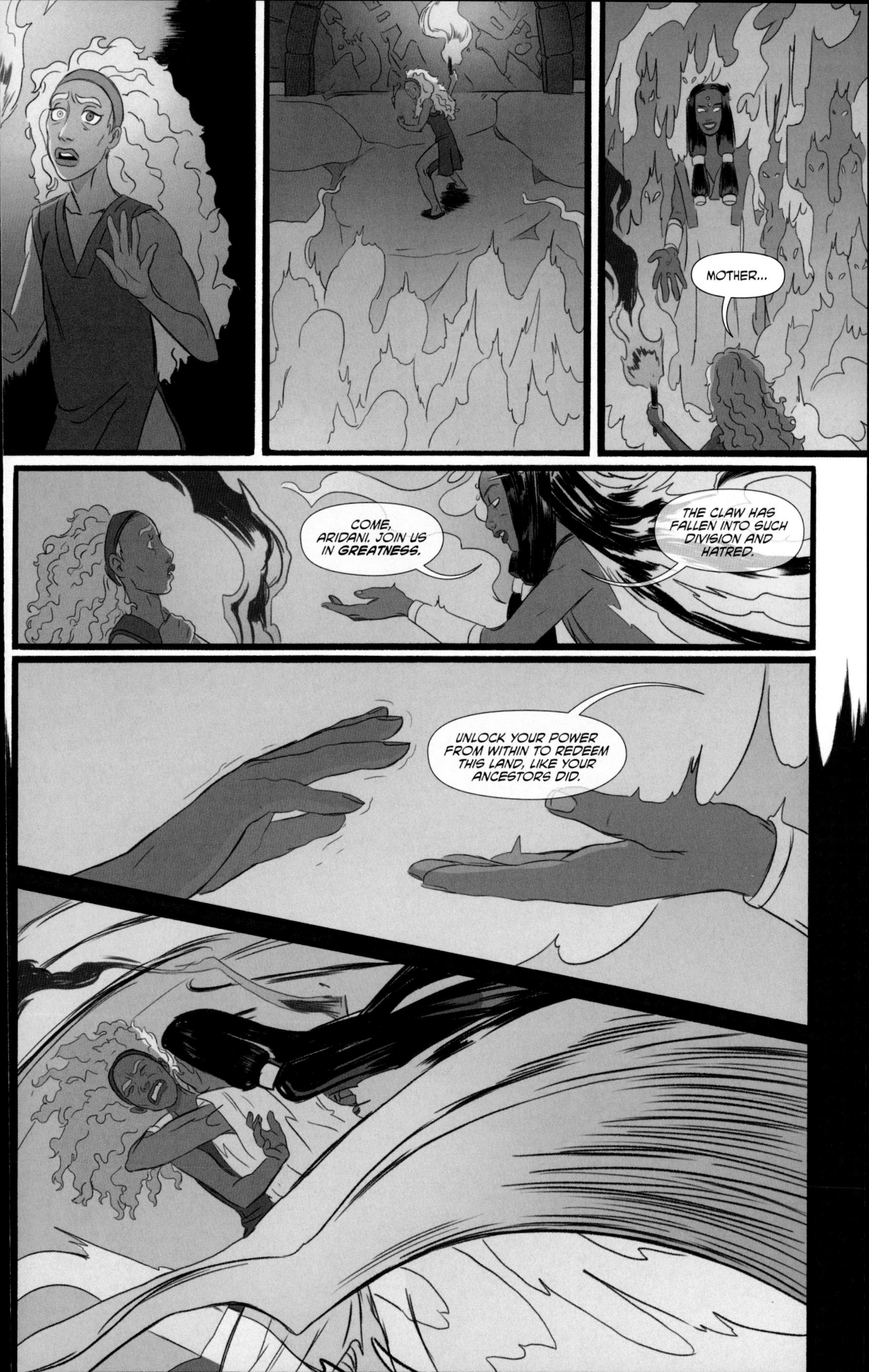
MOTHER...
COME, ARIDANI. JOIN US IN GREATNESS.
THE CLAW HAS FALLEN INTO SUCH DIVISION AND HATRED.
UNLOCK YOUR POWER FROM WITHIN TO REDEEM THIS LAND, LIKE YOUR ANCESTORS DID.

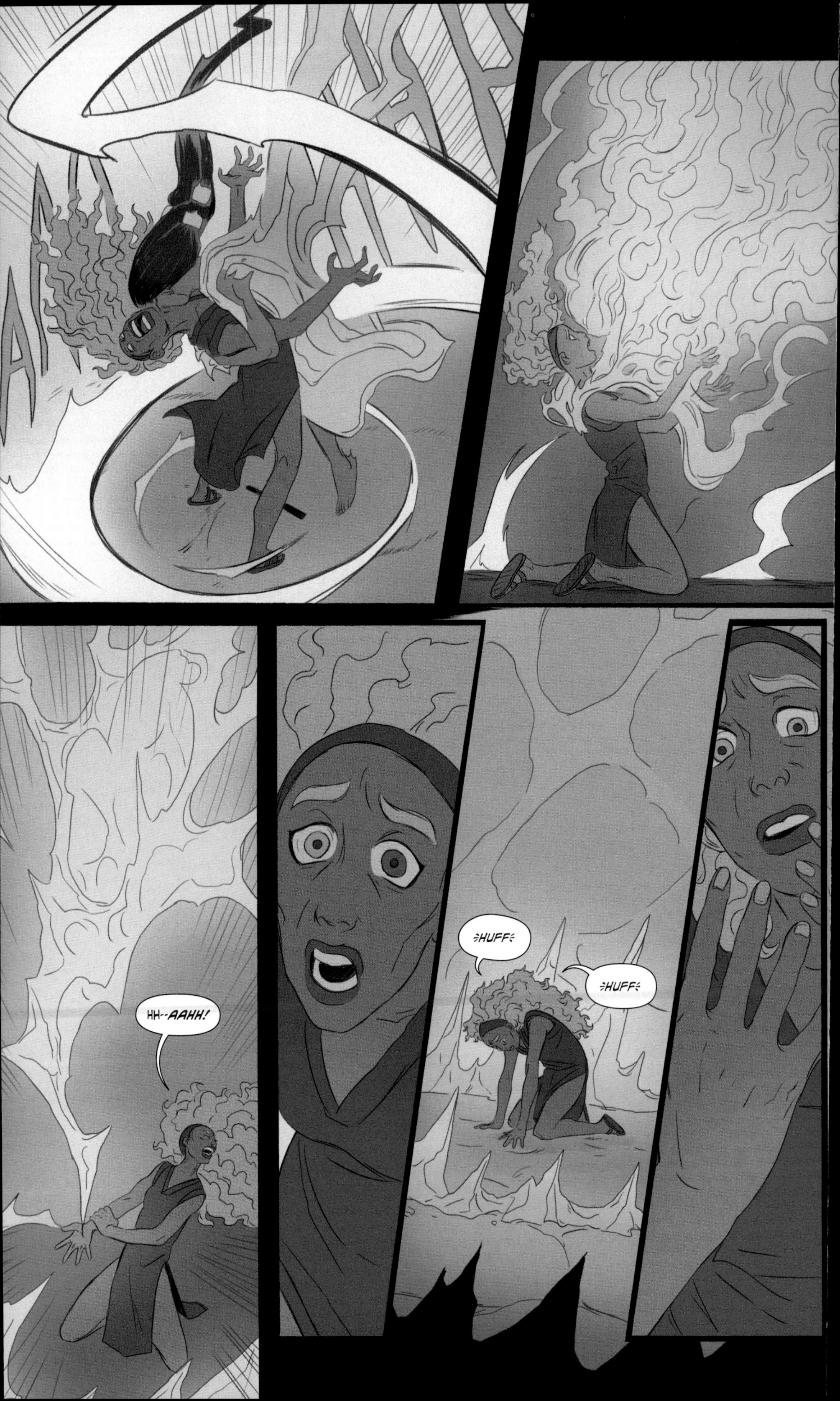
HH--AAHH!
HUFF
HUFF

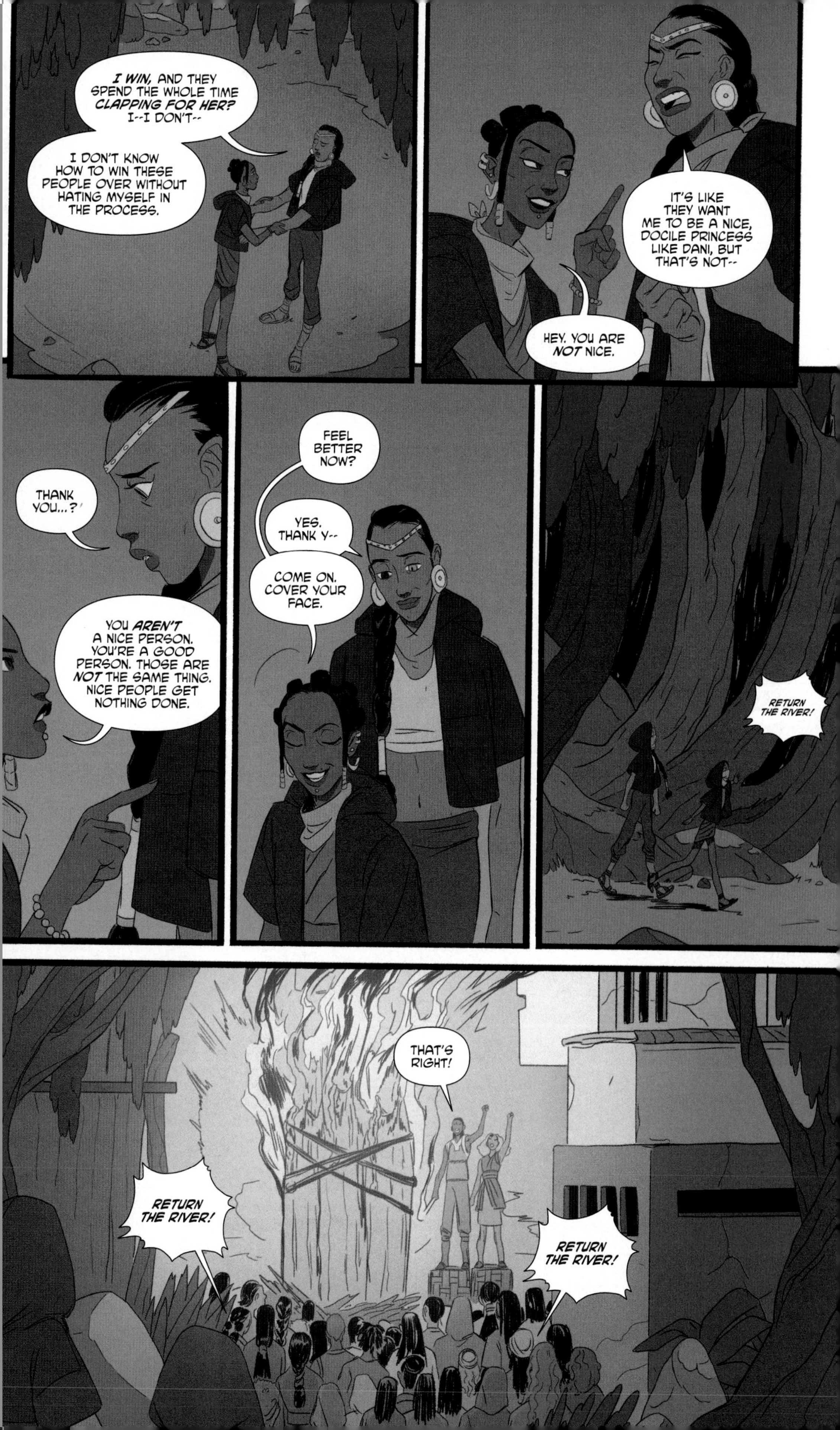
I WIN, AND THEY SPEND THE WHOLE TIME CLAPPING FOR HER? I--I DON'T--
I DON'T KNOW HOW TO WIN THESE PEOPLE OVER WITHOUT HATING MYSELF IN THE PROCESS.
IT'S LIKE THEY WANT ME TO BE A NICE, DOCILE PRINCESS LIKE DANI, BUT THAT'S NOT--
HEY. YOU ARE NOT NICE.
THANK YOU...?
YOU AREN'T A NICE PERSON. YOU'RE A GOOD PERSON. THOSE ARE NOT THE SAME THING. NICE PEOPLE GET NOTHING DONE.
FEEL BETTER NOW?
YES. THANK Y--
COME ON. COVER YOUR FACE.
RETURN THE RIVER!
THAT'S RIGHT!
RETURN THE RIVER!
RETURN THE RIVER!

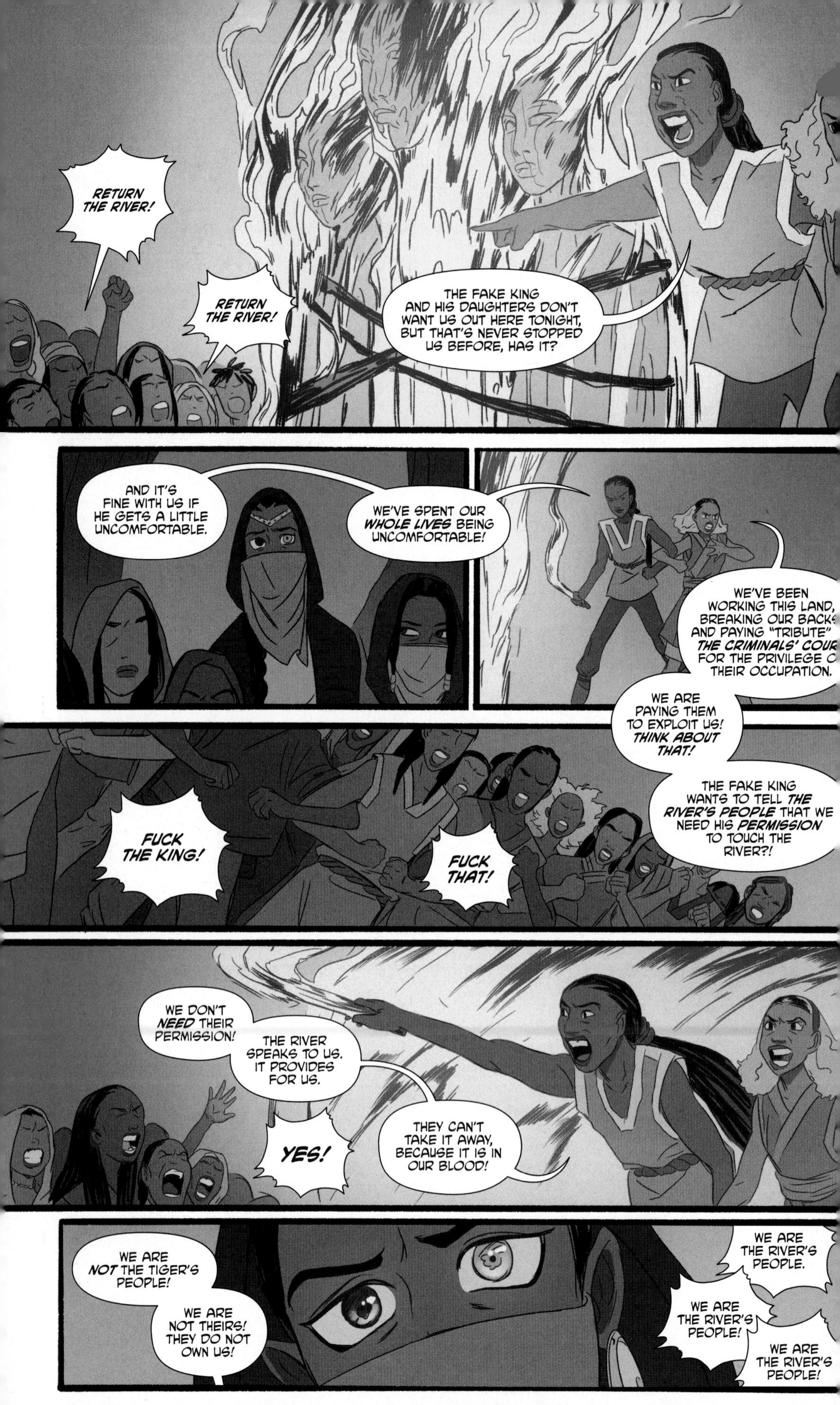
RETURN THE RIVER!
RETURN THE RIVER!
THE FAKE KING AND HIS DAUGHTERS DON'T WANT US OUT HERE TONIGHT, BUT THAT'S NEVER STOPPED US BEFORE, HAS IT?
AND IT'S FINE WITH US IF HE GETS A LITTLE UNCOMFORTABLE.
WE'VE SPENT OUR WHOLE LIVES BEING UNCOMFORTABLE!
WE'VE BEEN WORKING THIS LAND, BREAKING OUR BACKS AND PAYING "TRIBUTE" THE CRIMINALS' COUR FOR THE PRIVILEGE O THEIR OCCUPATION.
WE ARE PAYING THEM TO EXPLOIT US! THINK ABOUT THAT!
FUCK THE KING!
FUCK THAT!
THE FAKE KING WANTS TO TELL THE RIVER'S PEOPLE THAT WE NEED HIS PERMISSION TO TOUCH THE RIVER?!
WE DON'T NEED THEIR PERMISSION!
THE RIVER SPEAKS TO US. IT PROVIDES FOR US.
YES!
THEY CAN'T TAKE IT AWAY, BECAUSE IT IS IN OUR BLOOD!
WE ARE NOT THE TIGER'S PEOPLE!
WE ARE NOT THEIRS! THEY DO NOT OWN US!
WE ARE THE RIVER'S PEOPLE.
WE ARE THE RIVER'S PEOPLE!
WE ARE THE RIVER'S PEOPLE!

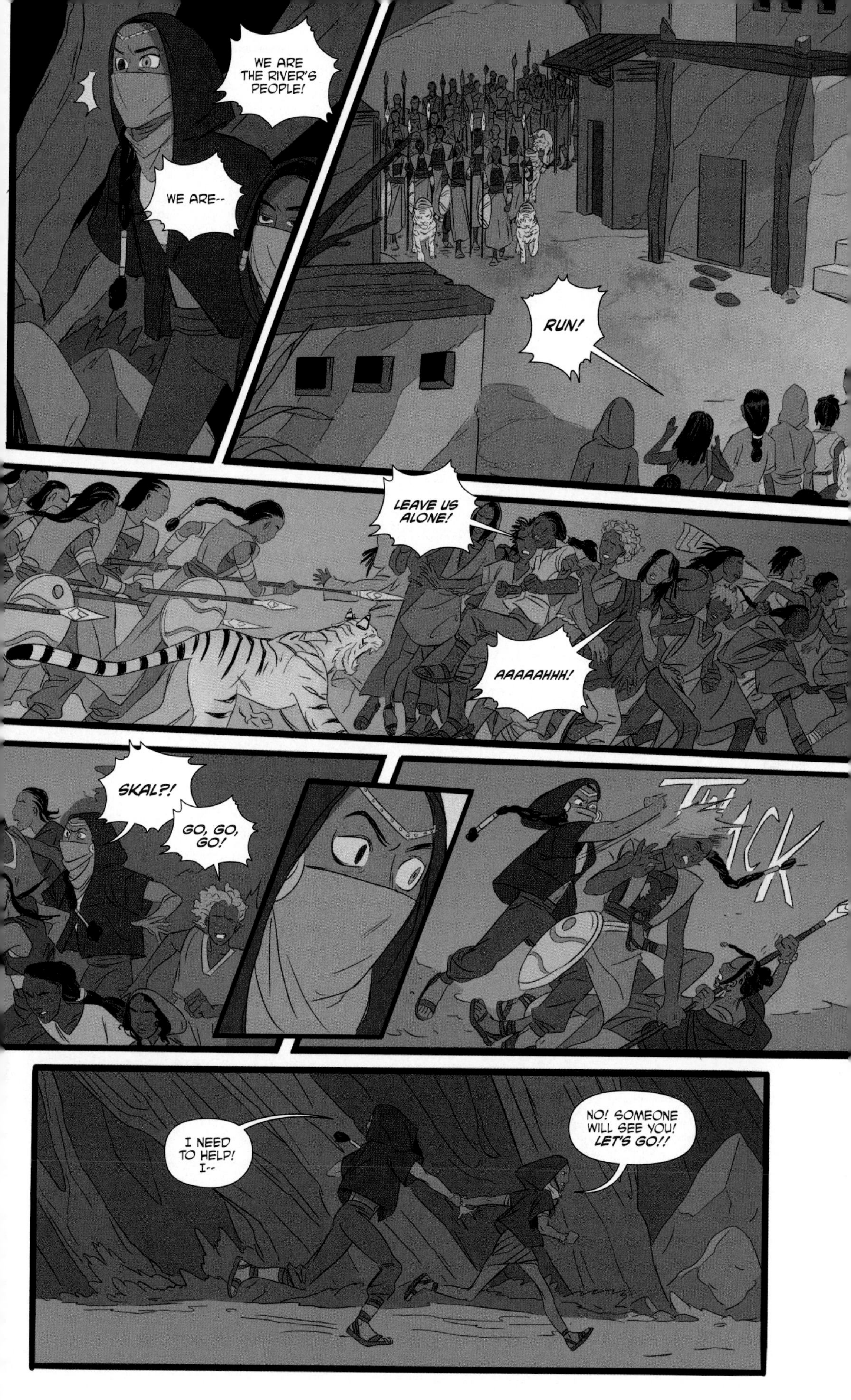
WE ARE THE RIVER'S PEOPLE!
WE ARE--
RUN!
LEAVE US ALONE!
AAAAAHHH!
SKAL?!
GO, GO, GO!
I NEED TO HELP! I--
NO! SOMEONE WILL SEE YOU! LET'S GO!!

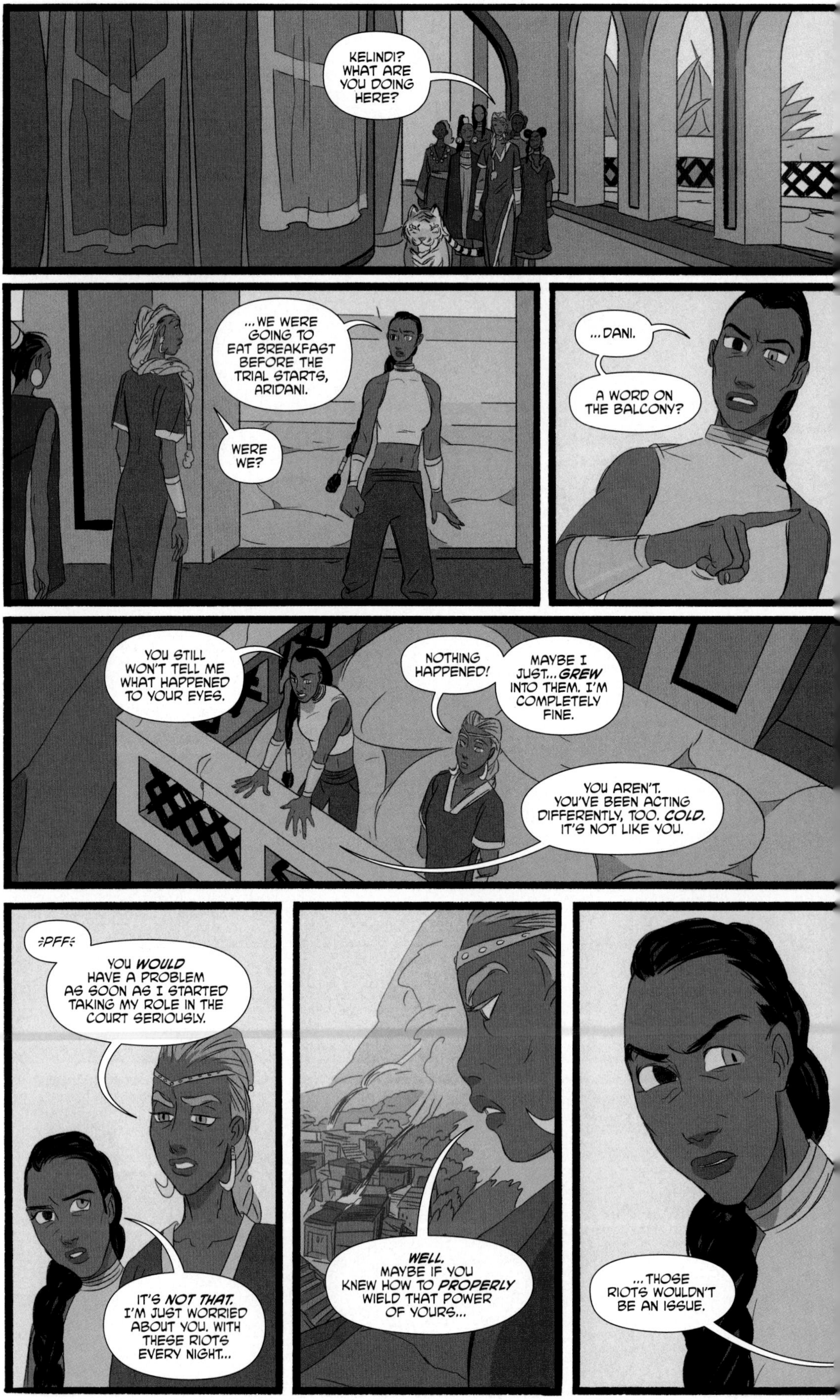
KELINDI? WHAT ARE YOU DOING HERE?
...WE WERE GOING TO EAT BREAKFAST BEFORE THE TRIAL STARTS, ARIDANI.
WERE WE?
...DANI.
A WORD ON THE BALCONY?
YOU STILL WON'T TELL ME WHAT HAPPENED TO YOUR EYES.
NOTHING HAPPENED!
MAYBE I JUST...GREW INTO THEM. I'M COMPLETELY FINE.
YOU AREN'T. YOU'VE BEEN ACTING DIFFERENTLY, TOO. COLD. IT'S NOT LIKE YOU.
PFF
YOU WOULD HAVE A PROBLEM AS SOON AS I STARTED TAKING MY ROLE IN THE COURT SERIOUSLY.
IT'S NOT THAT. I'M JUST WORRIED ABOUT YOU. WITH THESE RIOTS EVERY NIGHT...
WELL. MAYBE IF YOU KNEW HOW TO PROPERLY WIELD THAT POWER OF YOURS...
...THOSE RIOTS WOULDN'T BE AN ISSUE.

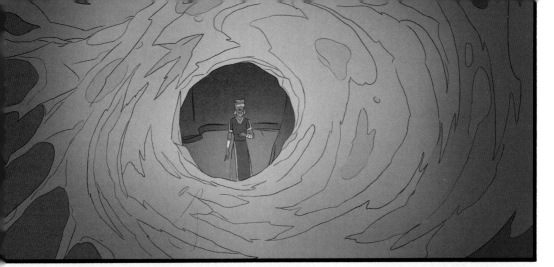

CHEER

HA!

LOOKS LIKE OUR GIRL JUST MADE THIS GAME *VERY* INTERESTING.

CONGRATULATONS, DAUGHTER.

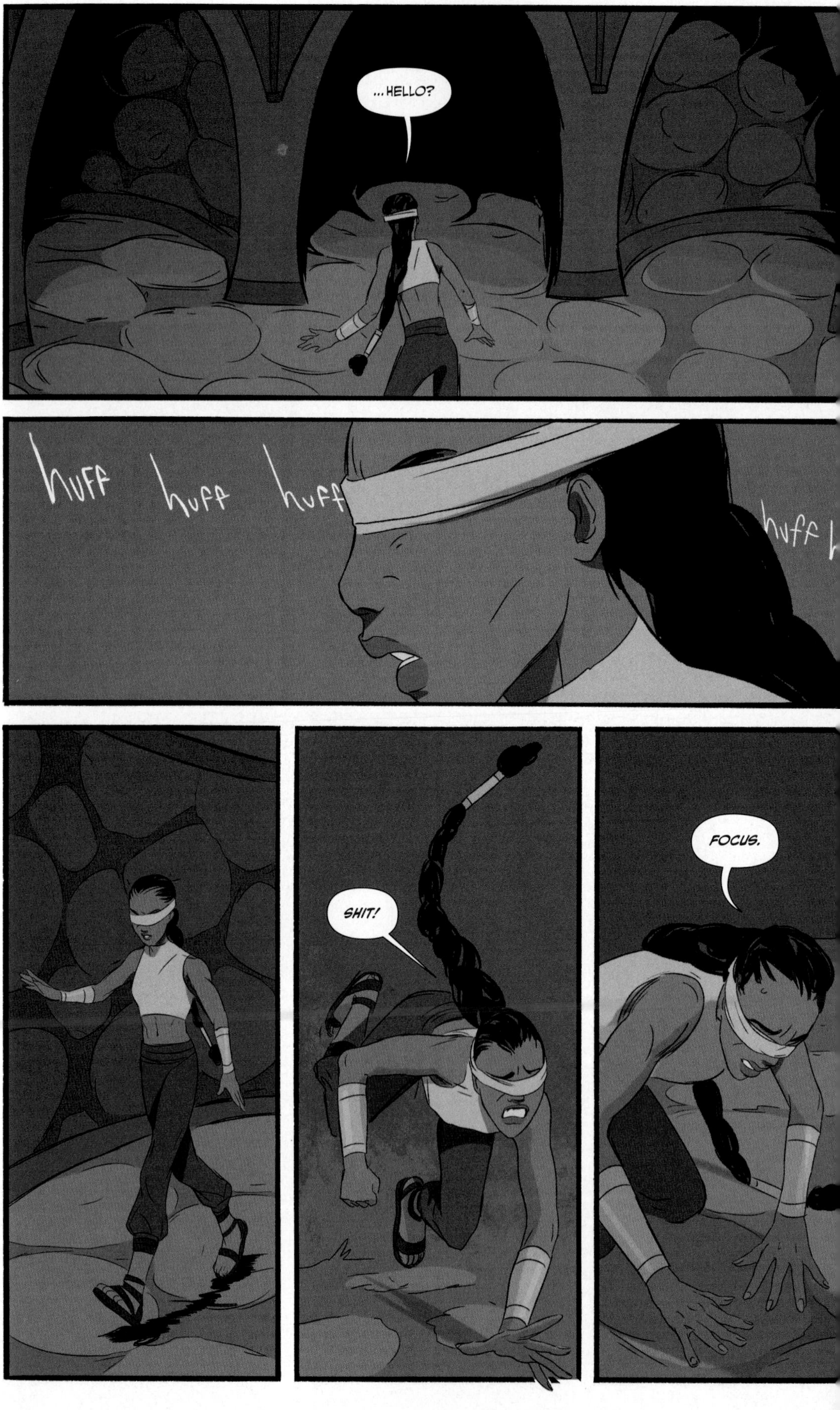
...HELLO?
huff huff huff
huff h
SHIT!
FOCUS.

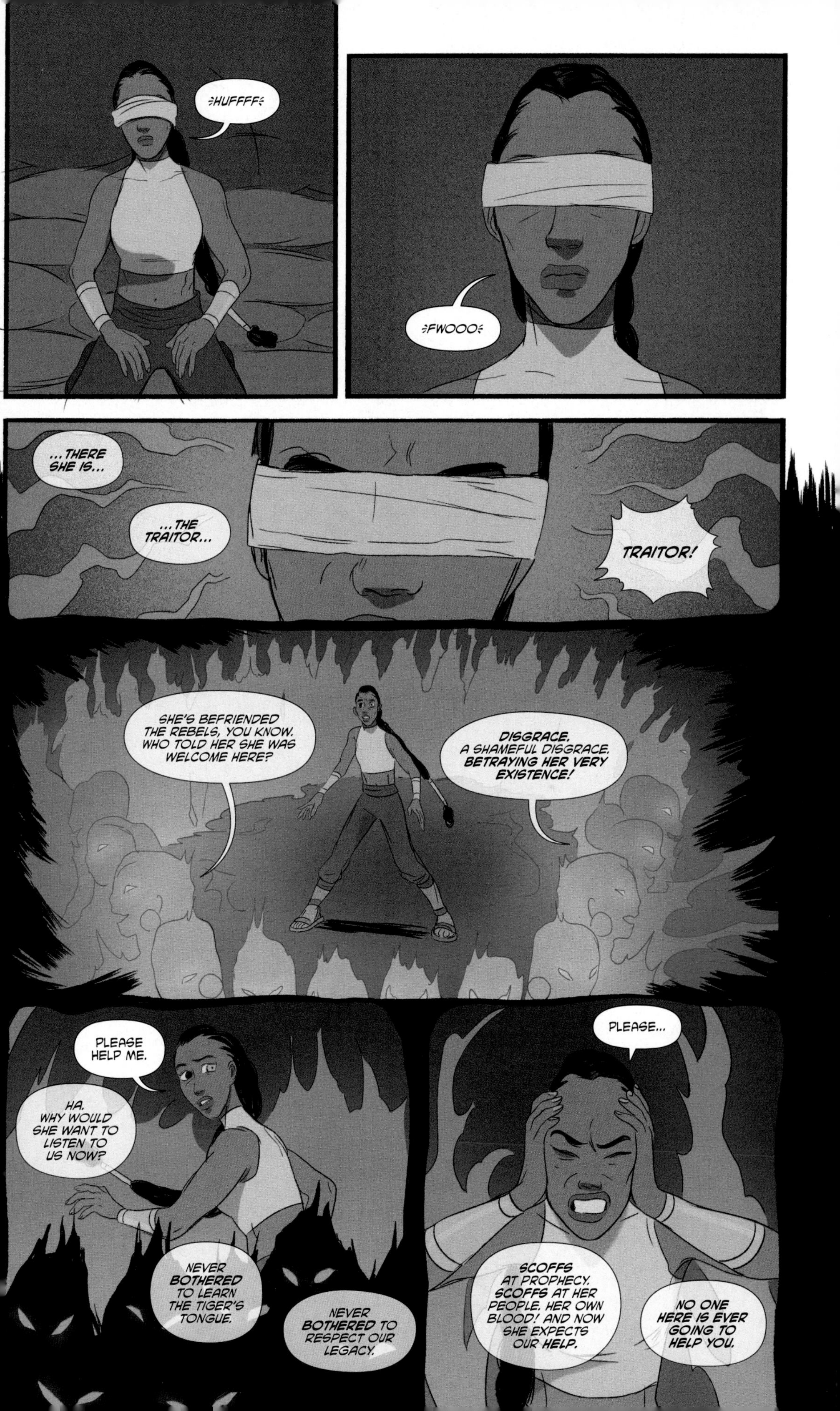

HUFFFF
FWOOO
...THERE SHE IS...
...THE TRAITOR...
TRAITOR!
SHE'S BEFRIENDED THE REBELS, YOU KNOW. WHO TOLD HER SHE WAS WELCOME HERE?
DISGRACE. A SHAMEFUL DISGRACE. BETRAYING HER VERY EXISTENCE!
PLEASE HELP ME.
HA. WHY WOULD SHE WANT TO LISTEN TO US NOW?
NEVER BOTHERED TO LEARN THE TIGER'S TONGUE.
NEVER BOTHERED TO RESPECT OUR LEGACY.
PLEASE...
SCOFFS AT PROPHECY. SCOFFS AT HER PEOPLE. HER OWN BLOOD! AND NOW SHE EXPECTS OUR HELP.
NO ONE HERE IS EVER GOING TO HELP YOU.

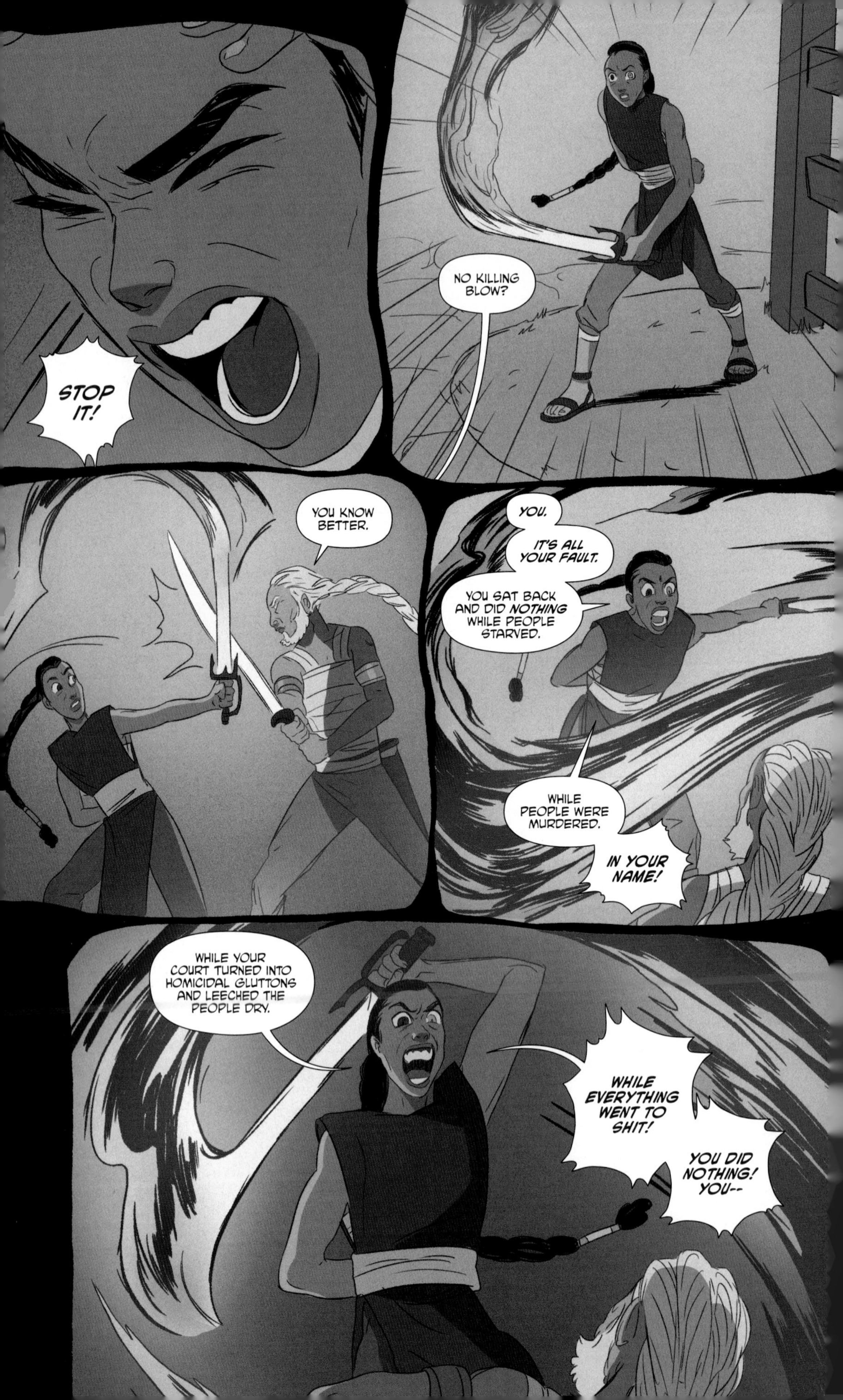
STOP IT!
NO KILLING BLOW?
YOU KNOW BETTER.
YOU.
IT'S ALL YOUR FAULT.
YOU SAT BACK AND DID NOTHING WHILE PEOPLE STARVED.
WHILE PEOPLE WERE MURDERED.
IN YOUR NAME!
WHILE YOUR COURT TURNED INTO HOMICIDAL GLUTTONS AND LEECHED THE PEOPLE DRY.
WHILE EVERYTHING WENT TO SHIT!
YOU DID NOTHING! YOU--

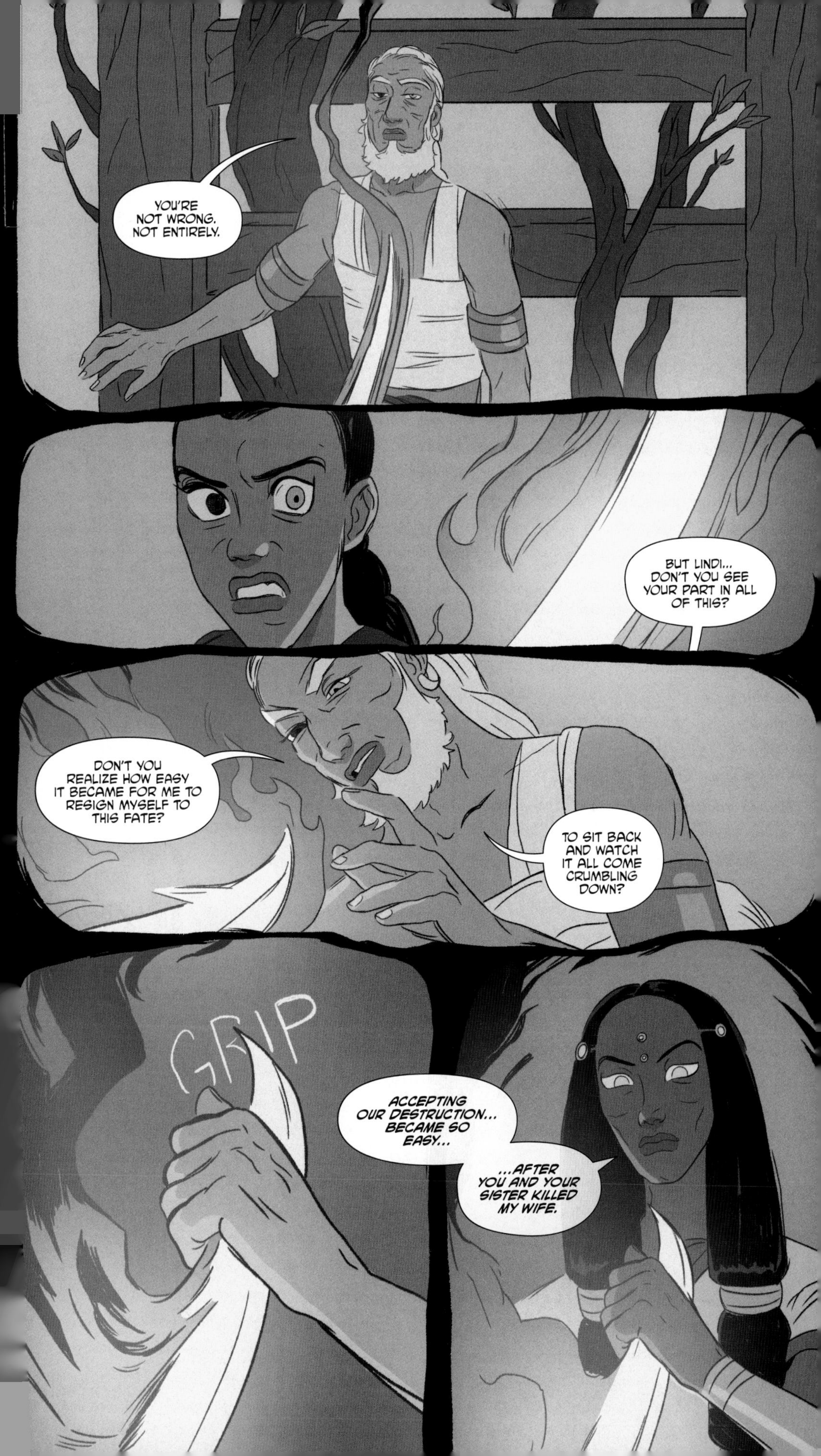
YOU'RE NOT WRONG. NOT ENTIRELY.
BUT LINDI... DON'T YOU SEE YOUR PART IN ALL OF THIS?
DON'T YOU REALIZE HOW EASY IT BECAME FOR ME TO RESIGN MYSELF TO THIS FATE?
TO SIT BACK AND WATCH IT ALL COME CRUMBLING DOWN?
GRIP
ACCEPTING OUR DESTRUCTION... BECAME SO EASY...
...AFTER YOU AND YOUR SISTER KILLED MY WIFE.

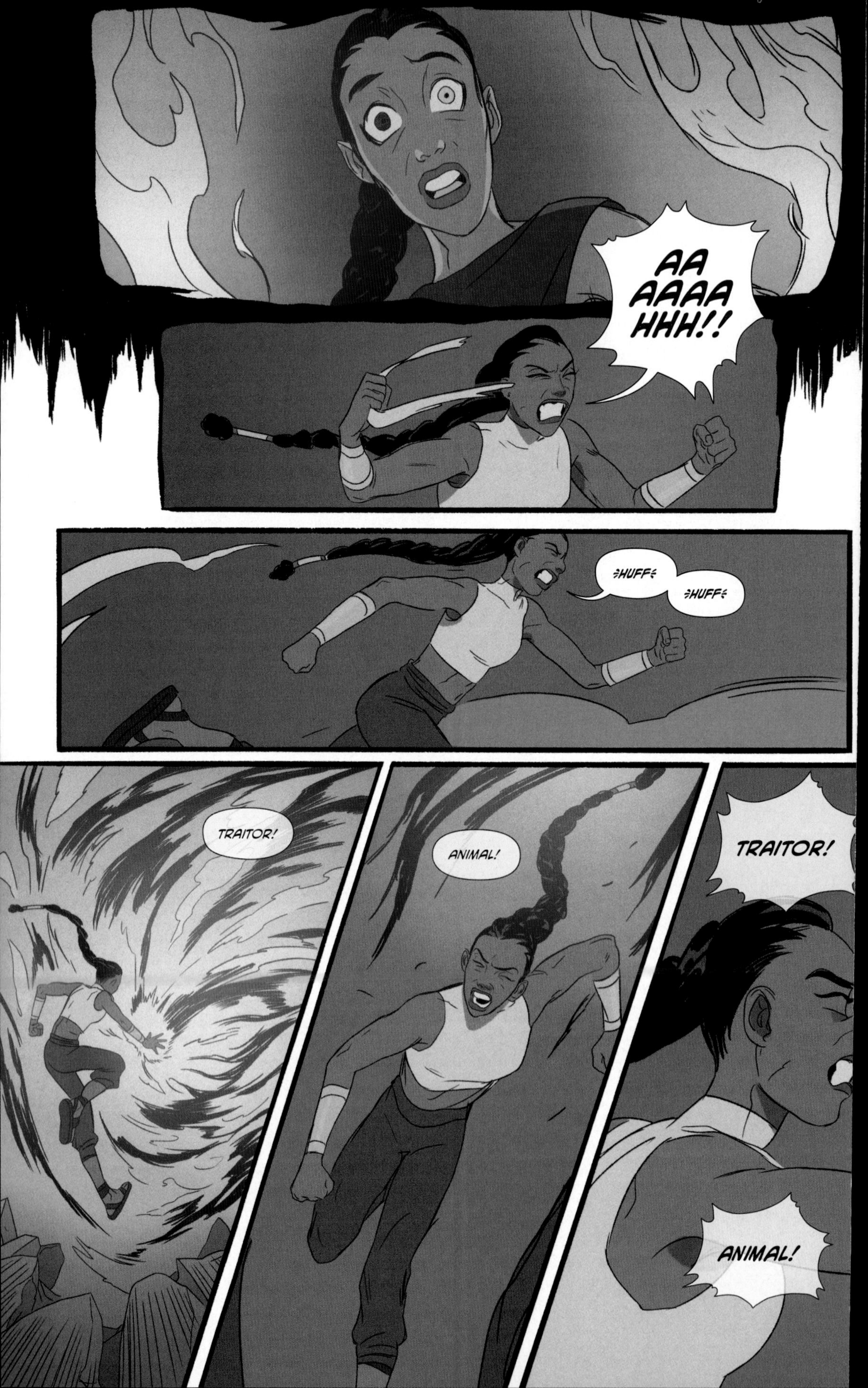
AA AAAA HHH!!
HUFF
HUFF
TRAITOR!
ANIMAL!
TRAITOR!
ANIMAL!

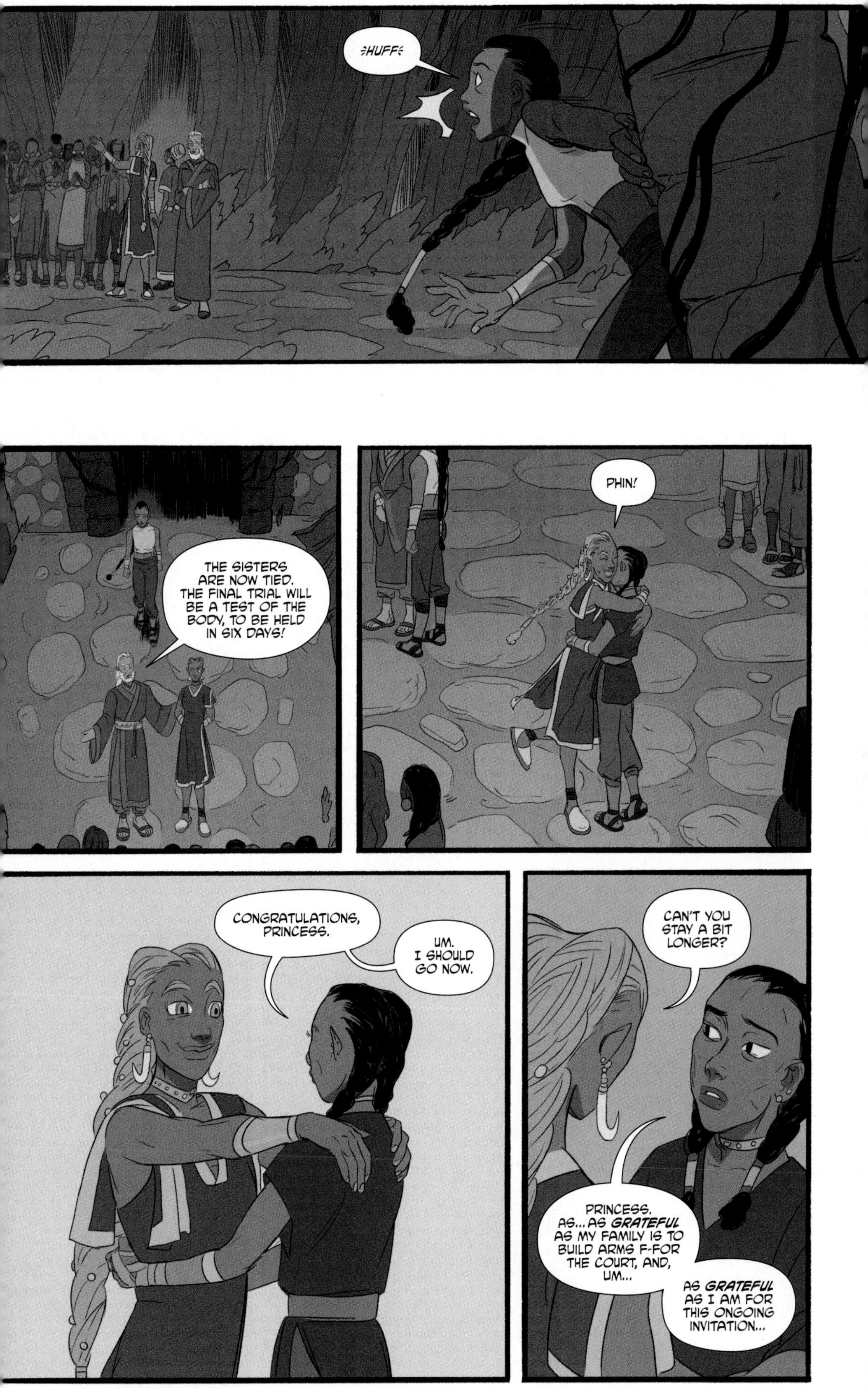

⚡HUFF⚡
THE SISTERS ARE NOW TIED. THE FINAL TRIAL WILL BE A TEST OF THE BODY, TO BE HELD IN SIX DAYS!
PHIN!
CONGRATULATIONS, PRINCESS.
UM. I SHOULD GO NOW.
CAN'T YOU STAY A BIT LONGER?
PRINCESS. AS...AS *GRATEFUL* AS MY FAMILY IS TO BUILD ARMS F-FOR THE COURT, AND, UM...
AS *GRATEFUL* AS I AM FOR THIS ONGOING INVITATION...

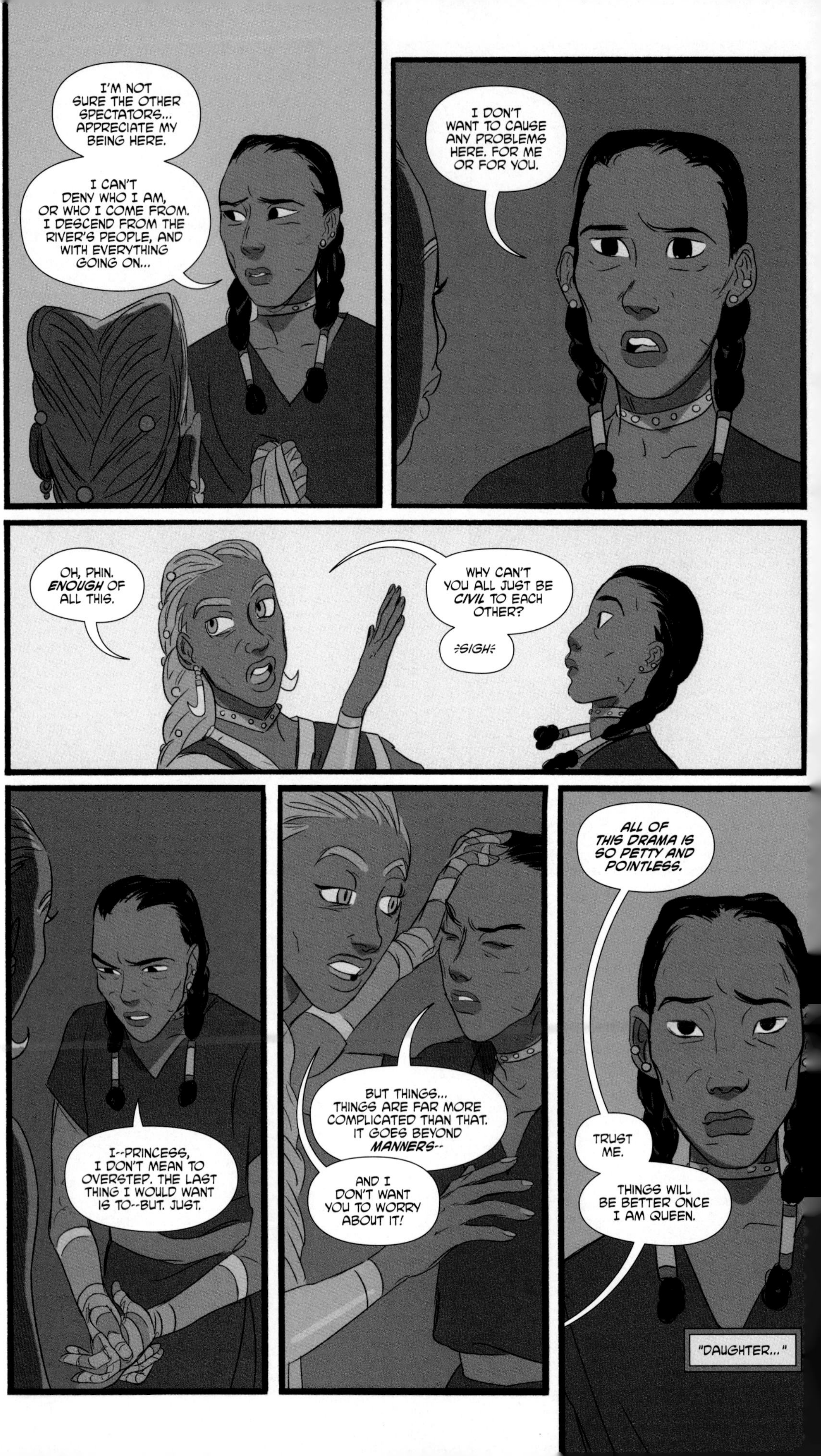
I'M NOT SURE THE OTHER SPECTATORS... APPRECIATE MY BEING HERE.
I CAN'T DENY WHO I AM, OR WHO I COME FROM. I DESCEND FROM THE RIVER'S PEOPLE, AND WITH EVERYTHING GOING ON...
I DON'T WANT TO CAUSE ANY PROBLEMS HERE. FOR ME OR FOR YOU.
OH, PHIN. *ENOUGH* OF ALL THIS.
WHY CAN'T YOU ALL JUST BE *CIVIL* TO EACH OTHER?
SIGH
I--PRINCESS, I DON'T MEAN TO OVERSTEP. THE LAST THING I WOULD WANT IS TO--BUT. JUST.
BUT THINGS... THINGS ARE FAR MORE COMPLICATED THAN THAT. IT GOES BEYOND *MANNERS*--
AND I DON'T WANT YOU TO WORRY ABOUT IT!
ALL OF THIS DRAMA IS SO PETTY AND POINTLESS.
TRUST ME.
THINGS WILL BE BETTER ONCE I AM QUEEN.
"DAUGHTER..."

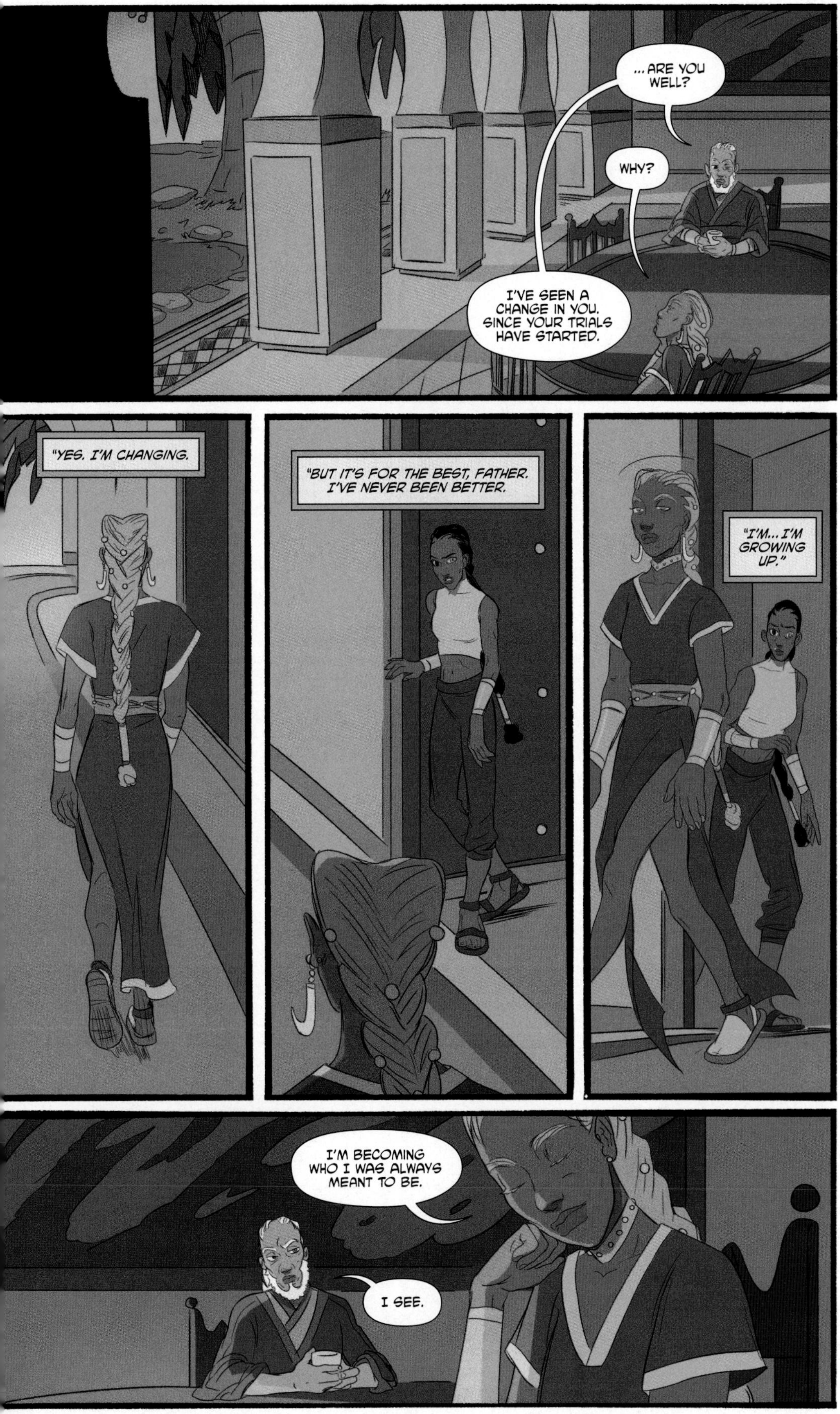
...ARE YOU WELL?
WHY?
I'VE SEEN A CHANGE IN YOU. SINCE YOUR TRIALS HAVE STARTED.
"YES. I'M CHANGING.
"BUT IT'S FOR THE BEST, FATHER. I'VE NEVER BEEN BETTER.
"I'M... I'M GROWING UP."
I'M BECOMING WHO I WAS ALWAYS MEANT TO BE.
I SEE.

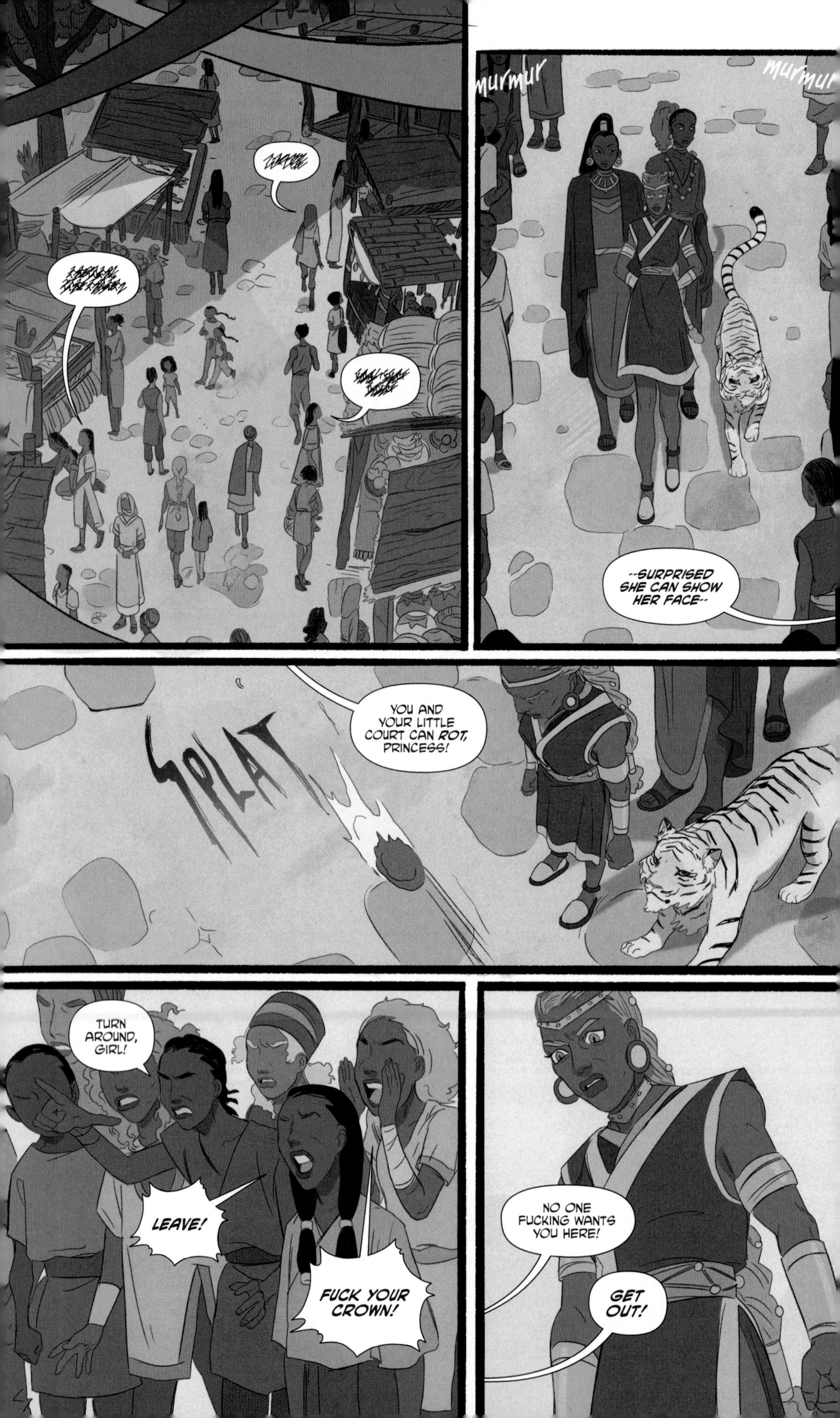
murmur
murmur
--SURPRISED SHE CAN SHOW HER FACE--
SPLAT
YOU AND YOUR LITTLE COURT CAN *ROT*, PRINCESS!
TURN AROUND, GIRL!
LEAVE!
FUCK YOUR CROWN!
NO ONE FUCKING WANTS YOU HERE!
GET OUT!

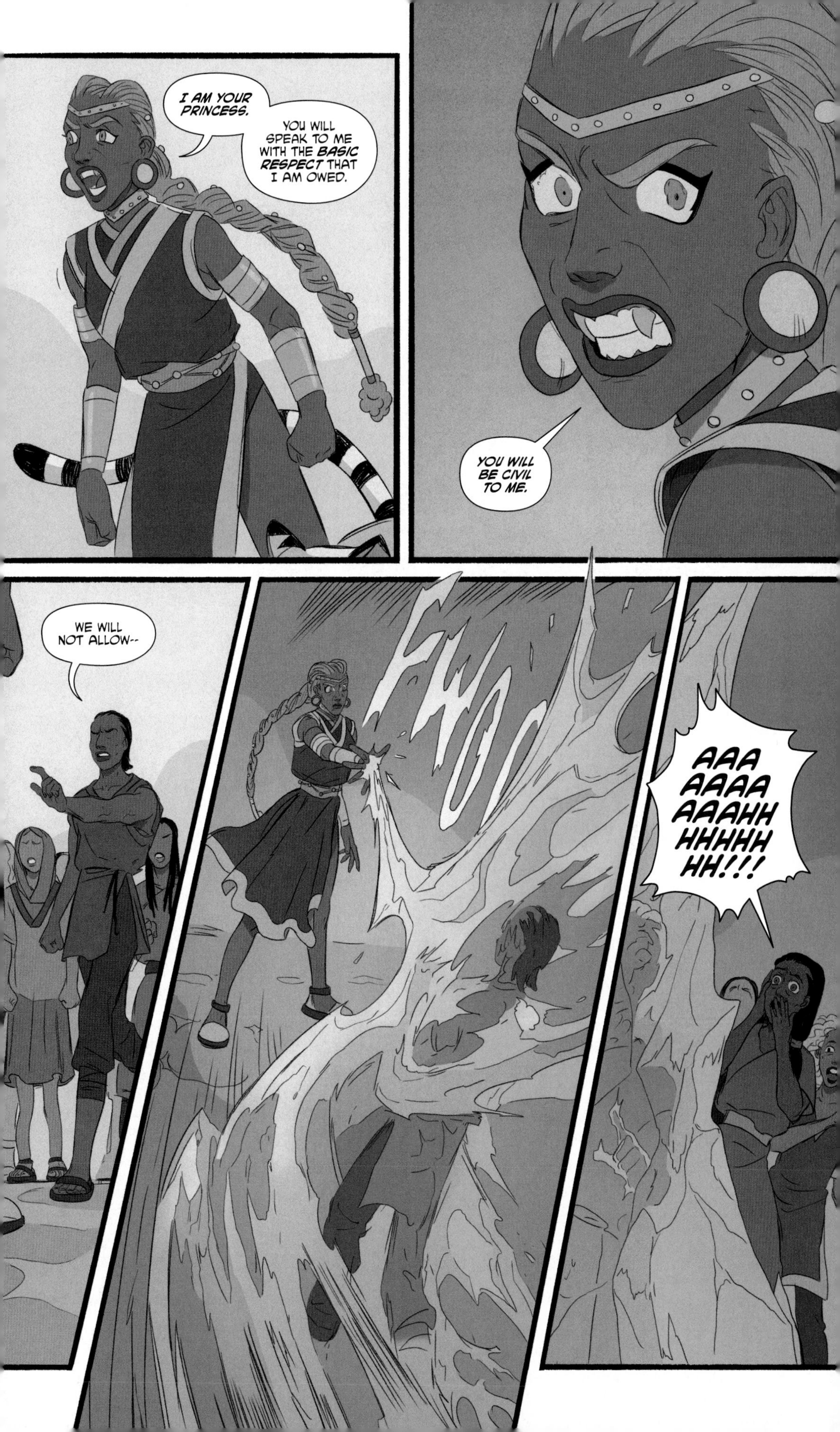
I AM YOUR PRINCESS.
YOU WILL SPEAK TO ME WITH THE BASIC RESPECT THAT I AM OWED.
YOU WILL BE CIVIL TO ME.
WE WILL NOT ALLOW--
FWOOO
AAAAAAAAAAHHHHHHH!!!

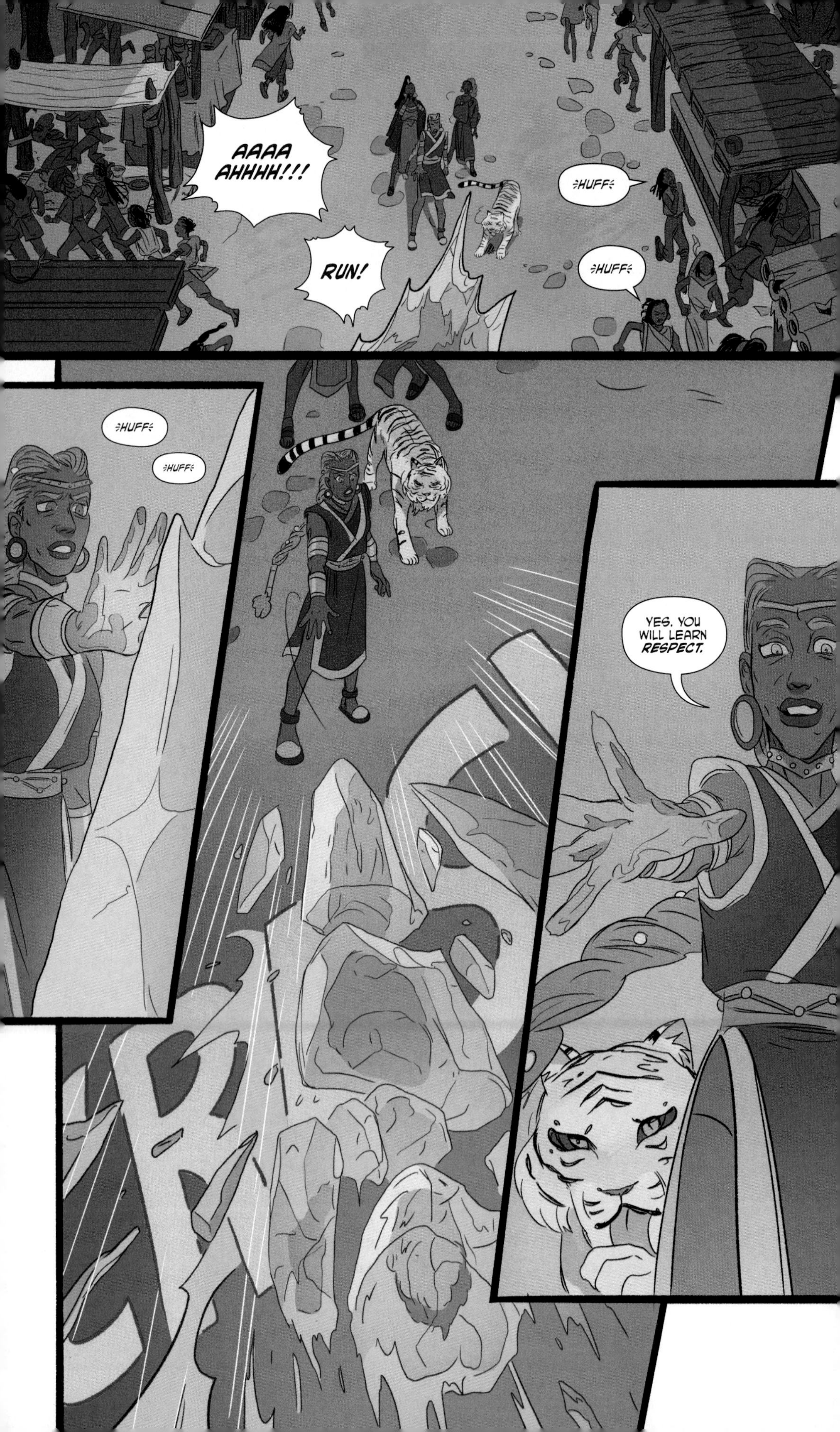
AAAA AHHHH!!!
RUN!
HUFF
HUFF
HUFF
HUFF
YES. YOU WILL LEARN *RESPECT.*

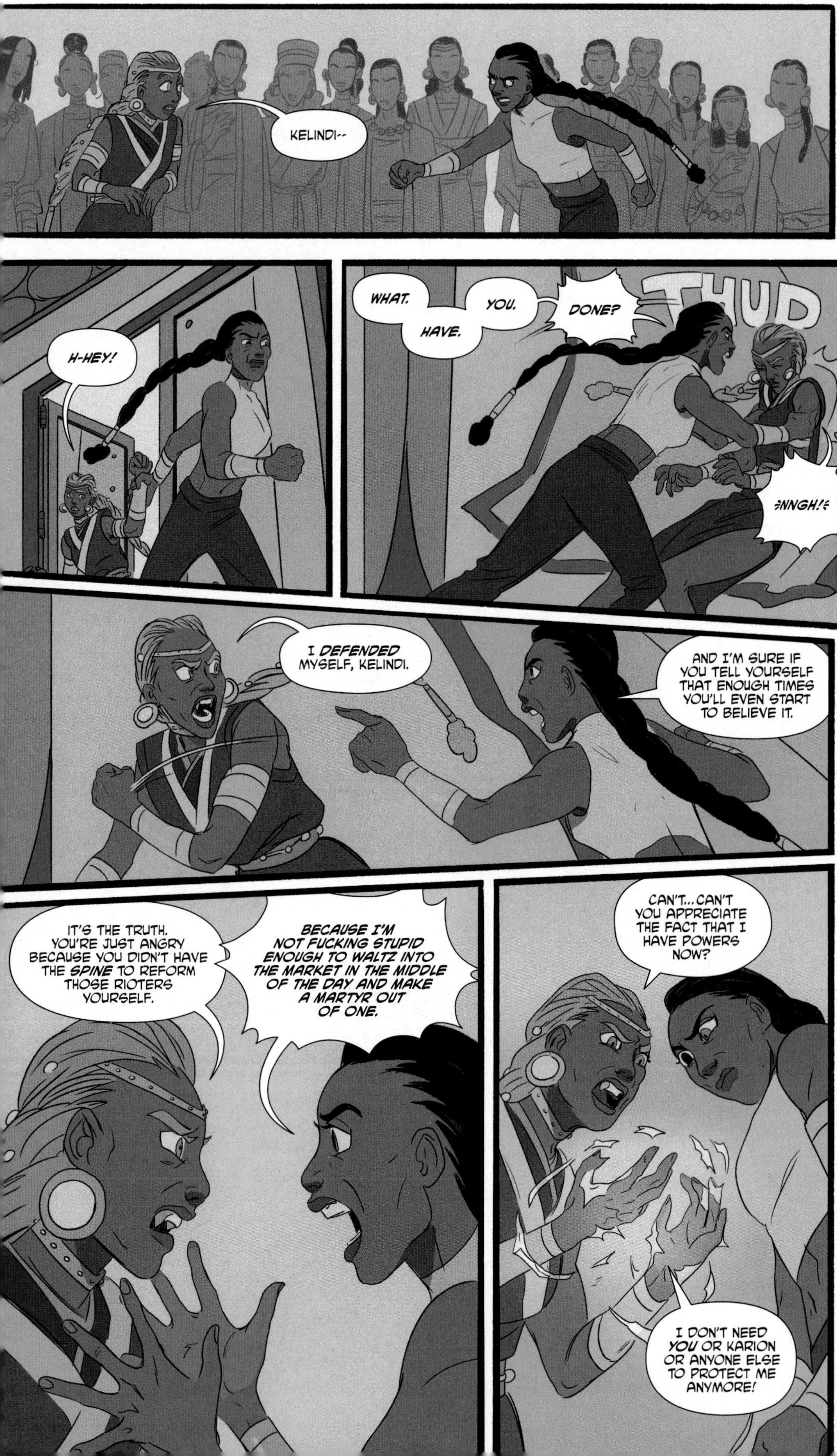
KELINDI--
H-HEY!
WHAT.
HAVE.
YOU.
DONE?
THUD
NNGH!
I *DEFENDED* MYSELF, KELINDI.
AND I'M SURE IF YOU TELL YOURSELF THAT ENOUGH TIMES YOU'LL EVEN START TO BELIEVE IT.
IT'S THE TRUTH. YOU'RE JUST ANGRY BECAUSE YOU DIDN'T HAVE THE *SPINE* TO REFORM THOSE RIOTERS YOURSELF.
BECAUSE I'M NOT FUCKING STUPID ENOUGH TO WALTZ INTO THE MARKET IN THE MIDDLE OF THE DAY AND MAKE A MARTYR OUT OF ONE.
CAN'T...CAN'T YOU APPRECIATE THE FACT THAT I HAVE POWERS NOW?
I DON'T NEED *YOU* OR KARION OR ANYONE ELSE TO PROTECT ME ANYMORE!

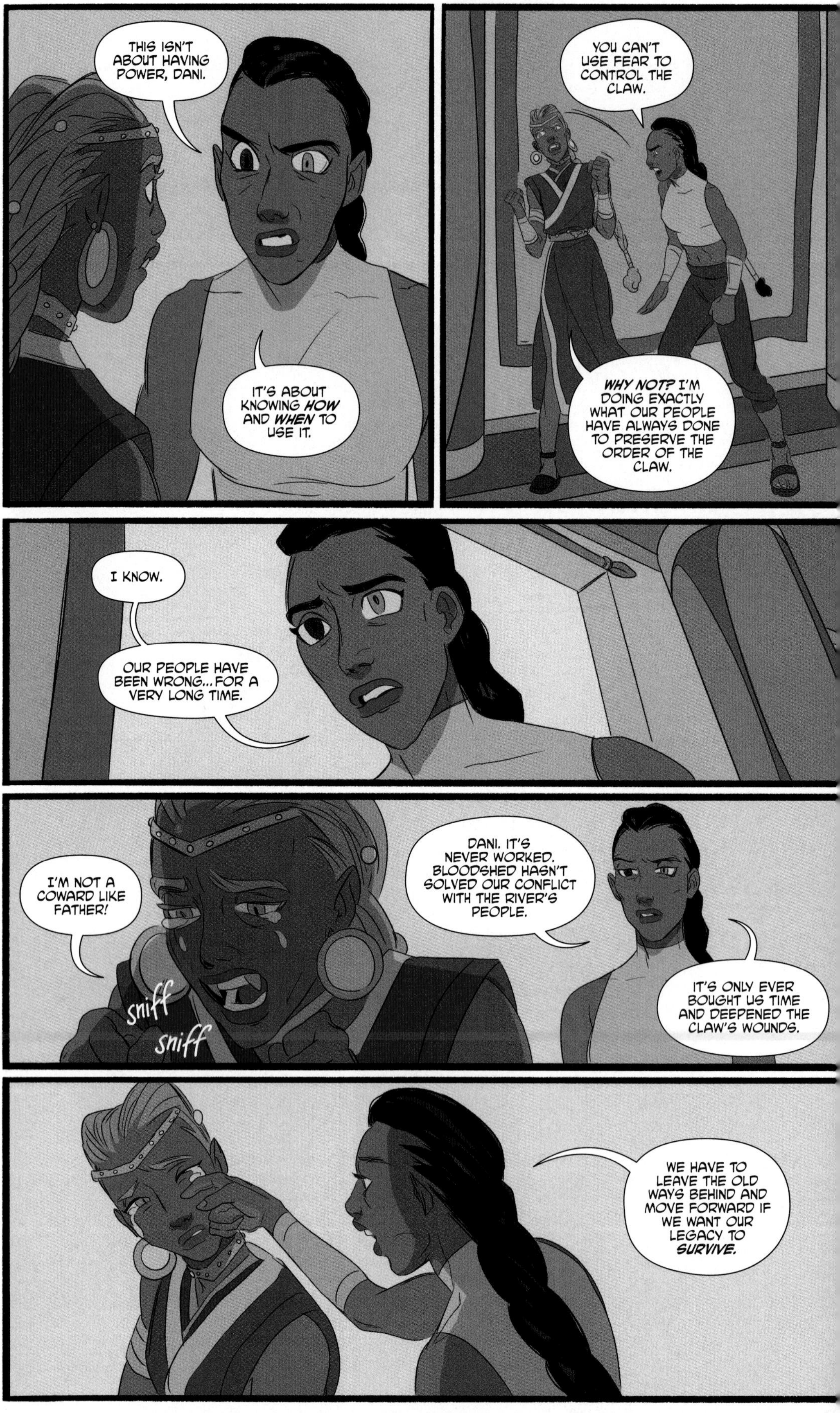
THIS ISN'T ABOUT HAVING POWER, DANI.
IT'S ABOUT KNOWING *HOW* AND *WHEN* TO USE IT.
YOU CAN'T USE FEAR TO CONTROL THE CLAW.
WHY NOT? I'M DOING EXACTLY WHAT OUR PEOPLE HAVE ALWAYS DONE TO PRESERVE THE ORDER OF THE CLAW.
I KNOW.
OUR PEOPLE HAVE BEEN WRONG...FOR A VERY LONG TIME.
I'M NOT A COWARD LIKE FATHER!
sniff
sniff
DANI. IT'S NEVER WORKED. BLOODSHED HASN'T SOLVED OUR CONFLICT WITH THE RIVER'S PEOPLE.
IT'S ONLY EVER BOUGHT US TIME AND DEEPENED THE CLAW'S WOUNDS.
WE HAVE TO LEAVE THE OLD WAYS BEHIND AND MOVE FORWARD IF WE WANT OUR LEGACY TO *SURVIVE.*

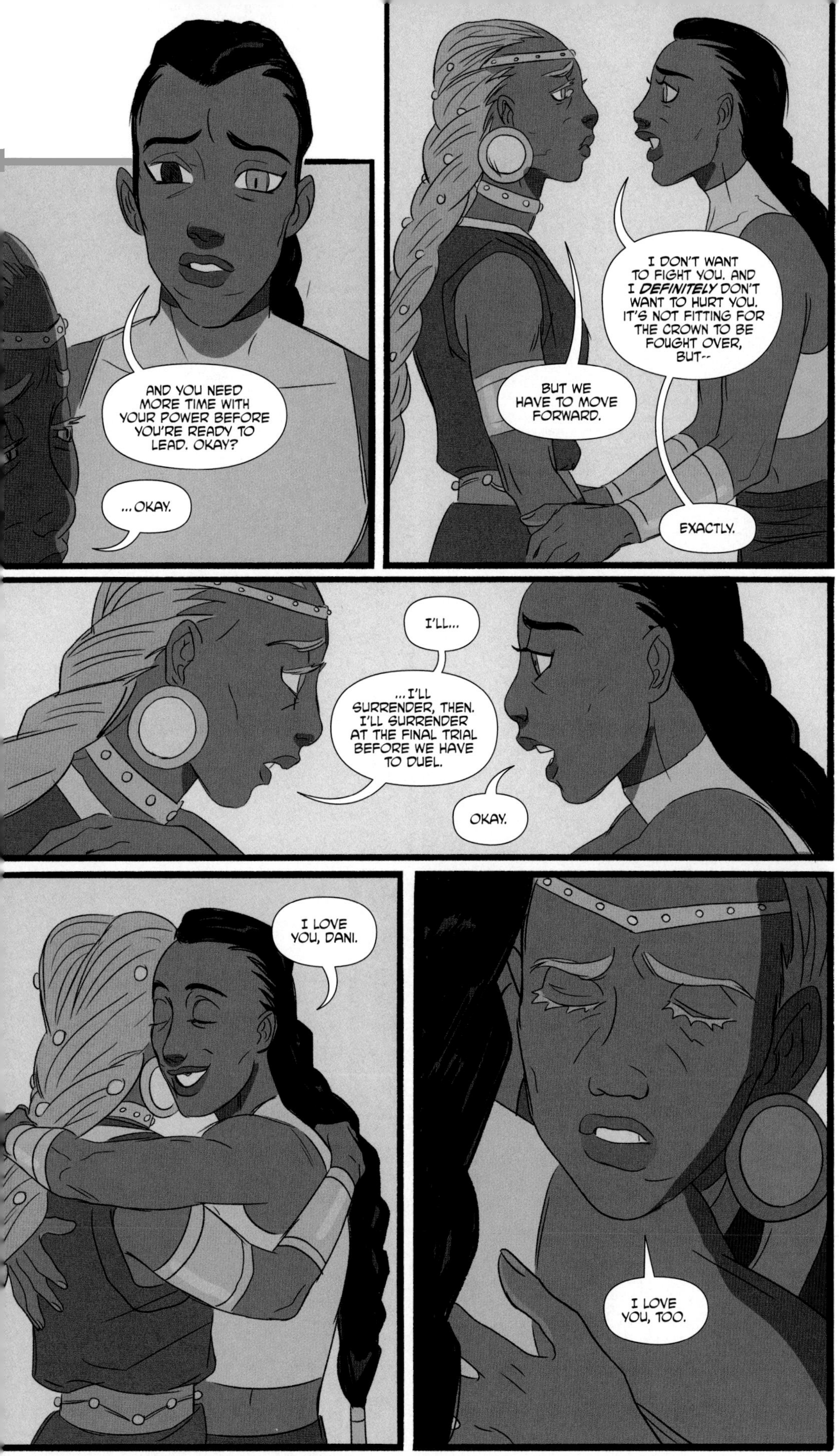
AND YOU NEED MORE TIME WITH YOUR POWER BEFORE YOU'RE READY TO LEAD. OKAY?
...OKAY.
I DON'T WANT TO FIGHT YOU. AND I *DEFINITELY* DON'T WANT TO HURT YOU. IT'S NOT FITTING FOR THE CROWN TO BE FOUGHT OVER, BUT--
BUT WE HAVE TO MOVE FORWARD.
EXACTLY.
I'LL...
...I'LL SURRENDER, THEN. I'LL SURRENDER AT THE FINAL TRIAL BEFORE WE HAVE TO DUEL.
OKAY.
I LOVE YOU, DANI.
I LOVE YOU, TOO.

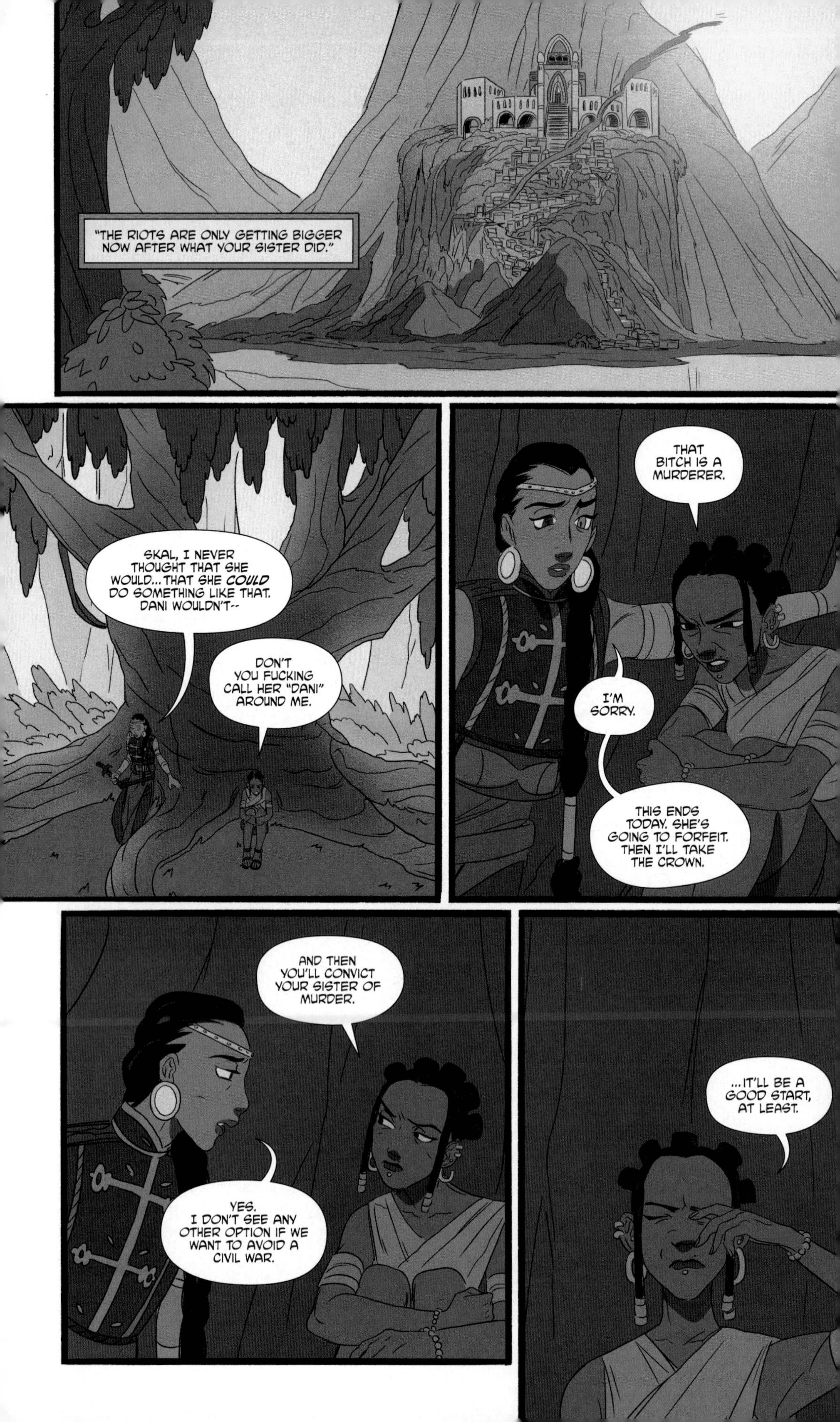
"THE RIOTS ARE ONLY GETTING BIGGER NOW AFTER WHAT YOUR SISTER DID."
SKAL, I NEVER THOUGHT THAT SHE WOULD... THAT SHE *COULD* DO SOMETHING LIKE THAT. DANI WOULDN'T--
DON'T YOU FUCKING CALL HER "DANI" AROUND ME.
THAT BITCH IS A MURDERER.
I'M SORRY.
THIS ENDS TODAY. SHE'S GOING TO FORFEIT. THEN I'LL TAKE THE CROWN.
AND THEN YOU'LL CONVICT YOUR SISTER OF MURDER.
YES. I DON'T SEE ANY OTHER OPTION IF WE WANT TO AVOID A CIVIL WAR.
...IT'LL BE A GOOD START, AT LEAST.

"JUST BEAR WITH ME, SKAL. I'LL HAVE ALL OF THIS UNDER CONTROL SOON."

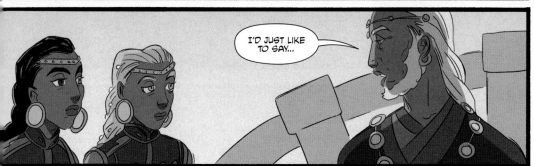

I'D JUST LIKE TO SAY...

...HOW DEEPLY I CARE FOR YOU, KELINDI AND ARIDANI.

AND TODAY'S OUTCOME WON'T CHANGE THAT.

THERE IS MUCH WORK TO BE DONE IN THE CLAW.

WORK THAT YOU'VE INHERITED FROM ME, REGRETTABLY.

BUT THIS IS THE TIME THAT OUR FAMILY MUST COME TOGETHER...

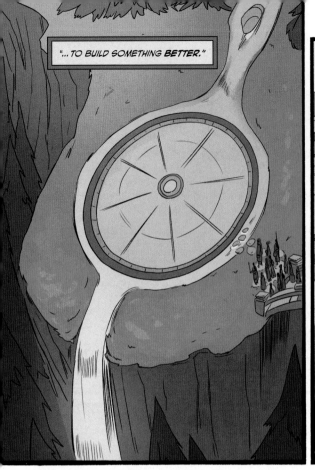

"...TO BUILD SOMETHING *BETTER*."

PHYSICAL STRENGTH HAS ALWAYS BEEN THE GREATEST TOOL OF THE TIGER'S PEOPLE.

"THE TIGER'S CLAW WAS BORN FROM THAT STRENGTH."

"WE USE IT TO SHAPE OUR PARADISE, AS WELL AS OUR FUTURE."

TODAY'S TRIAL, THE FINAL TRIAL, WILL BE ONE OF THE BODY. A TEST OF STRENGTH, ENDURANCE, AND TENACITY.

THE DUEL WILL END WHEN ONE PARTY RELENTS.

AND AFTER, WE WILL CROWN OUR NEW QUEEN.

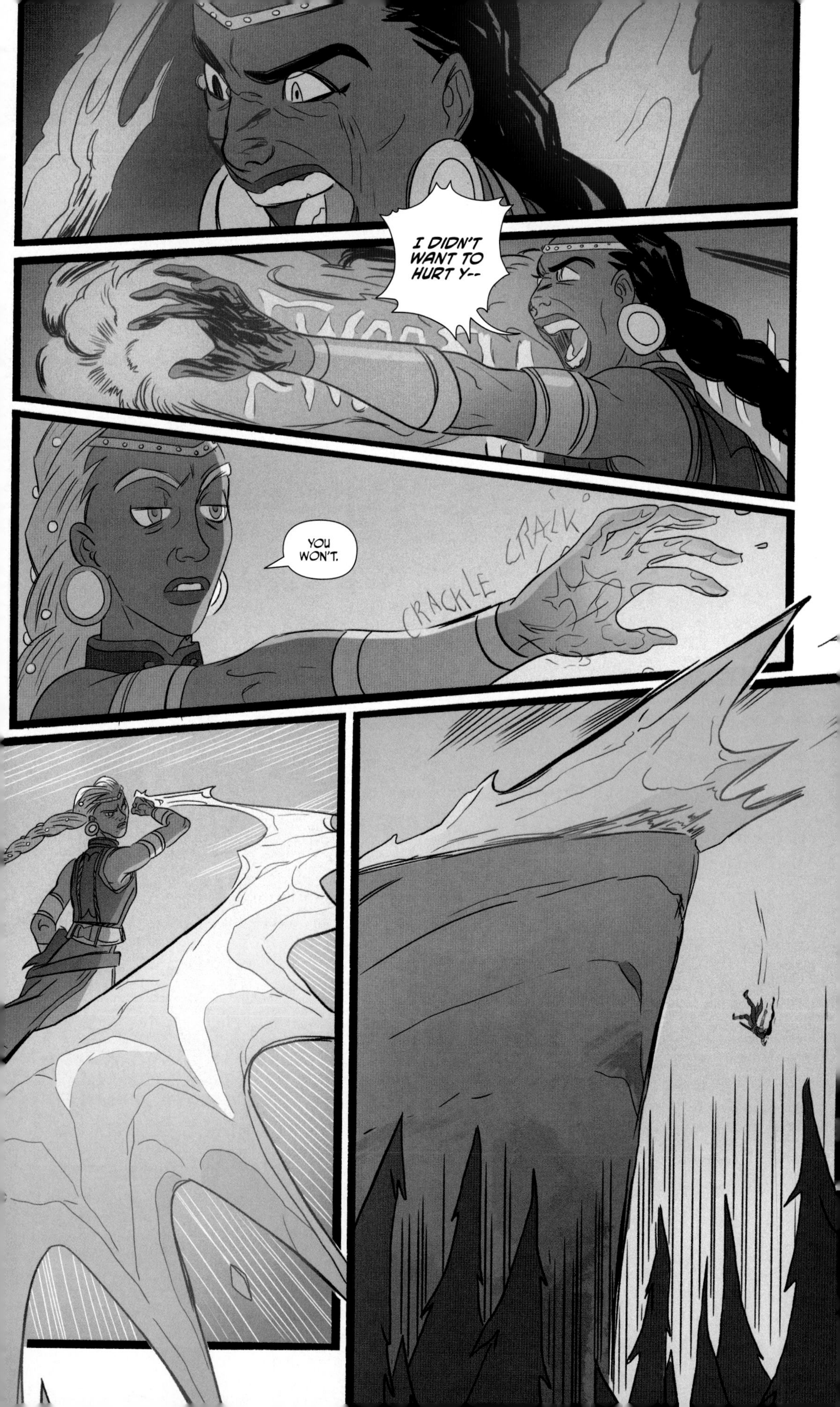
I DIDN'T WANT TO HURT Y--
YOU WON'T.
CRACKLE
CRACK

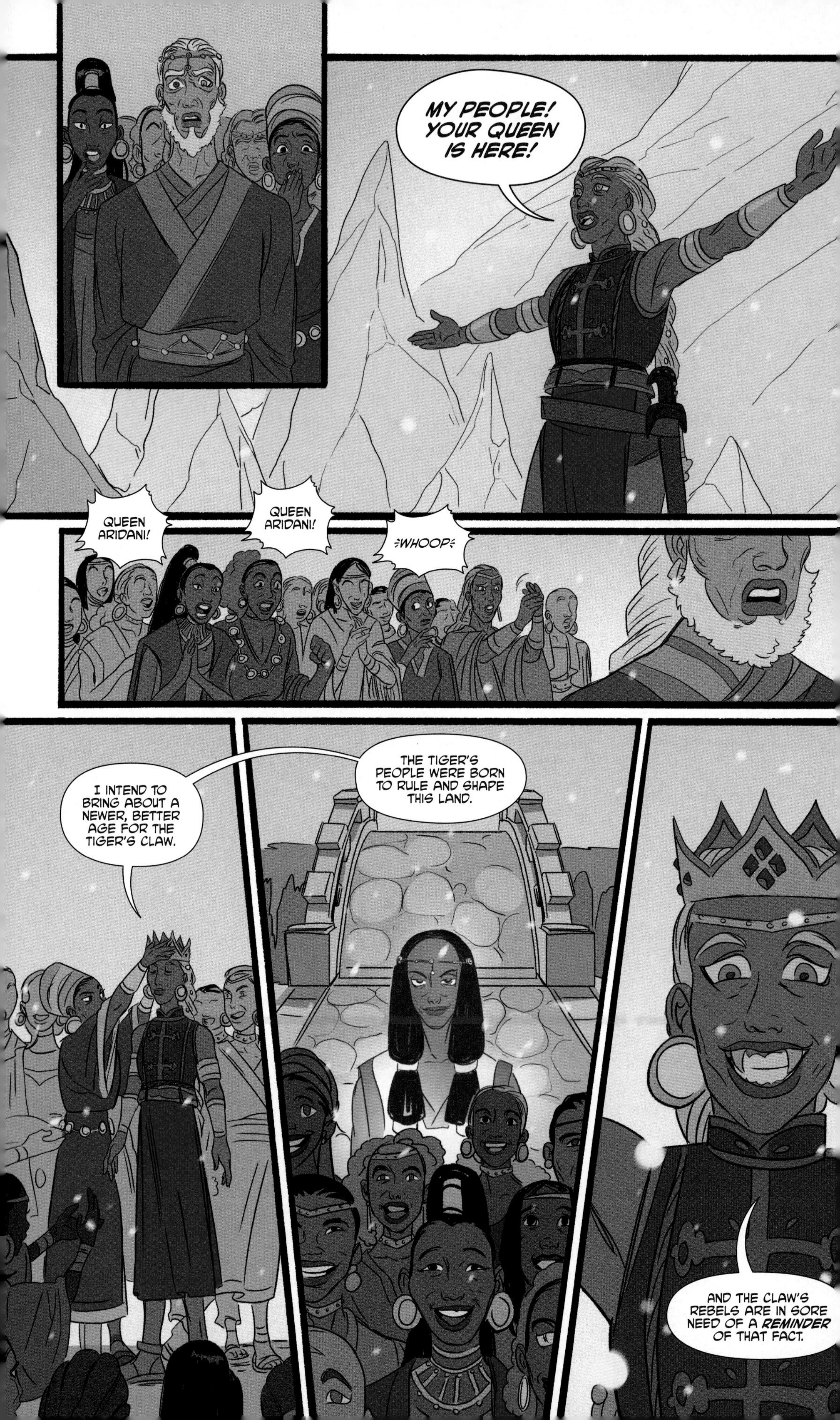
MY PEOPLE! YOUR QUEEN IS HERE!
QUEEN ARIDANI!
QUEEN ARIDANI!
WHOOP
I INTEND TO BRING ABOUT A NEWER, BETTER AGE FOR THE TIGER'S CLAW.
THE TIGER'S PEOPLE WERE BORN TO RULE AND SHAPE THIS LAND.
AND THE CLAW'S REBELS ARE IN SORE NEED OF A *REMINDER* OF THAT FACT.

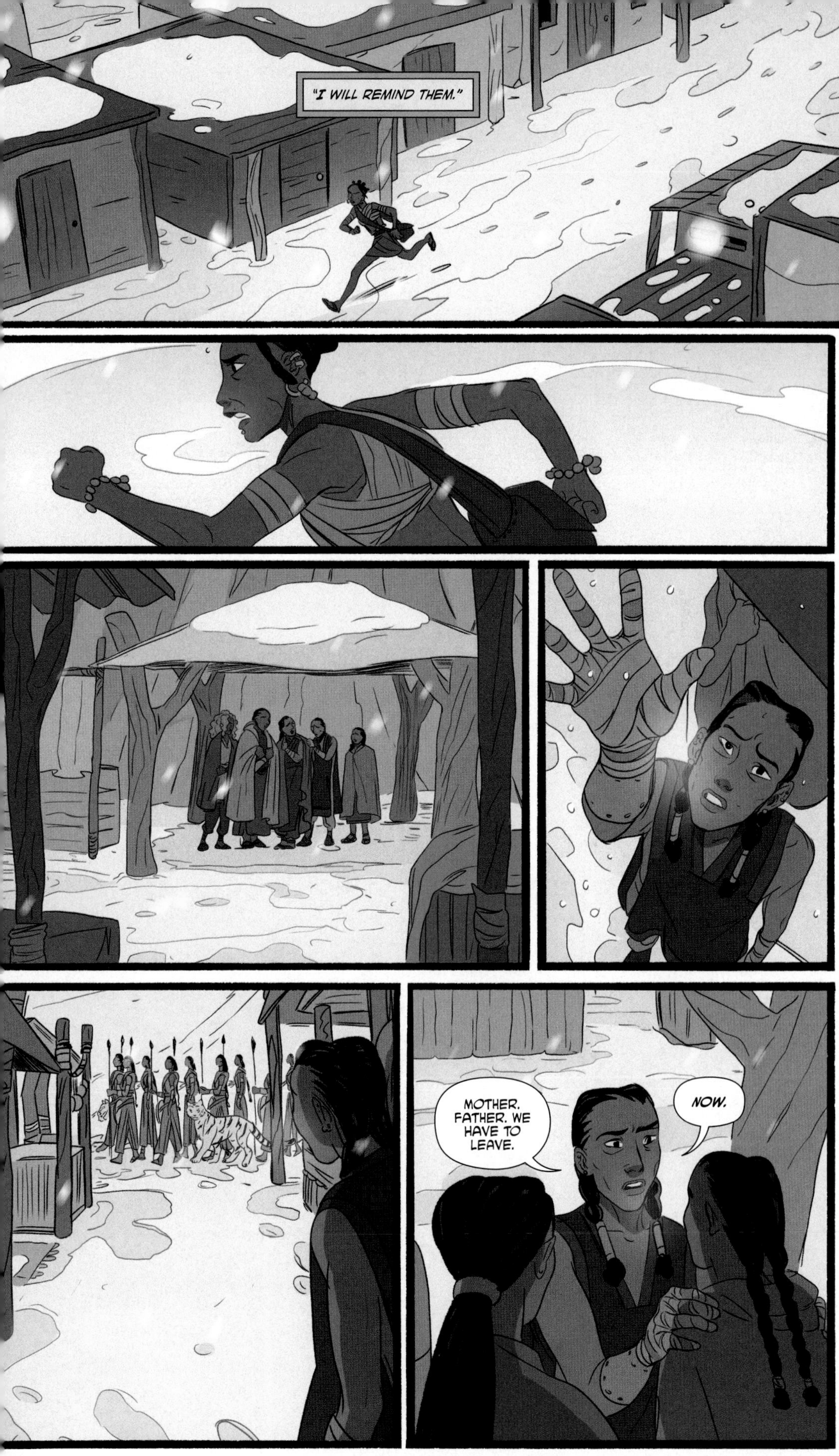
"I WILL REMIND THEM."
MOTHER. FATHER. WE HAVE TO LEAVE.
NOW.

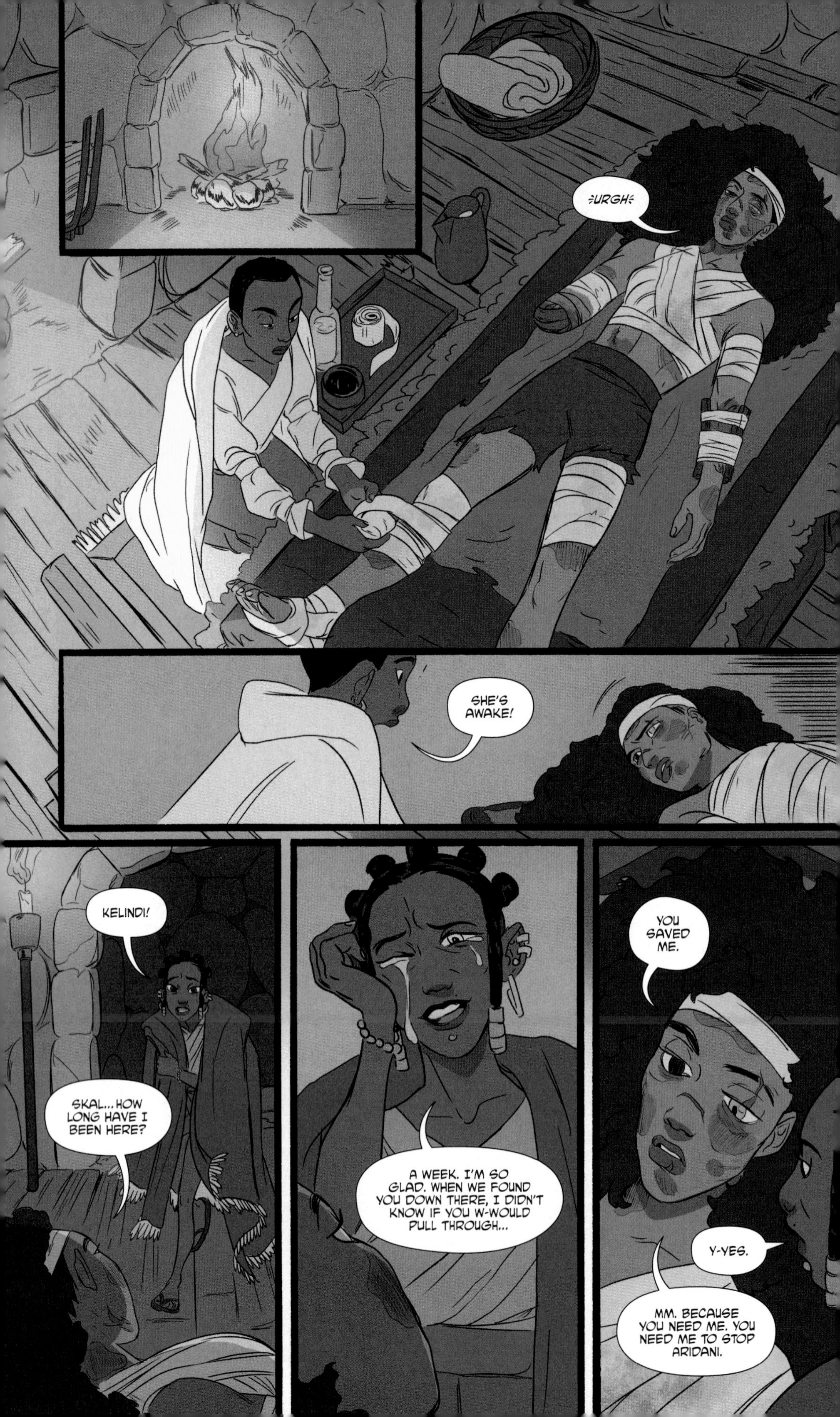

URGH
SHE'S AWAKE!
KELINDI!
SKAL... HOW LONG HAVE I BEEN HERE?
A WEEK. I'M SO GLAD. WHEN WE FOUND YOU DOWN THERE, I DIDN'T KNOW IF YOU W-WOULD PULL THROUGH...
YOU SAVED ME.
Y-YES.
MM. BECAUSE YOU NEED ME. YOU NEED ME TO STOP ARIDANI.

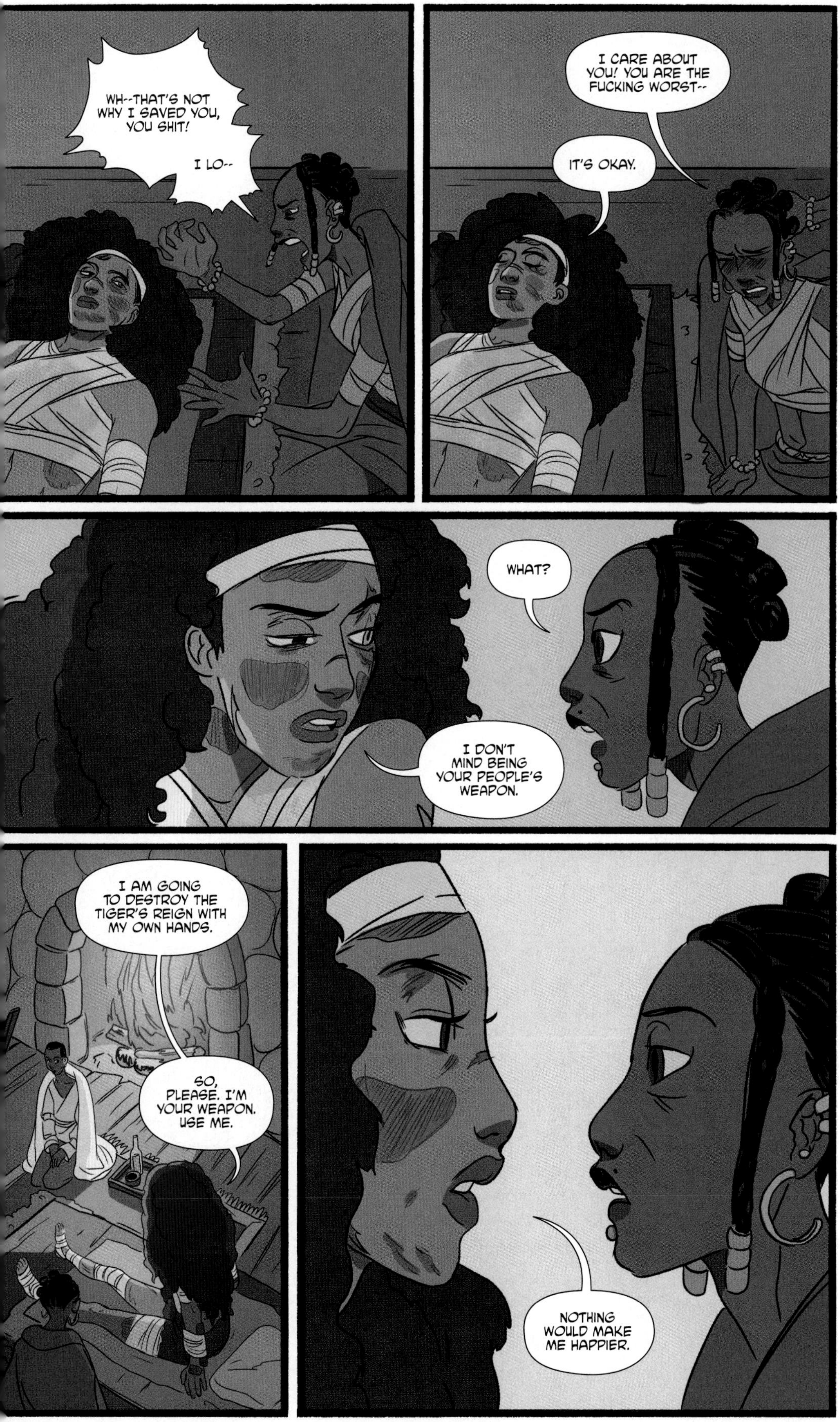
WH--THAT'S NOT WHY I SAVED YOU, YOU SHIT!
I LO--
I CARE ABOUT YOU! YOU ARE THE FUCKING WORST--
IT'S OKAY.
WHAT?
I DON'T MIND BEING YOUR PEOPLE'S WEAPON.
I AM GOING TO DESTROY THE TIGER'S REIGN WITH MY OWN HANDS.
SO, PLEASE. I'M YOUR WEAPON. USE ME.
NOTHING WOULD MAKE ME HAPPIER.

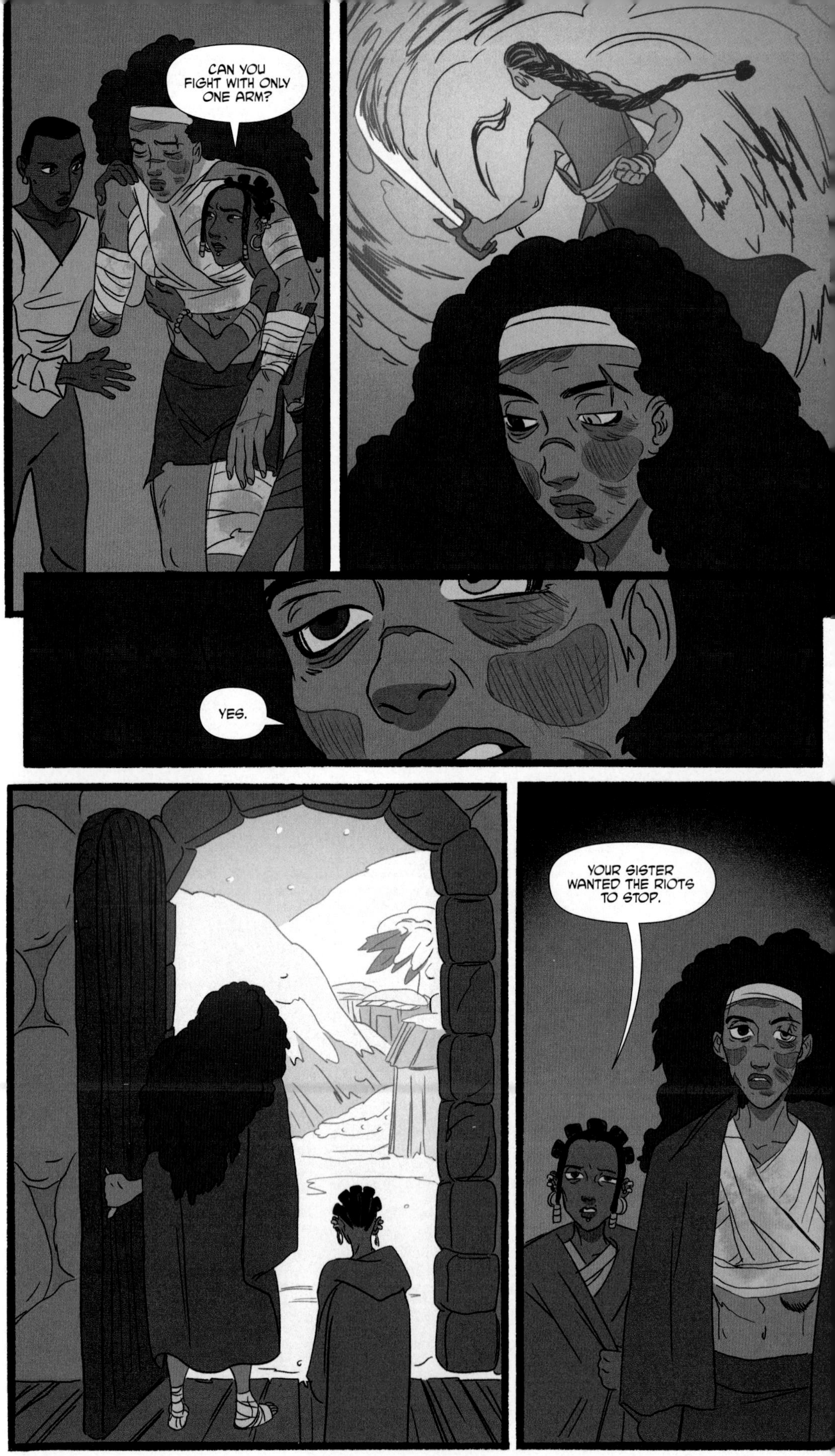
CAN YOU FIGHT WITH ONLY ONE ARM?
YES.
YOUR SISTER WANTED THE RIOTS TO STOP.

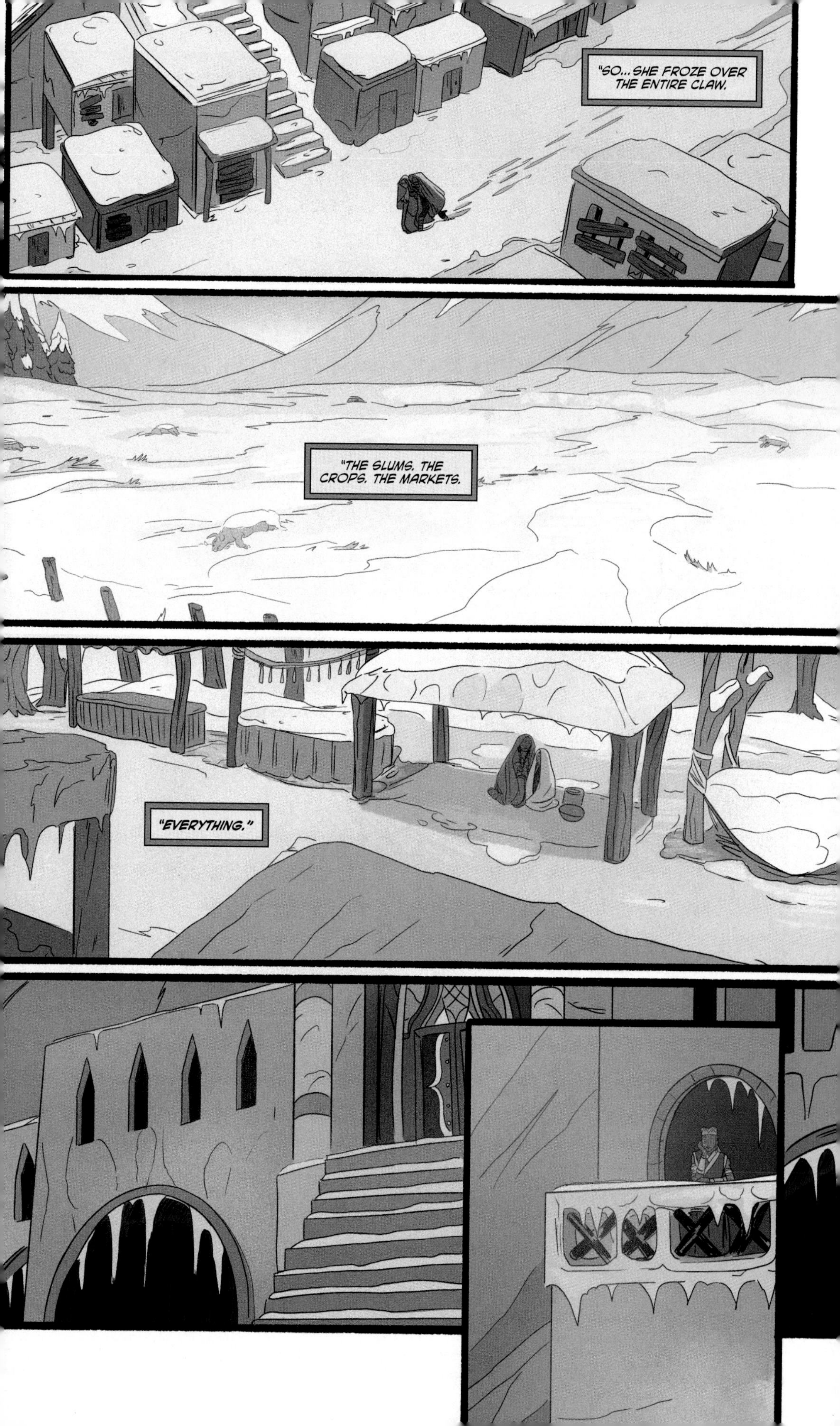
"SO... SHE FROZE OVER THE ENTIRE CLAW.
"THE SLUMS. THE CROPS. THE MARKETS.
"EVERYTHING."

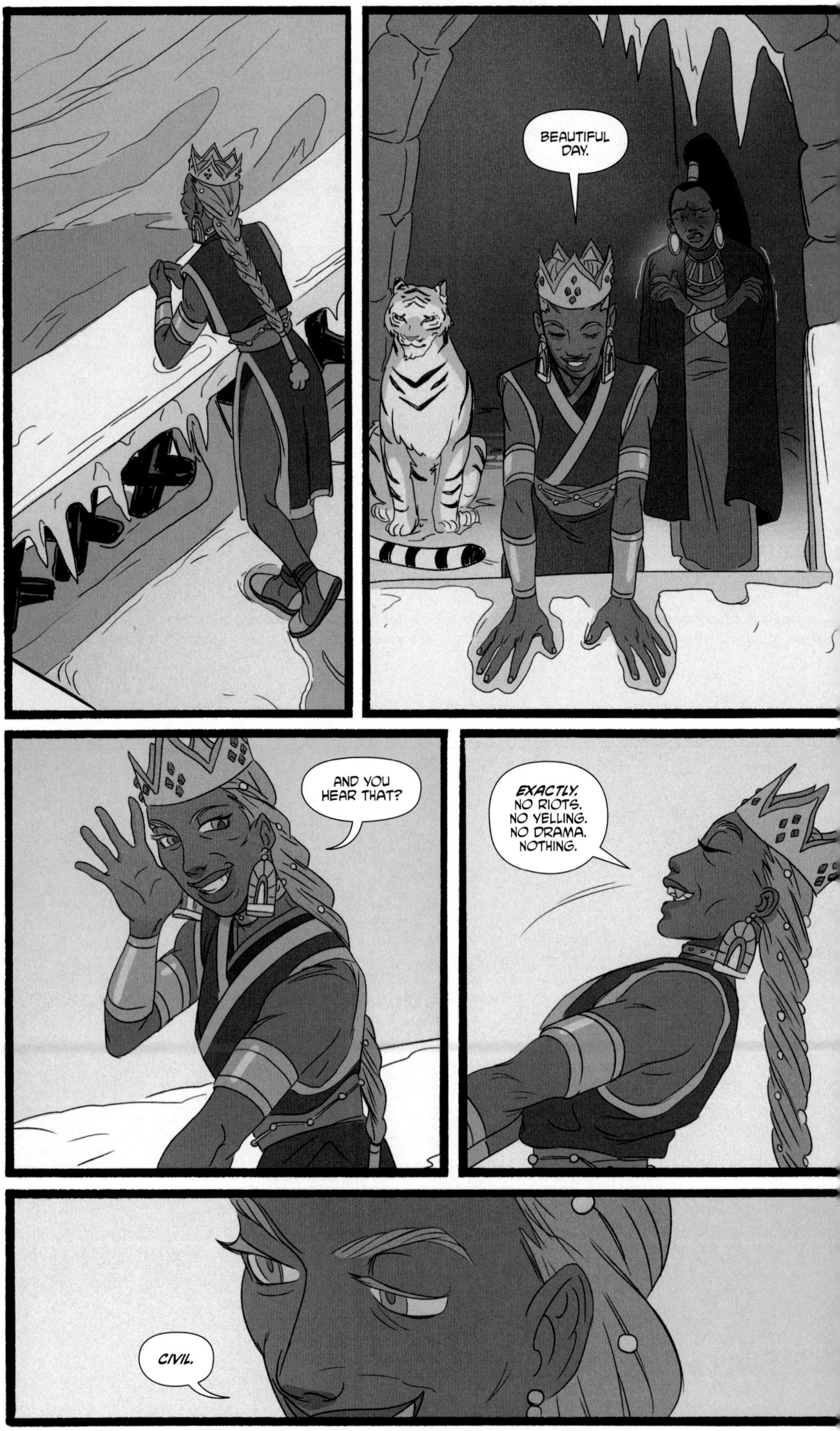
BEAUTIFUL DAY.
AND YOU HEAR THAT?
EXACTLY. NO RIOTS. NO YELLING. NO DRAMA. NOTHING.
CIVIL.

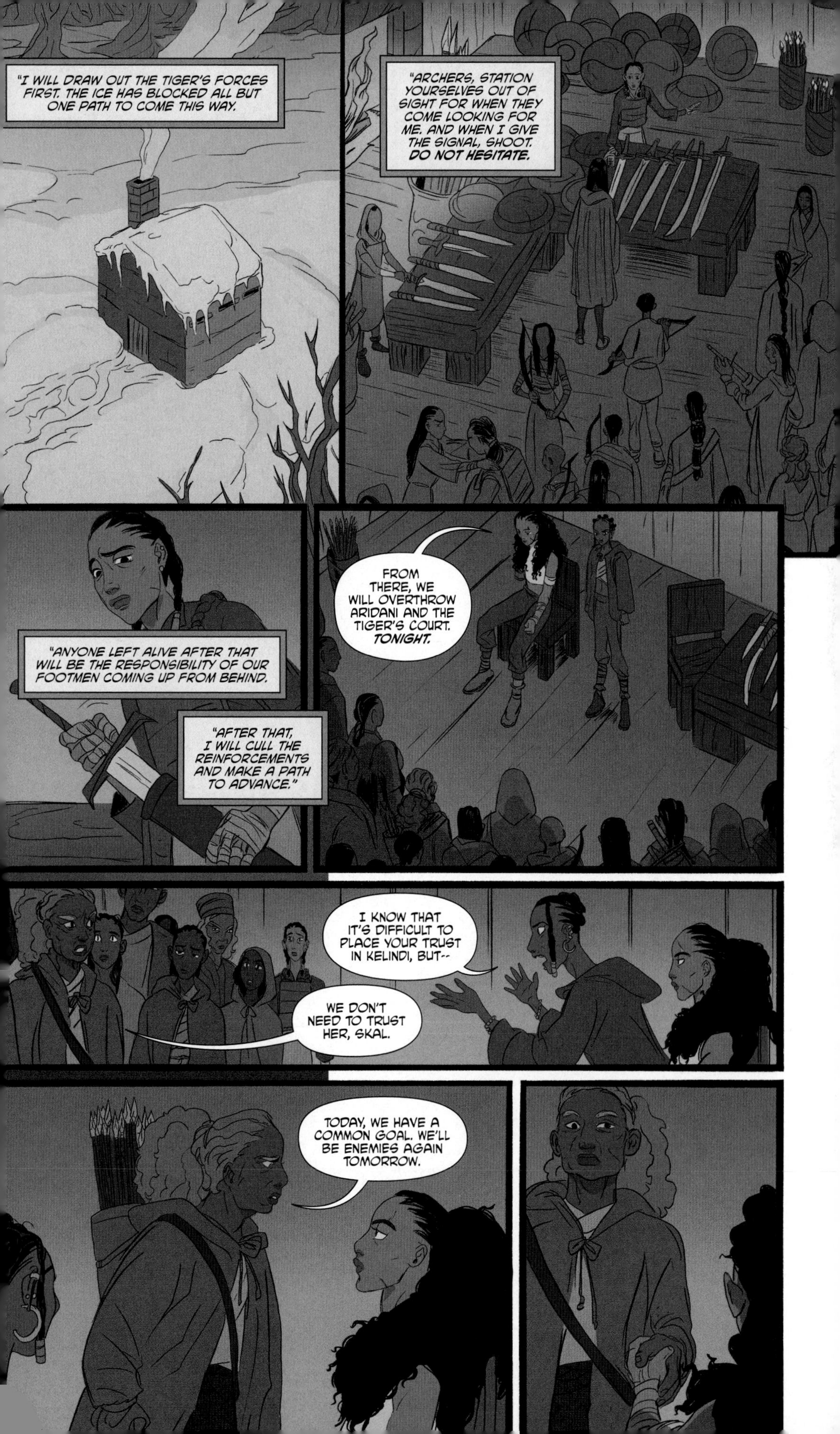
"I WILL DRAW OUT THE TIGER'S FORCES FIRST. THE ICE HAS BLOCKED ALL BUT ONE PATH TO COME THIS WAY.
"ARCHERS, STATION YOURSELVES OUT OF SIGHT FOR WHEN THEY COME LOOKING FOR ME. AND WHEN I GIVE THE SIGNAL, SHOOT. DO NOT HESITATE.
"ANYONE LEFT ALIVE AFTER THAT WILL BE THE RESPONSIBILITY OF OUR FOOTMEN COMING UP FROM BEHIND.
"AFTER THAT, I WILL CULL THE REINFORCEMENTS AND MAKE A PATH TO ADVANCE."
FROM THERE, WE WILL OVERTHROW ARIDANI AND THE TIGER'S COURT. TONIGHT.
I KNOW THAT IT'S DIFFICULT TO PLACE YOUR TRUST IN KELINDI, BUT--
WE DON'T NEED TO TRUST HER, SKAL.
TODAY, WE HAVE A COMMON GOAL. WE'LL BE ENEMIES AGAIN TOMORROW.

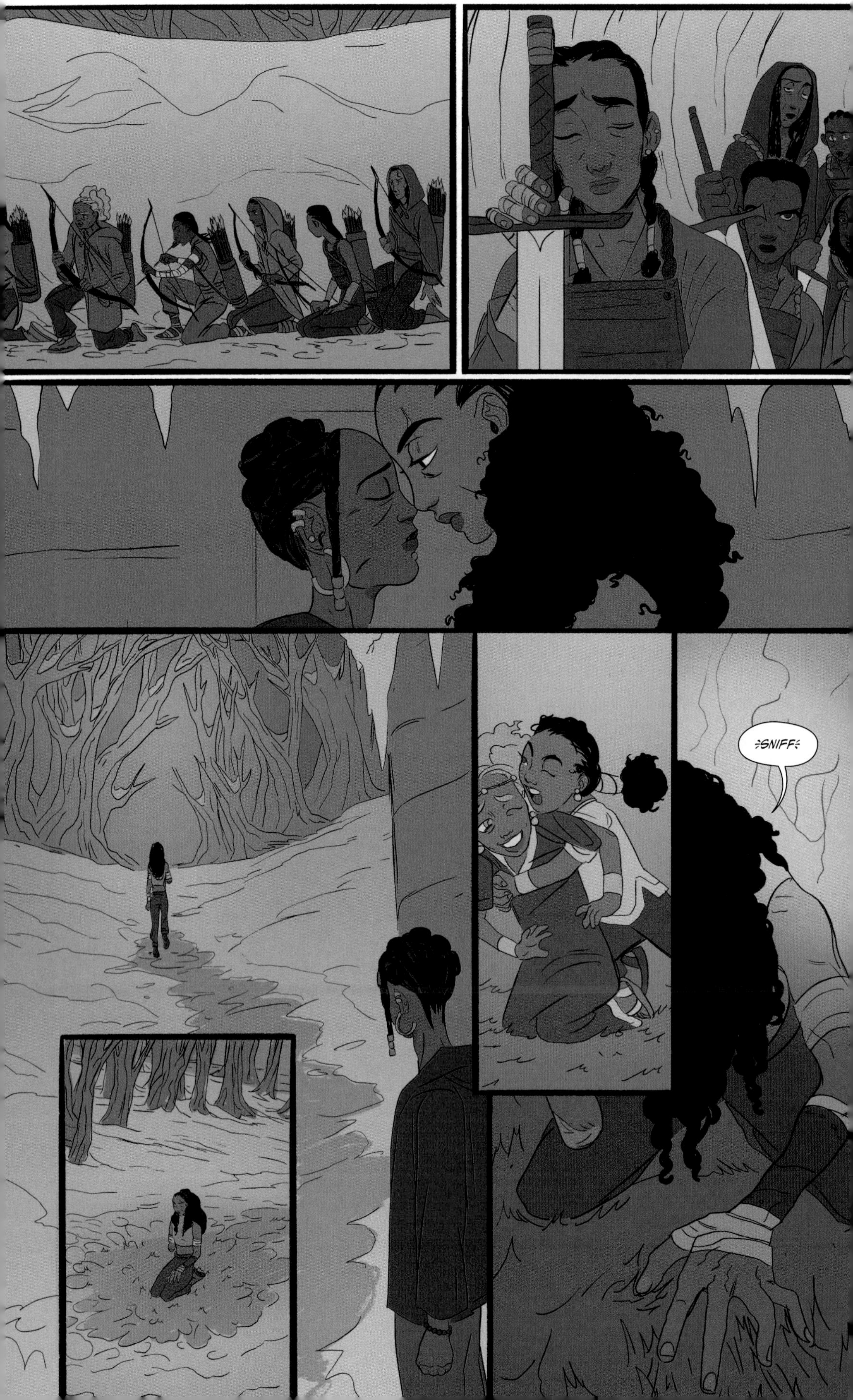
SNIFF

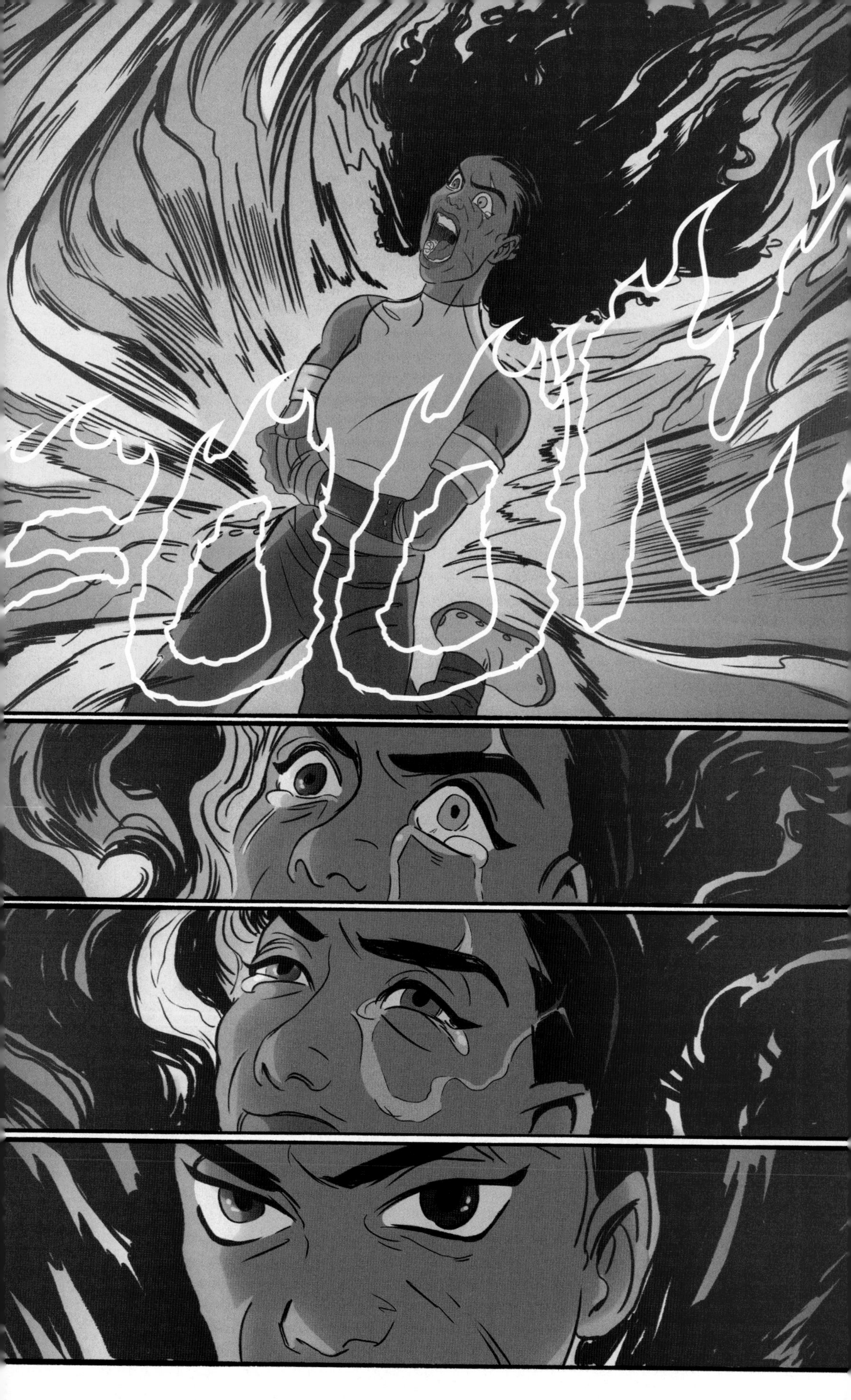

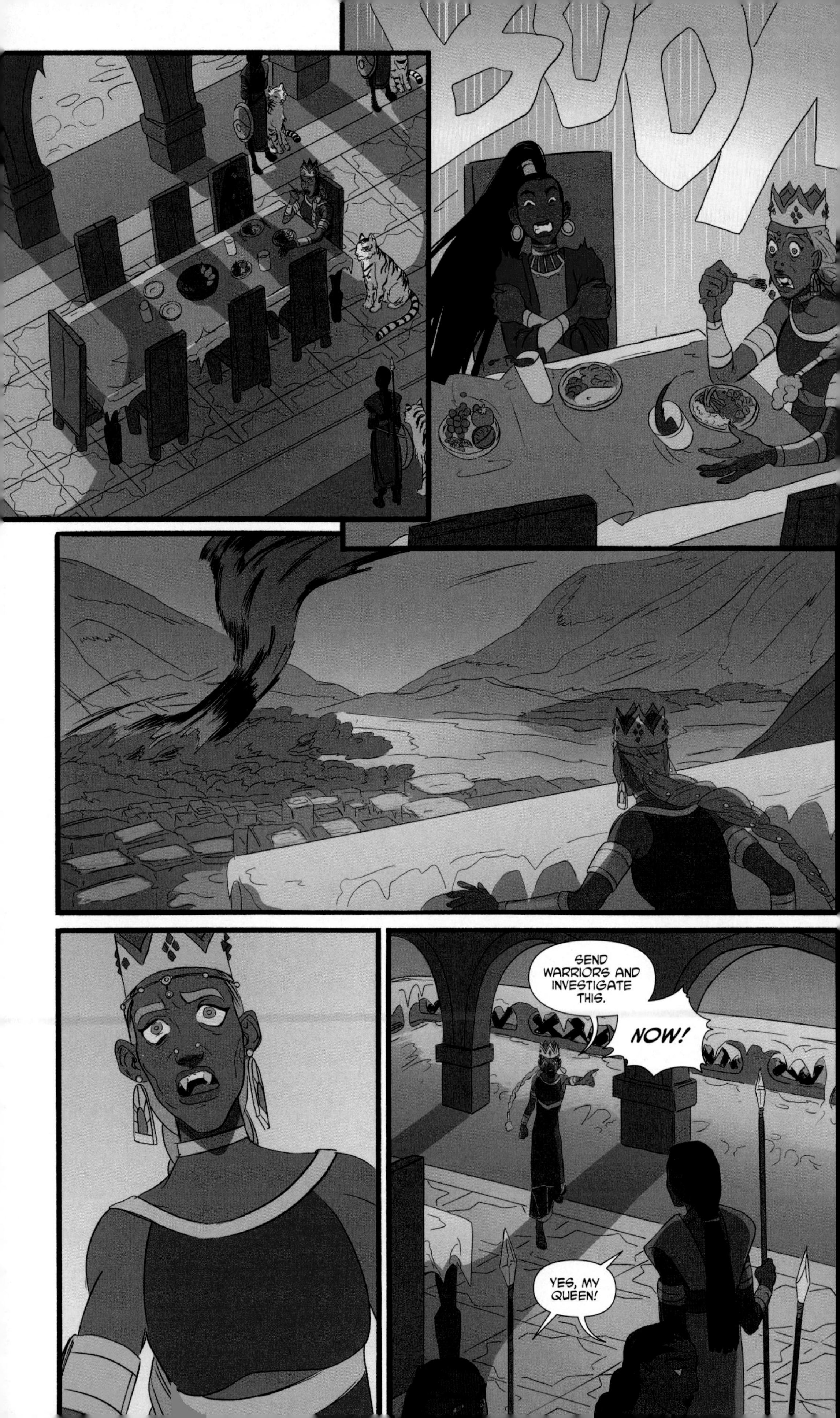
BOOM
SEND WARRIORS AND INVESTIGATE THIS.
NOW!
YES, MY QUEEN!

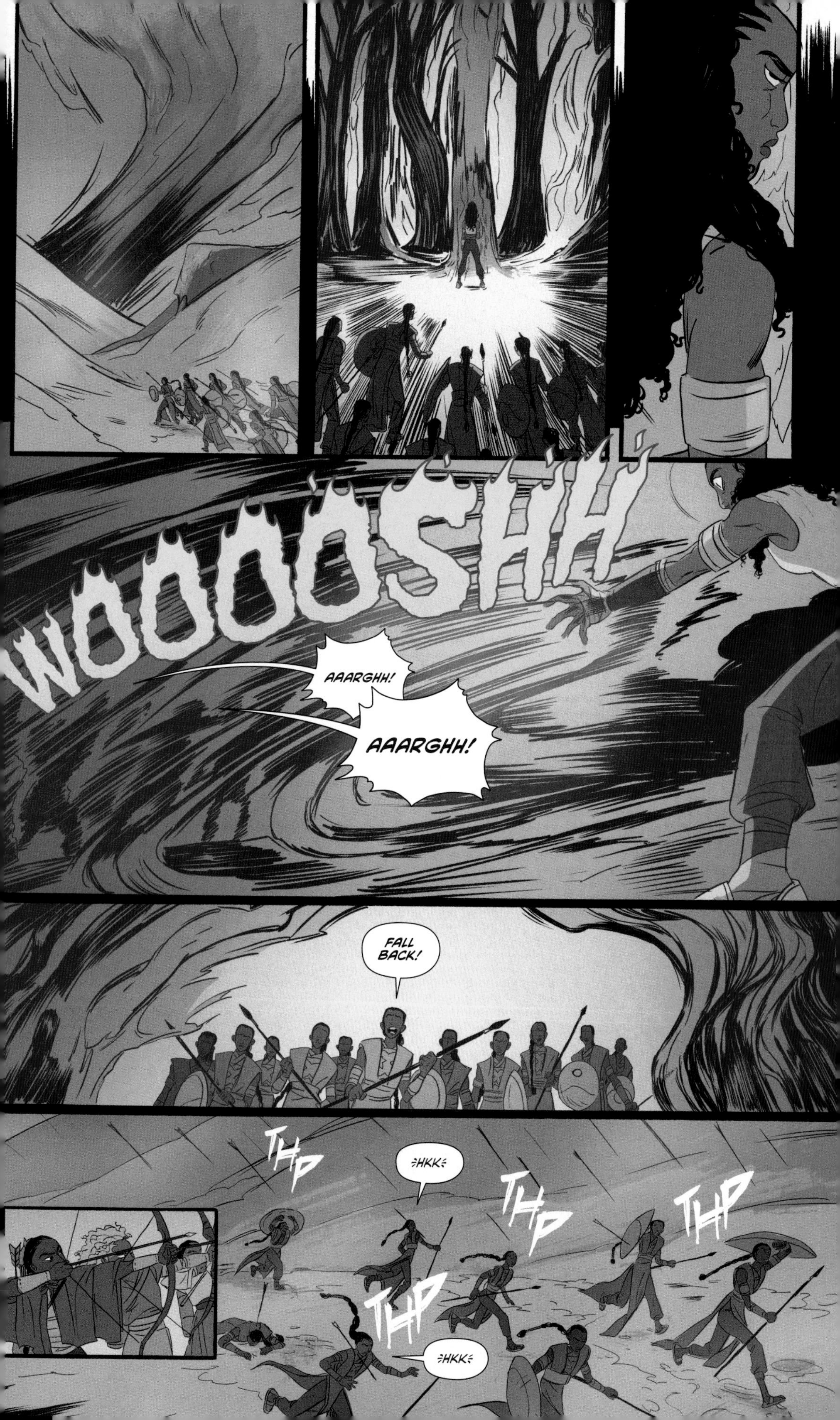
WOOOOSHH
AAARGHH!
AAARGHH!
FALL BACK!
THP
HKK
THP
THP
THP
HKK

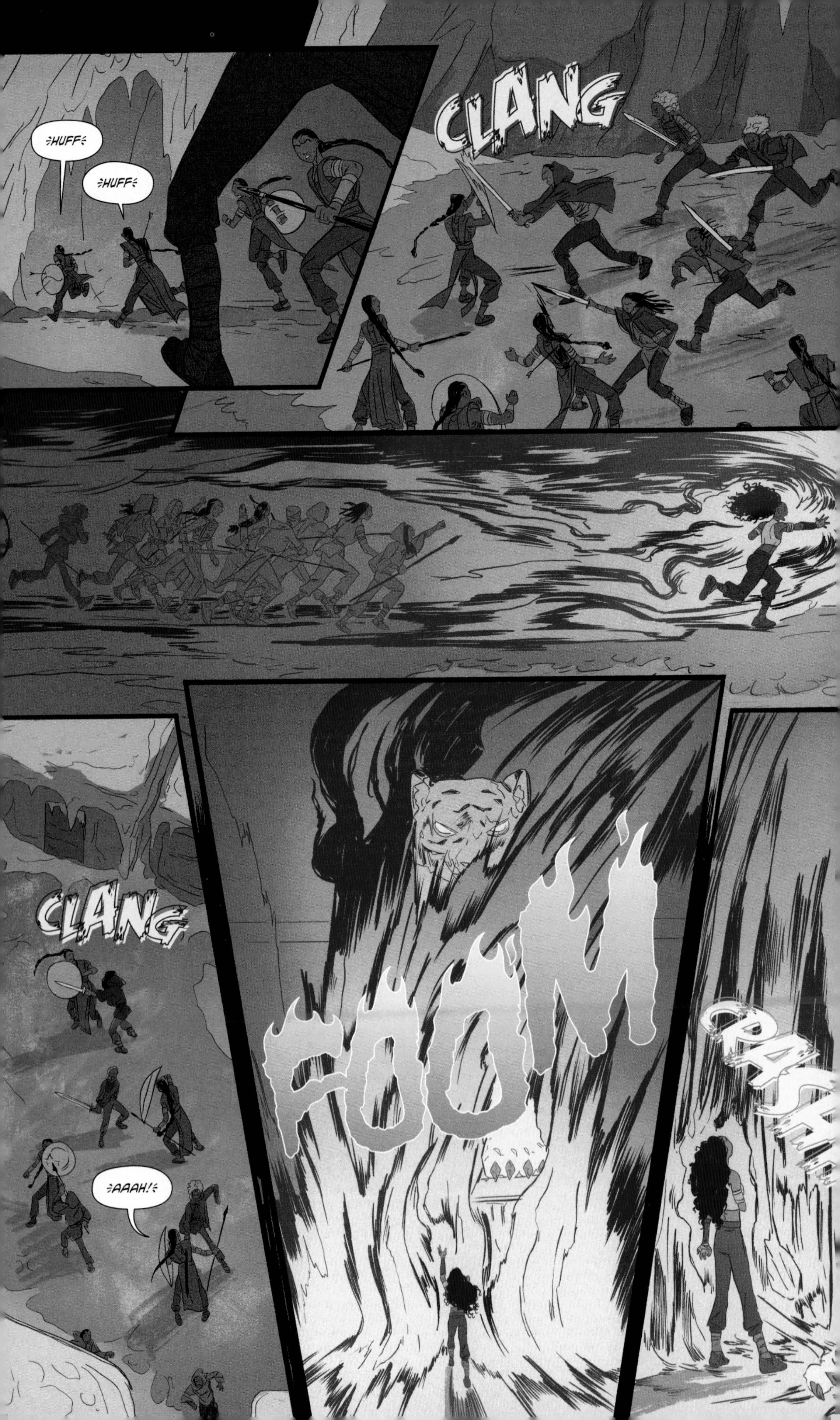
HUFF
HUFF
CLANG
CLANG
AAAH!
FOOM
CRASH

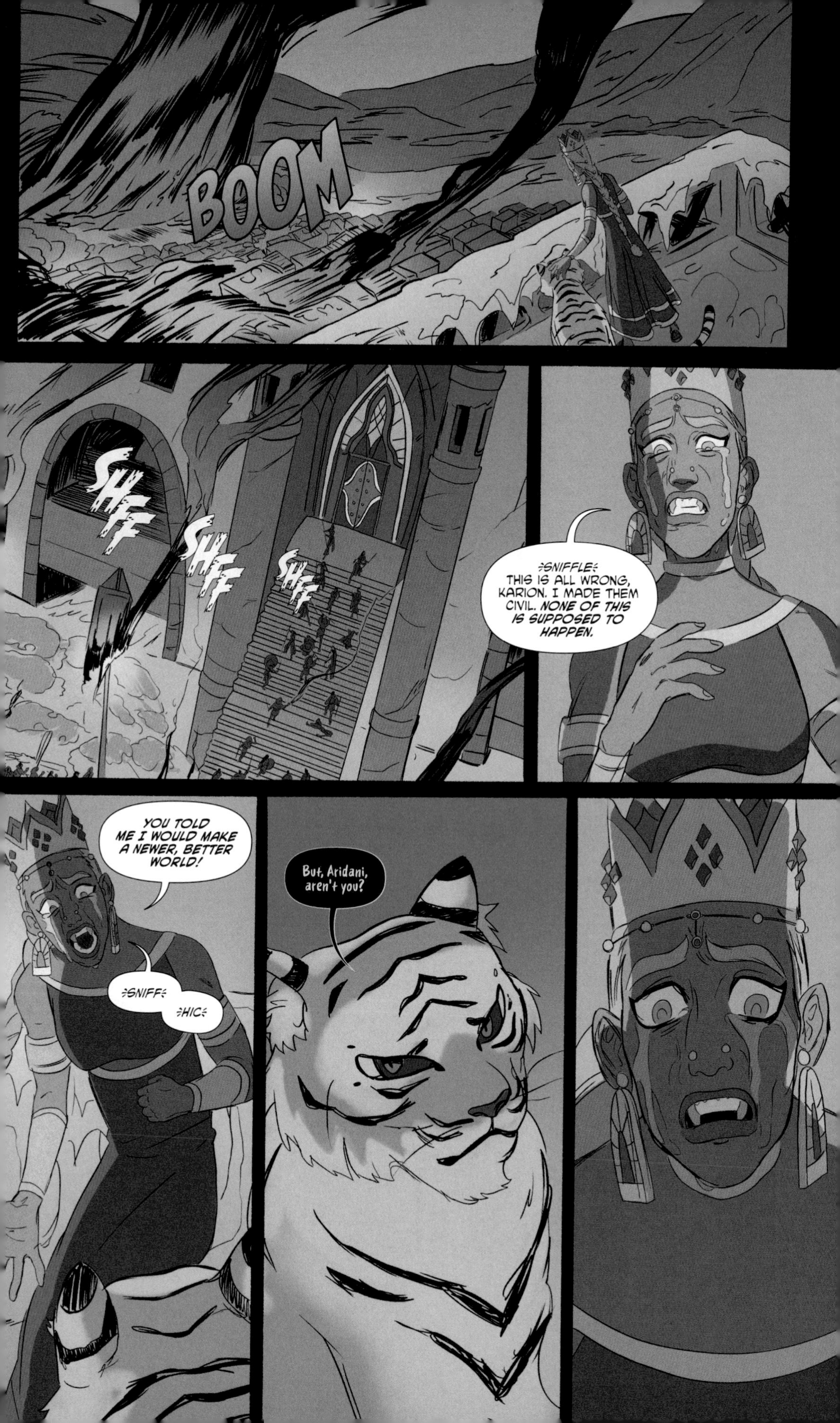
BOOM
SHFF
SHFF
SHFF
⊰SNIFFLE⊱ THIS IS ALL WRONG, KARION. I MADE THEM CIVIL. NONE OF THIS IS SUPPOSED TO HAPPEN.
YOU TOLD ME I WOULD MAKE A NEWER, BETTER WORLD!
⊰SNIFF⊱
⊰HIC⊱
But, Aridani, aren't you?

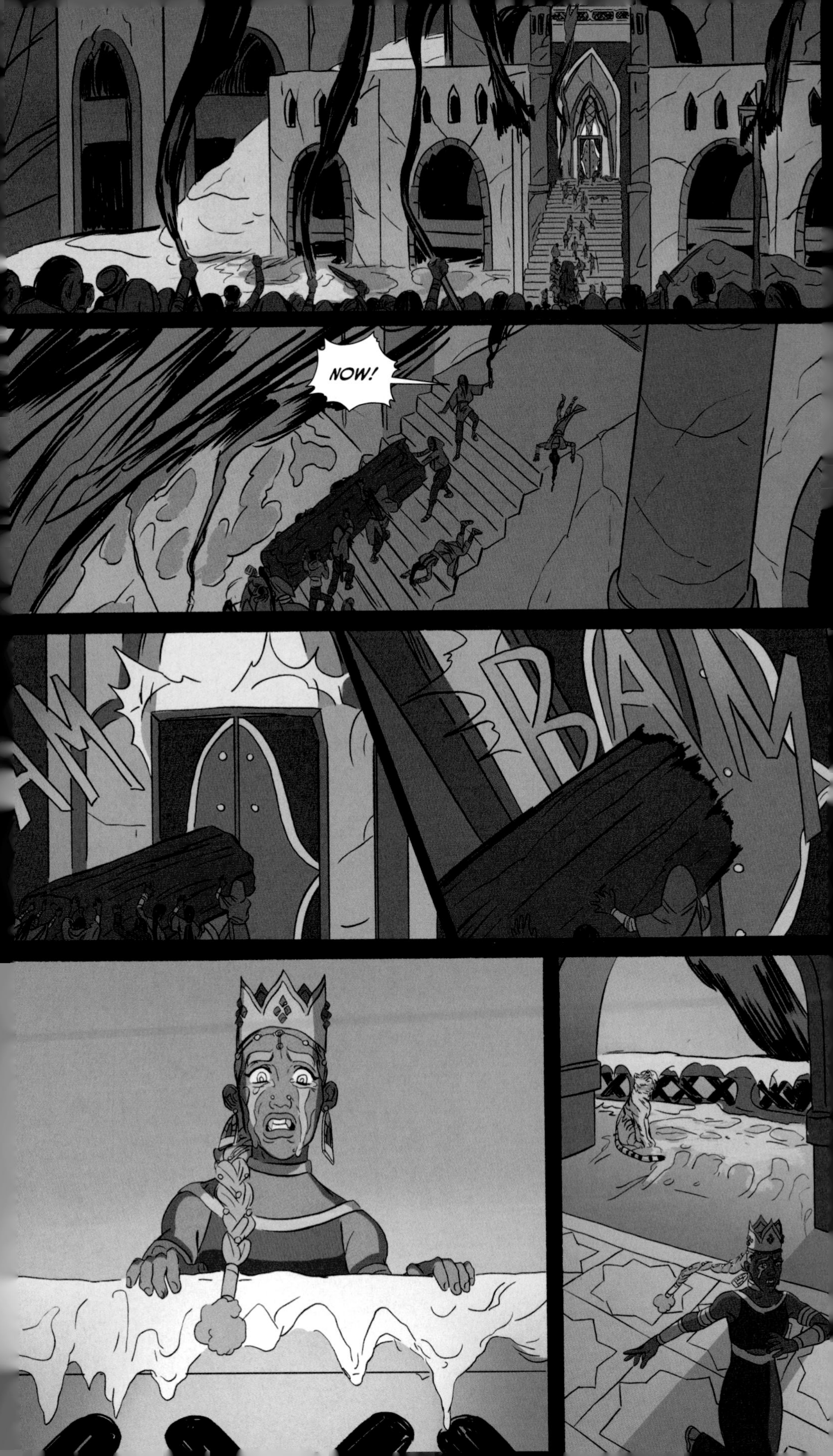
NOW!
BAM

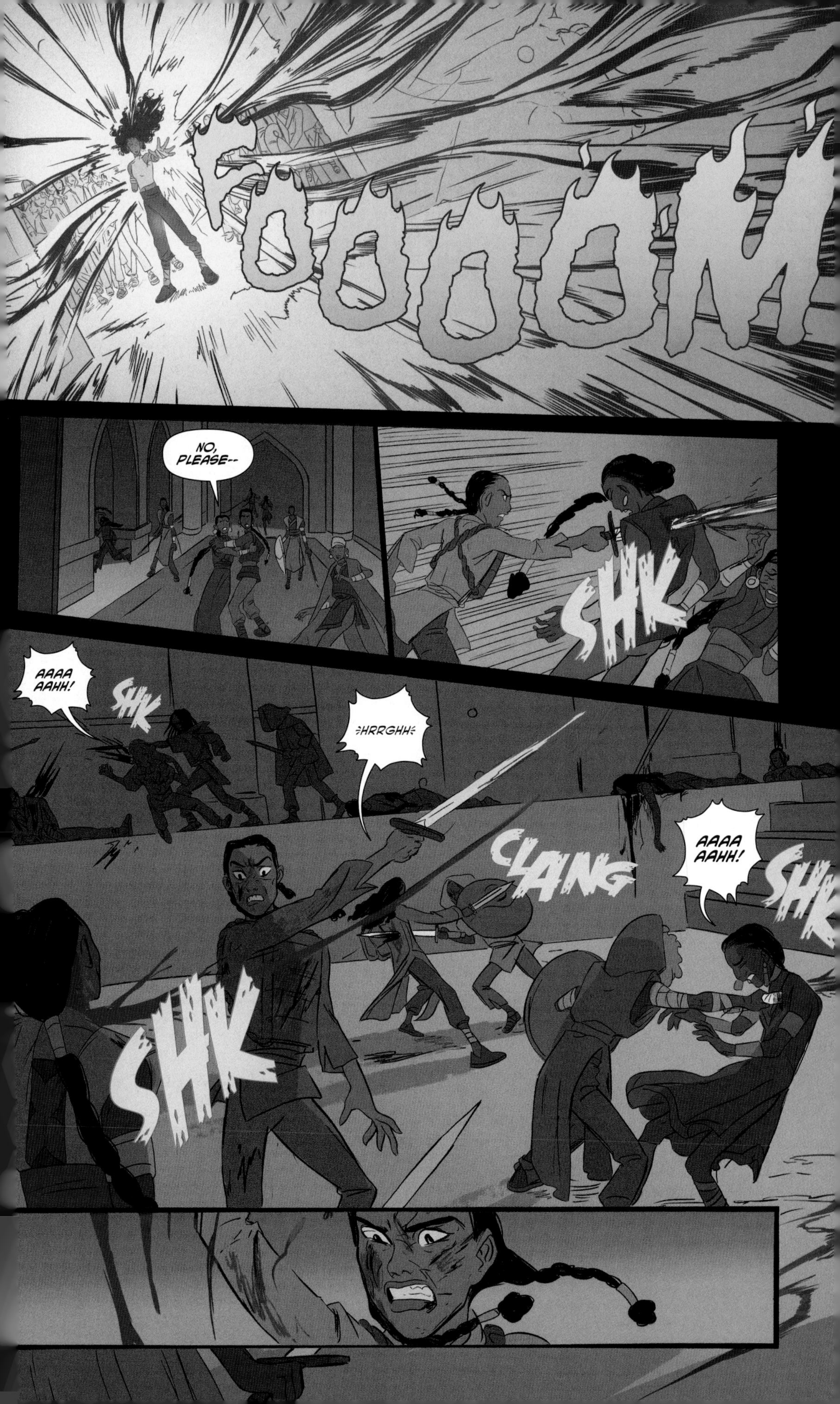

FOOOOOM!
NO, PLEASE--
SHK
AAAA AAHH!
SHK
HRRGHH
CLANG
AAAA AAHH!
SHK
SHK

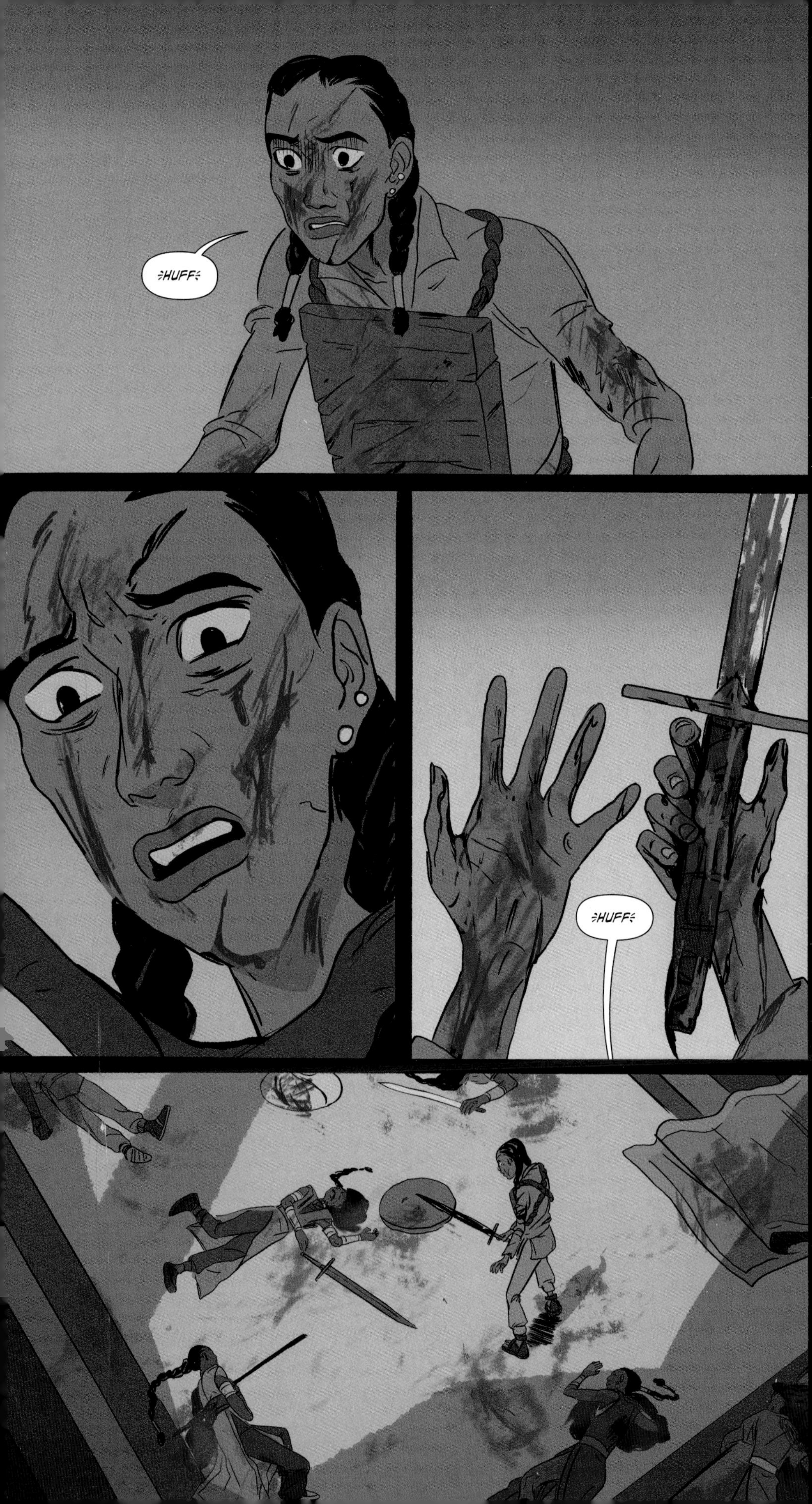
HUFF
HUFF

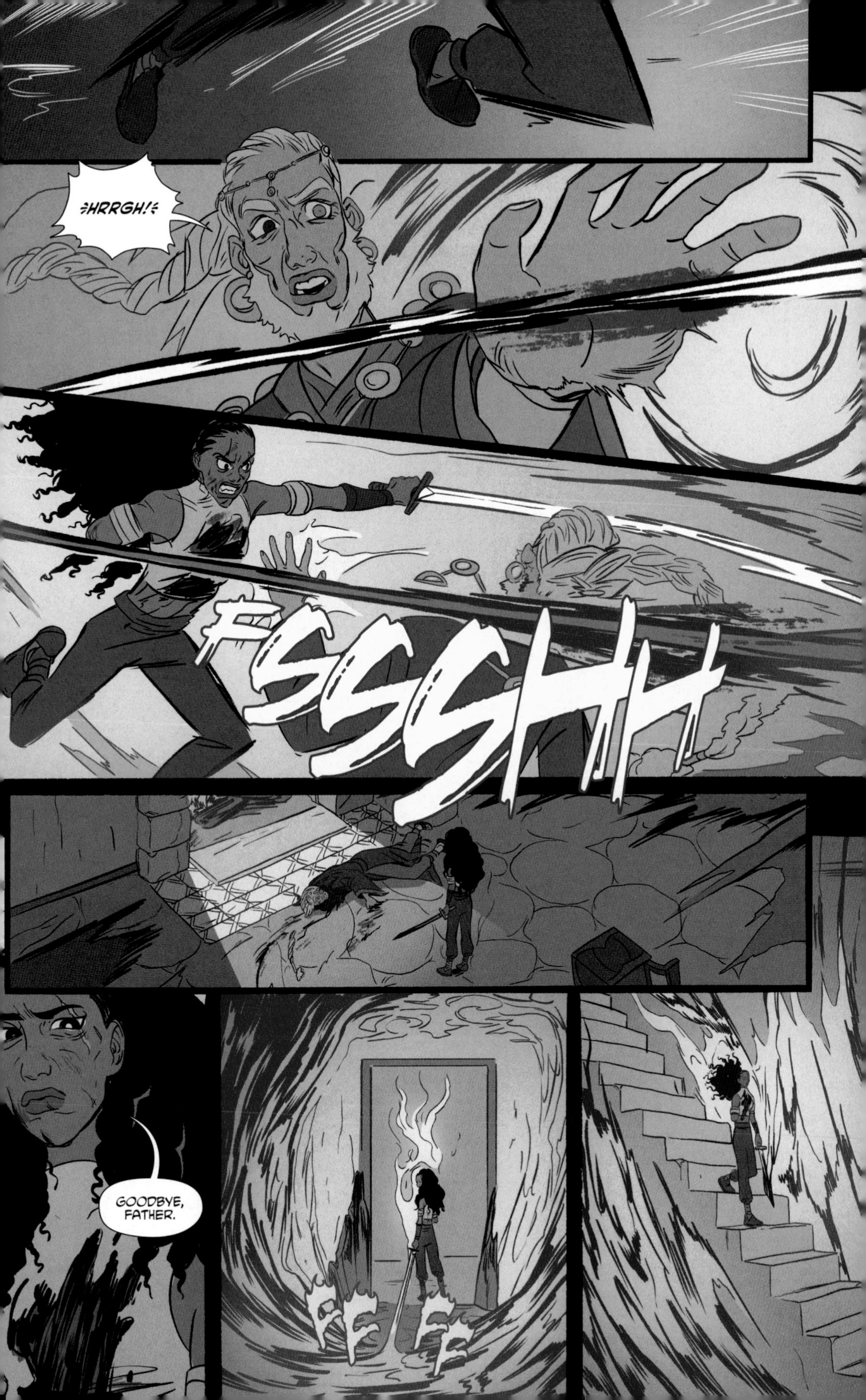
HRRGH!
FSSHH
GOODBYE, FATHER.

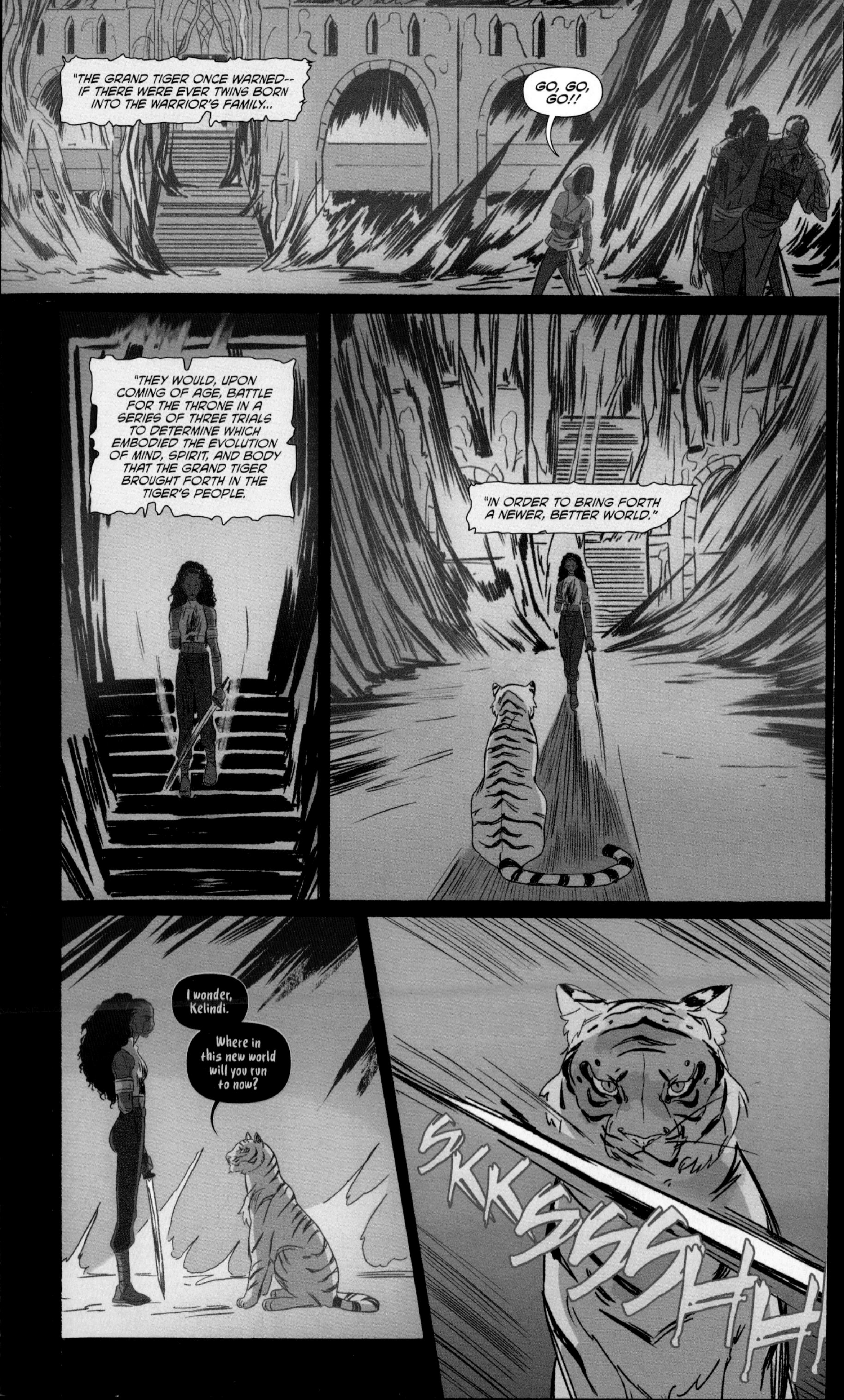
"THE GRAND TIGER ONCE WARNED-- IF THERE WERE EVER TWINS BORN INTO THE WARRIOR'S FAMILY...
GO, GO, GO!!
"THEY WOULD, UPON COMING OF AGE, BATTLE FOR THE THRONE IN A SERIES OF THREE TRIALS TO DETERMINE WHICH EMBODIED THE EVOLUTION OF MIND, SPIRIT, AND BODY THAT THE GRAND TIGER BROUGHT FORTH IN THE TIGER'S PEOPLE.
"IN ORDER TO BRING FORTH A NEWER, BETTER WORLD."
I wonder, Kelindi.
Where in this new world will you run to now?
SKKSSSHHH

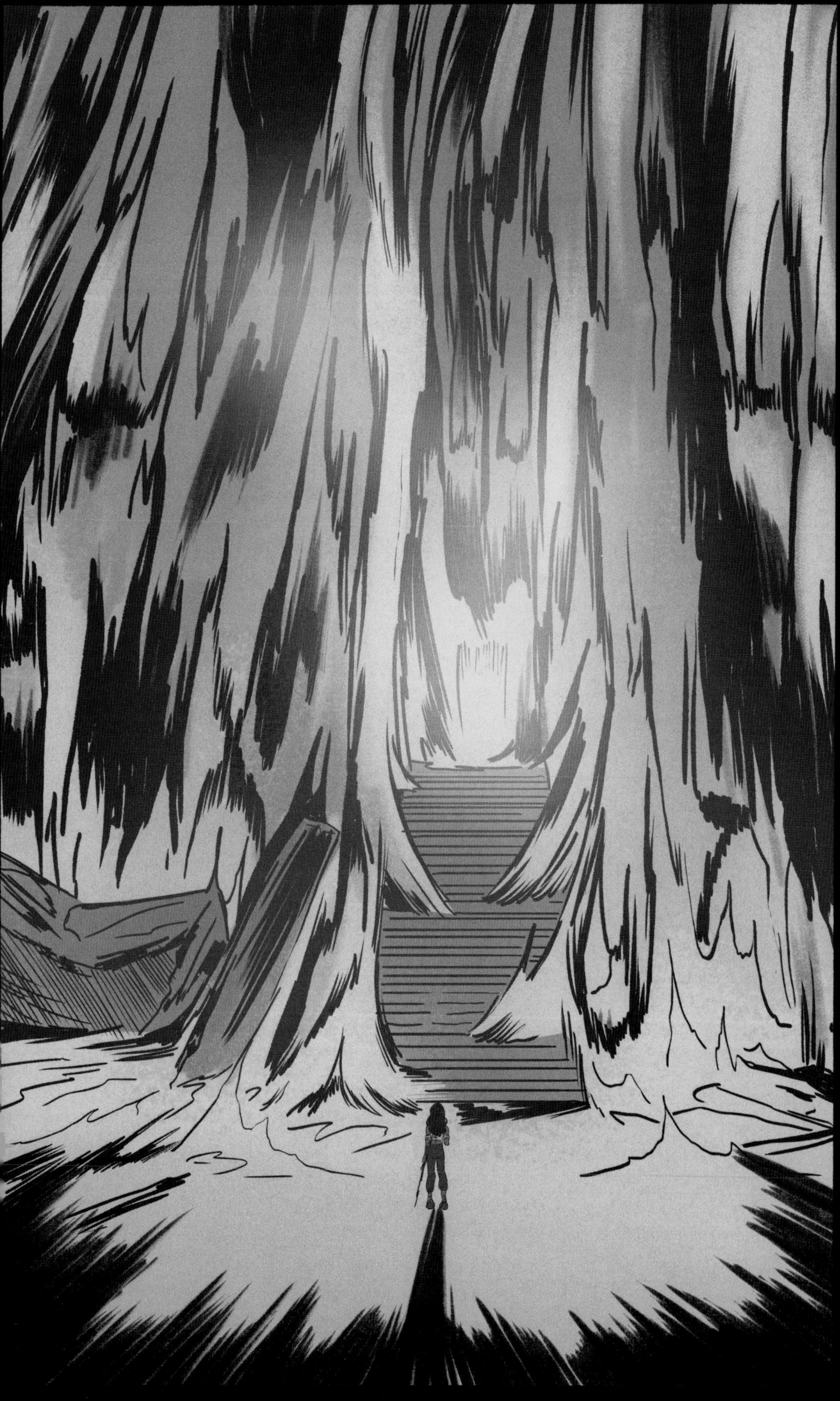

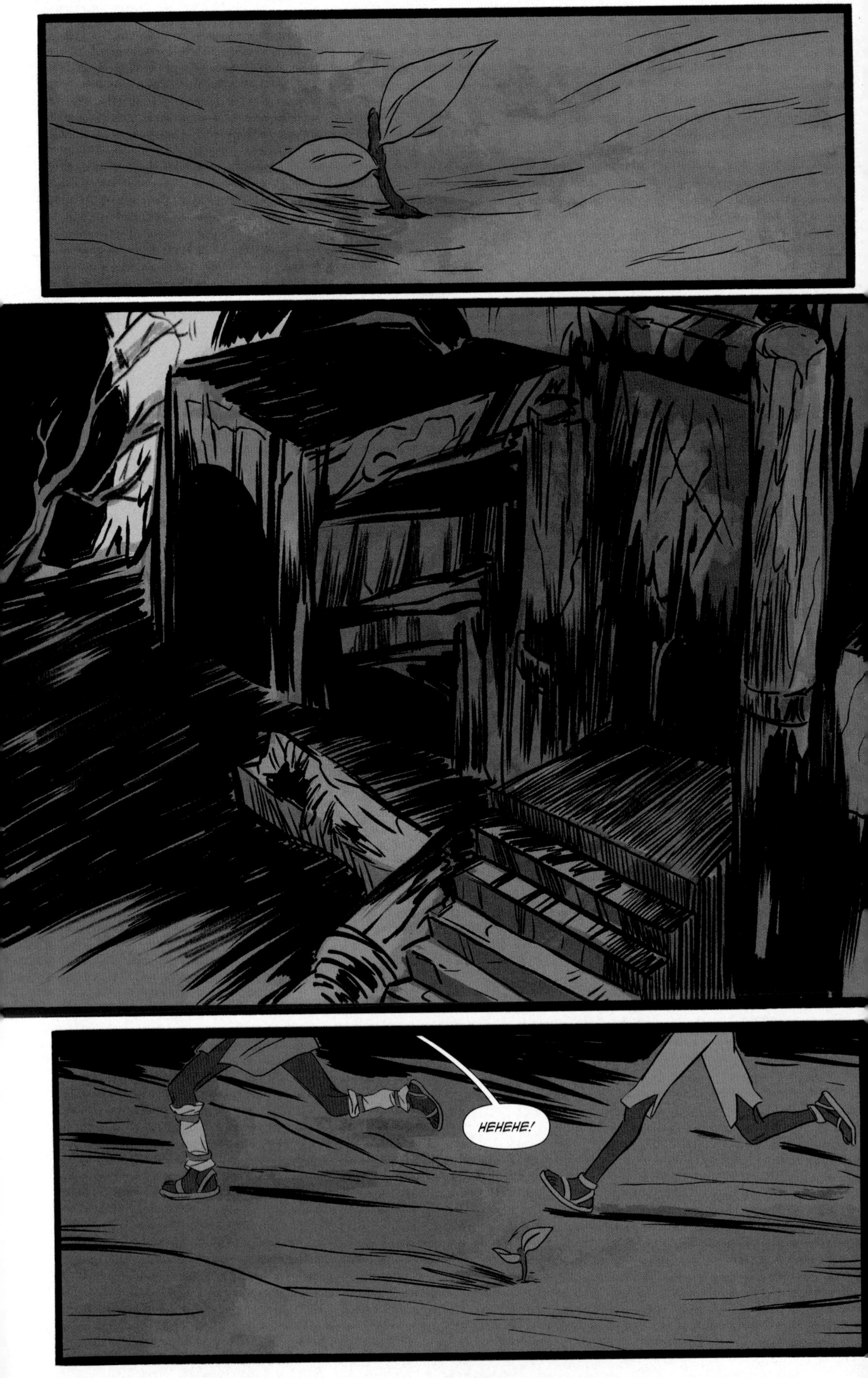
HEHEHE!

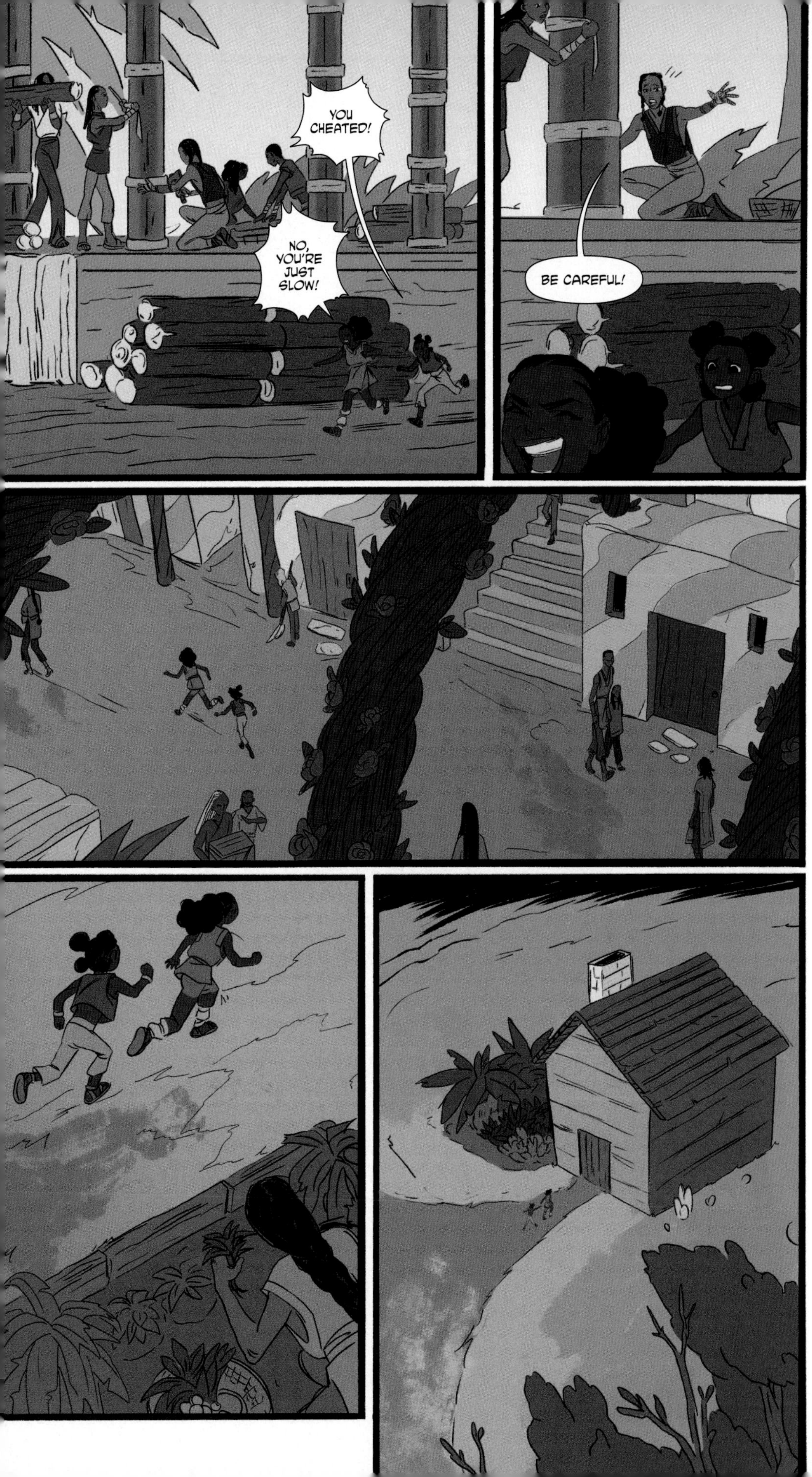
YOU CHEATED!
NO, YOU'RE JUST SLOW!
BE CAREFUL!

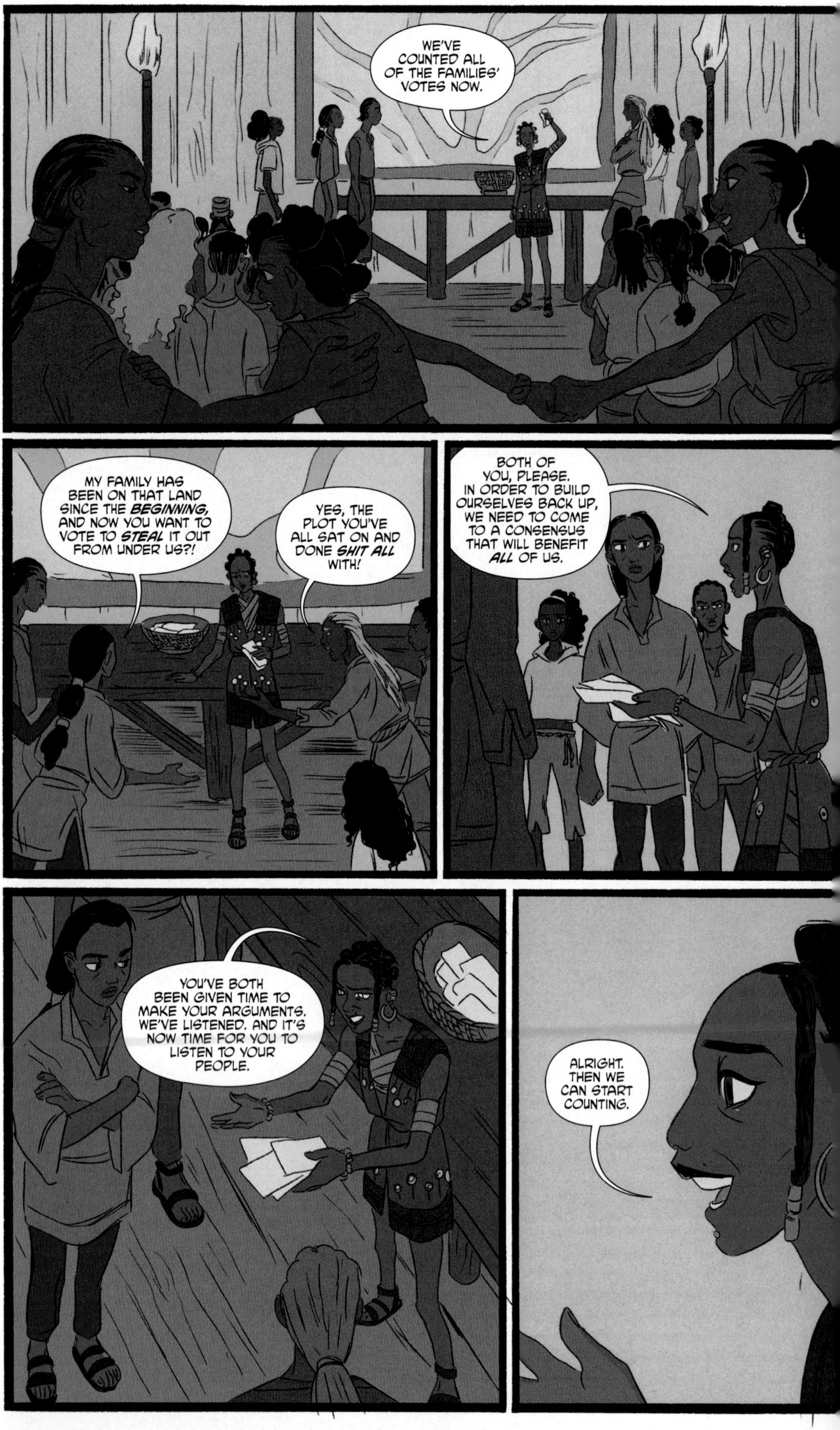
WE'VE COUNTED ALL OF THE FAMILIES' VOTES NOW.
MY FAMILY HAS BEEN ON THAT LAND SINCE THE BEGINNING, AND NOW YOU WANT TO VOTE TO STEAL IT OUT FROM UNDER US?!
YES, THE PLOT YOU'VE ALL SAT ON AND DONE SHIT ALL WITH!
BOTH OF YOU, PLEASE. IN ORDER TO BUILD OURSELVES BACK UP, WE NEED TO COME TO A CONSENSUS THAT WILL BENEFIT ALL OF US.
YOU'VE BOTH BEEN GIVEN TIME TO MAKE YOUR ARGUMENTS. WE'VE LISTENED. AND IT'S NOW TIME FOR YOU TO LISTEN TO YOUR PEOPLE.
ALRIGHT. THEN WE CAN START COUNTING.

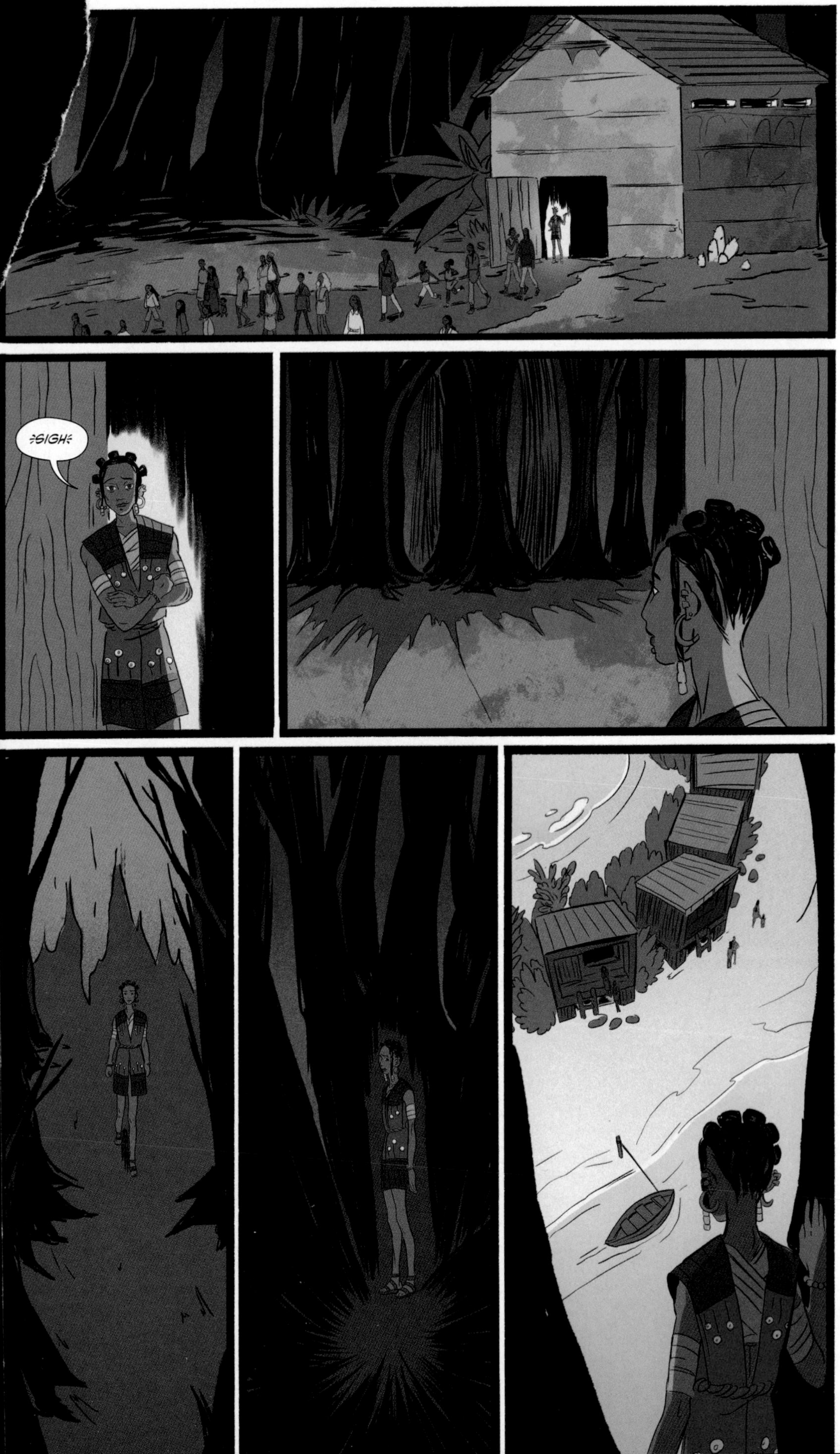
SIGH

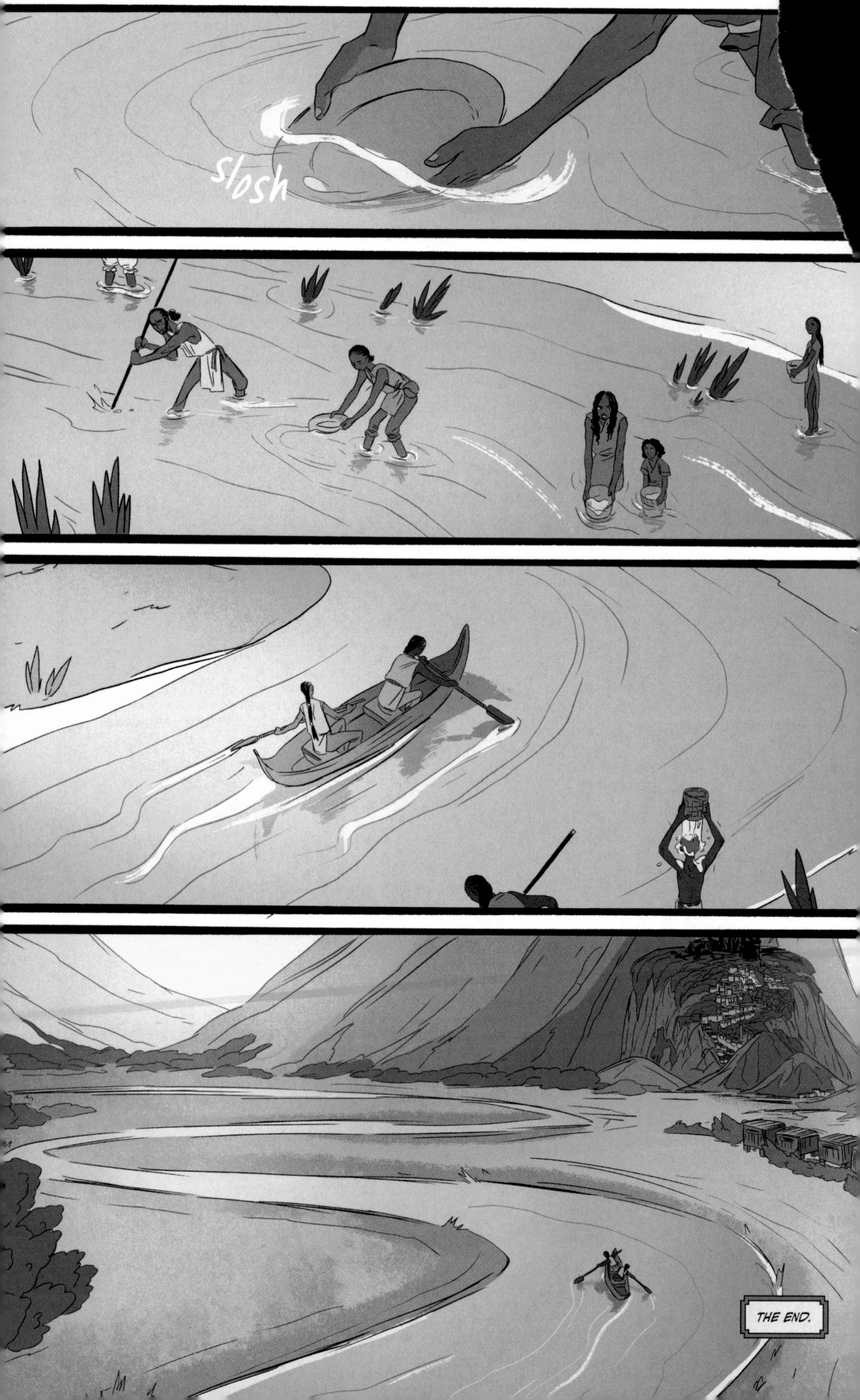
slosh
THE END.

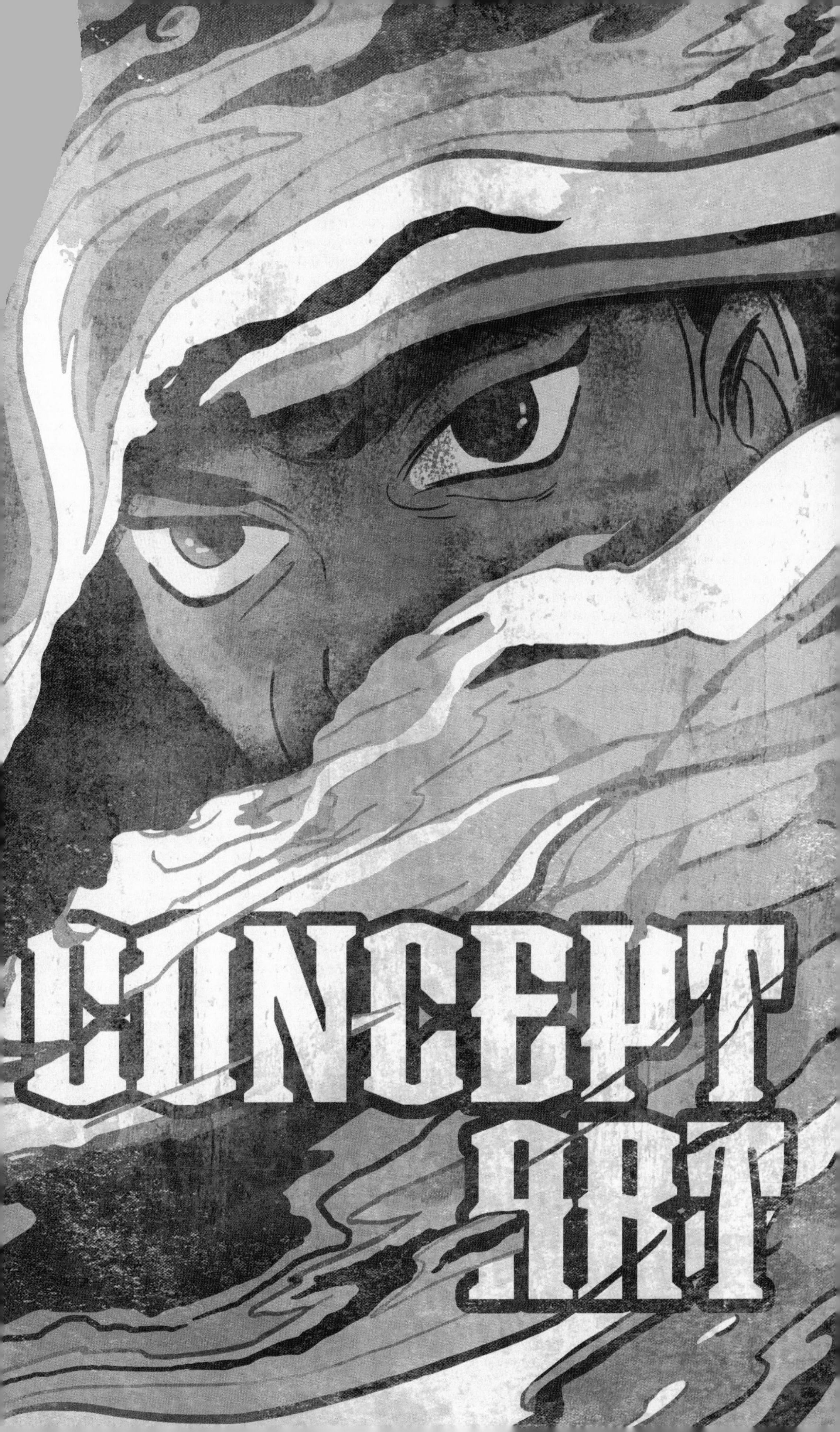
CONCEPT
ART

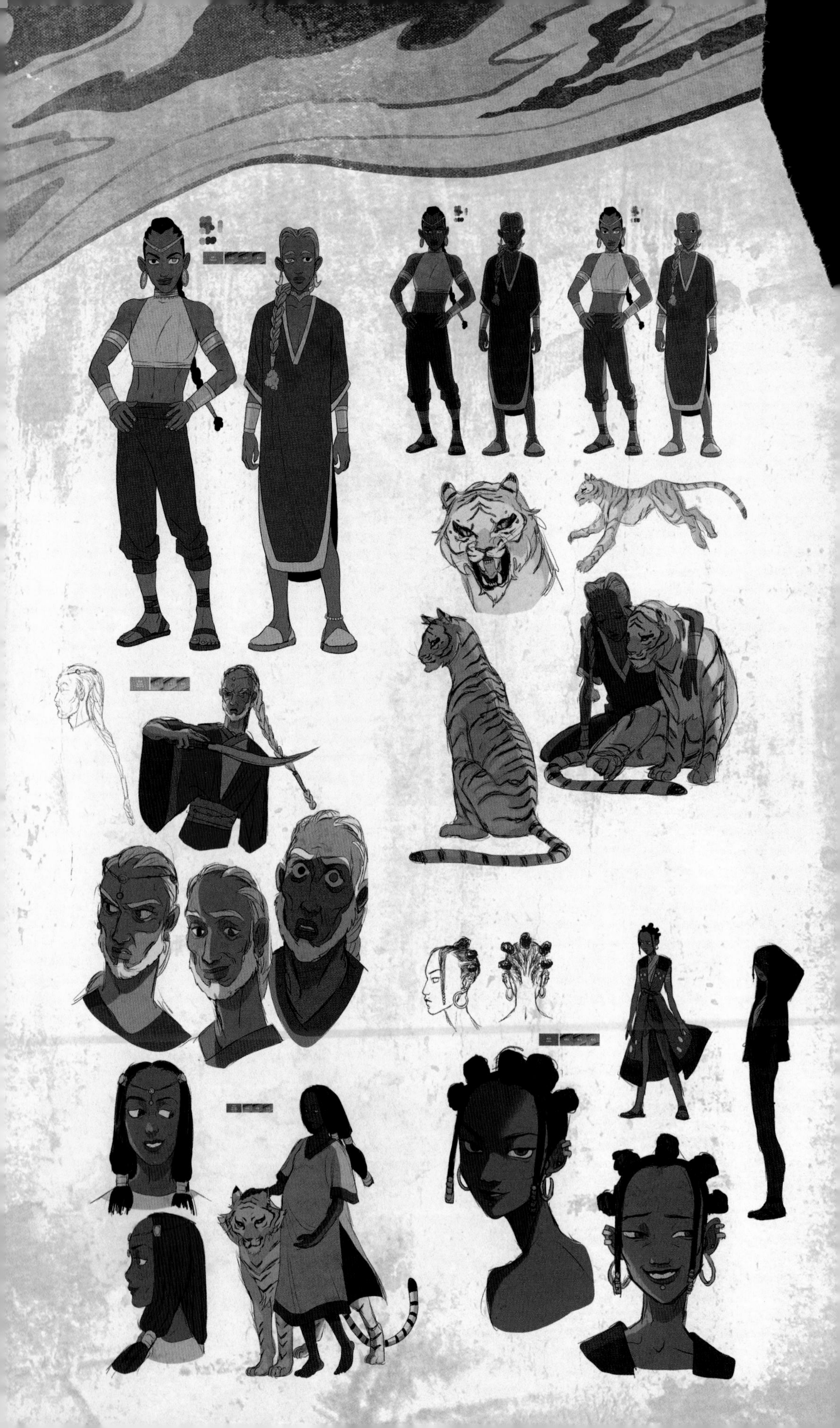

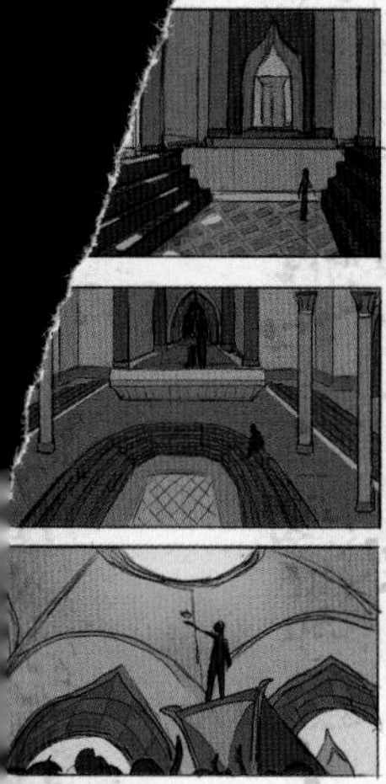

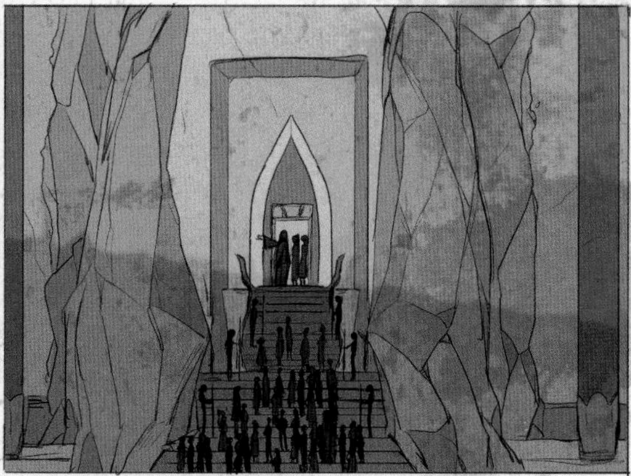

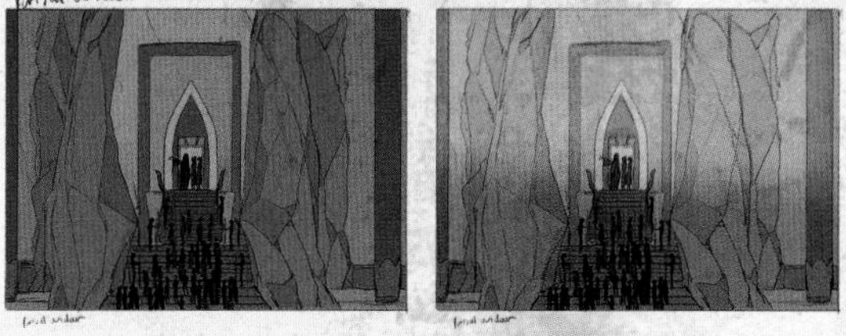

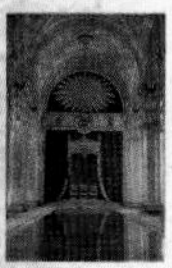
Interior colour Ref

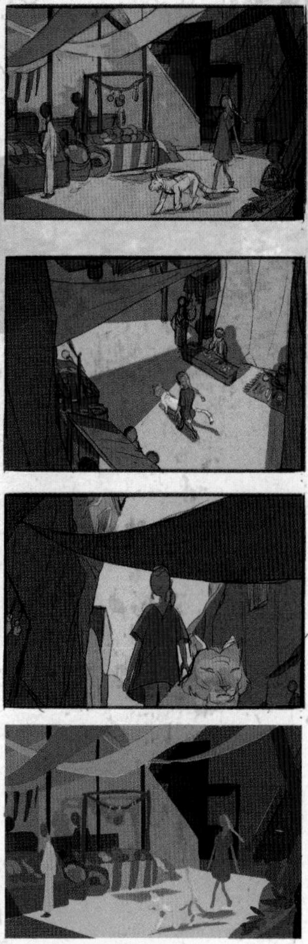

e Tiger's Claw setting environment concept

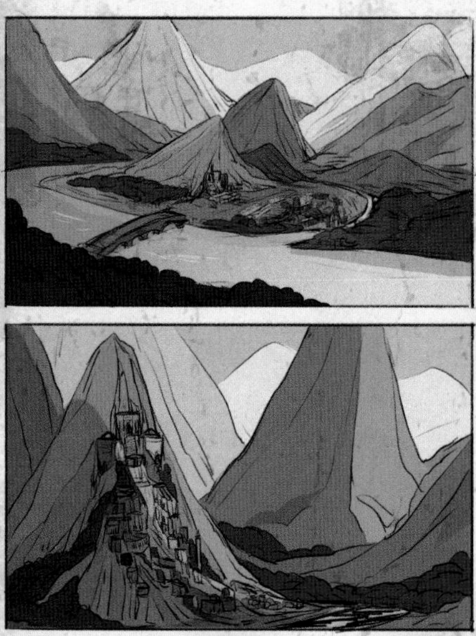

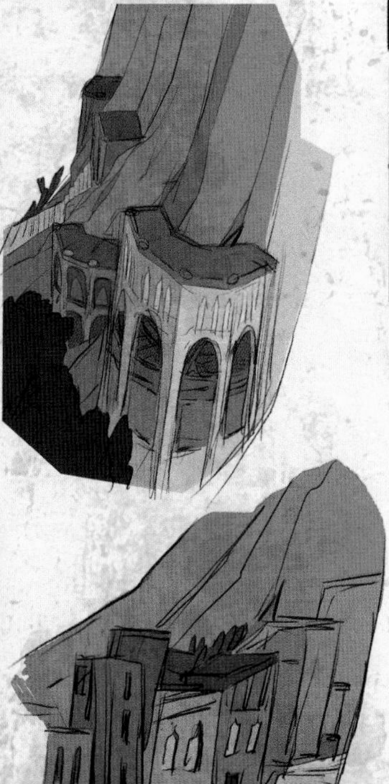

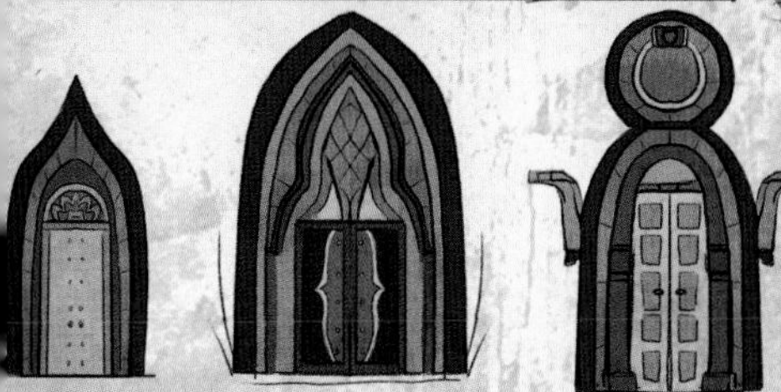
Palace Door

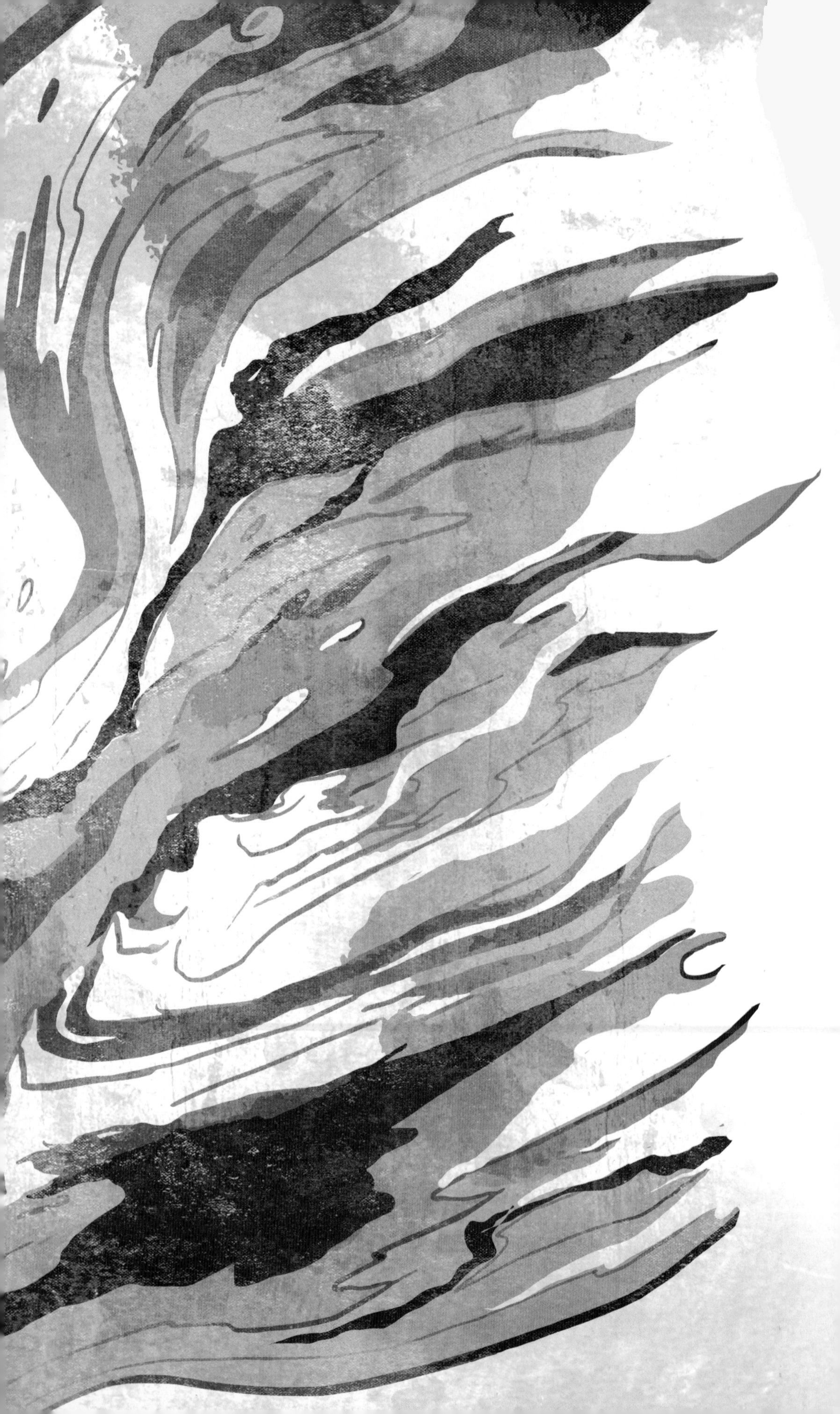